Provincial America, 1600-1763

SOURCES IN AMERICAN HISTORY

GENERAL EDITOR: *George H. Knoles*

Professor of History and Director of
the Institute of American History,
Stanford University

Provincial America
1600-1763

Edited by Bradley Chapin

*State University of New York
at Buffalo*

The Free Press, New York
Collier-Macmillan Limited, London

Preface

DEAN CHAPIN HAS PREPARED A STIMULATING COL-
lection of readings for the opening volume in this
series, *Provincial America, 1600-1763.* It is no simple task to assemble an essay and a score or more documents covering almost
two hundred years of American history. It is sometimes argued
that the colonial period of American history involved so few
people—the first official federal census in 1790 numbered less than
four million—in comparison to the tens of millions living in twentieth-century America, that the student need not devote much
time to the study of the seventeenth and eighteenth centuries. On
the other hand, it can be observed that these years were years of
beginnings, years when the newly arrived immigrants from Europe and their descendents laid the foundations and the mud-sills
of nineteenth- and twentieth-century America and are therefore
worthy of as careful study as any later period of our history. "If
we carefully examine the social and political state of America,
after having studied its history," Alexis de Tocqueville noted in
1835, "we shall remain perfectly convinced that not an opinion,
not a custom, not a law, I may even say not an event, is upon
record which the origin of that people will not explain." Allowing
for the closeness to the period of origins when he wrote and allowing too for some hyperbole of statement, there still is truth in
de Tocqueville's judgment.

This volume brings together a number of documents reflecting
a wide range of colonial interests and directed toward a high-
lighting of the origins of the American people. From the very
beginning, Europeans were intensely concerned with the new
world and what its exploitation might mean for the old world. An
age of colonization succeeded an age of exploration. Dean Chapin's book ably directs the students' attention to many of the problems faced by the colonists and the colonizing power: How to
fabricate a government in a wilderness; How to organize a society

and how to provide a sound economic basis for its life; How to
develop adhesives and cements to bind communities of men and
women together within society; How, especially after the colonies
had grown in power and in wealth, to mold them into an empire
of mutually supporting units; How to regulate imperial trade and
how to use the colonies in the contests with other European
empires.

Periods of origins also witness the development of self-con-
sciousness within societies and among their leaders. Colonial
America experienced the dialectical pull between a religious ordering of life and a materialistic ordering of life. The tensions
generated by the conflict between these two produced an *American* attitude toward life, aspects of which are caught by the editor
of this volume.

Stanford University   GEORGE HARMON KNOLES

Contents

Provincial America, 1600-1763

Introduction:

Colonial Origins

THE FIRST ENGLISHMEN CAME TO AMERICA FOR various reasons, which ranged from strictly personal considerations to the highest levels of national policy. They came first as adventurers in Elizabeth's time (1558-1603), seeking the quick wealth of gold mines or routes to the Oriental trade. The physical facts of coastal North America guaranteed that they would be disappointed. To a very large degree, Elizabeth's efforts at settlement had been aspects of the queen's anti-Spanish diplomacy, and in that context, her work had been a success. Although the Queen refused to the end of her days to make peace with Spain, her successor did not. Under James I (1603-25), the opportunity for Englishmen to settle America north of the thirtieth parallel opened.

The forces that generated the trans-Atlantic migration of the English were both negative and positive. An uncertain religious settlement, a rapidly changing economy, and turbulent politics created the pressures that tended to force people out of England. Land, trading opportunities, the hope of religious freedom, and considerations of national prosperity and security were the positive factors that drew them out.

The most complete theory of the value of overseas migration and settlement was expressed by the advocates of mercantilism. Though mercantilism as a statutory system of economic control

was not installed in the English empire until the latter half of
the seventeenth century, the precedents for such a policy existed
before actual settlement began. The Elizabethan publicist, Richard Hakluyt, whose *Discourse Concerning Westerne Planting* is
included in this collection, was a prophet of mercantilism. The
theory advocated a planned economy that would guarantee economic well-being and national security. High on the list of
advantages of colonialism was the fact that regular transatlantic
commerce would stimulate shipping. The trade would not
only be profitable but would also result in a great expansion of
England's merchant fleet. In time of war the vessels could be
converted into fighting ships. Expanded oceanic trade also would
provide a valuable "nursery for seamen," which would train the
sailors who could man the ships of the line. By strengthening
naval potential, colonies would buttress the national defense.

Mercantilism was an expression of economic nationalism
that provided a formula for prosperity in an era of intense
commercial competition. Hakluyt described how colonies could
strengthen the English economy by acting as markets and
sources of supply. By the seventeenth century, the agricultural,
industrial and commercial well-being of England was bound
increasingly to the woolen industry. The production of woolen
cloth mounted steadily and created the demand for expanding
markets. Overseas settlements would provide such markets and
would do so on ideal terms because colonies could be reserved
as an exclusive, monopolized market for English manufactured
goods. In return for manufactured goods the colonies would
provide England with supplies previously imported from foreign
sources. As they speculated about the products of America, the
mercantilists' imagination ran into an extravagant vein. They expected the colonies to produce virtually every item known to
man.

As mercantilism developed, events in England created com-
pelling reasons for individual and group emigration. The en-
closure movements, which consolidated large tracts of land for
cultivation or for sheep pasture, broke up the stable pattern of
an agrarian, village society. Enclosures caused a severe disloca-
tion of population and a huge problem of rural unemployment.
Hakluyt saw in the western continent a place where these

"multitudes of loiterers and idle vagabonds" could be put to work profitably.

The English reformation created a series of religious groups that lived constantly with the fact or threat of persecution. Elizabeth had attempted to bring stability to English religious life by creating a national church in the middle ground between Roman Catholicism and extreme Protestantism. When the opportunity for overseas settlement presented itself, Elizabeth's compromise church had been in being for a generation, but it had failed to attract all Englishmen. At one side of the settlement, stood the unconverted Catholics, labeled "recusant." At all times, they lived under the ban of the law. A sudden shift in English diplomacy, a crisis with Spain or France, would activate persecution. Substantial numbers of Catholics were to seek asylum in America. For many Protestants, the Anglican Church represented an ungodly compromise with Rome. The largest group of nonconforming Protestants were the Puritans. Within the Church and in Parliament they worked for a further reformation of the religious establishment. Their fortunes hit nadir in the late 1620s when Charles I (1625-1647) repudiated the Petition of Right and launched his experiment in personal government. The great Puritan migration to New England, especially to Massachusetts Bay, coincided exactly with the period of ascendency of Archbishop William Laud and the Earl of Strafford.

A smaller group of Protestant nonconformists shared many of the religious ideas of the Puritans but advocated the separation of Church and State. These Separatists regarded a Church as a group of like-minded believers joined together by voluntary association. Such a group was the Pilgrims. In 1608 they emigrated to the Netherlands and twelve years later they came out to America and settled at Plymouth. William Bradford relates their odyssey in *Of Plymouth Plantation.*

Through the first decades the settlement of America was hard, costly and dangerous. Those who undertook migration were bold or desperate men. The crossing, either by the tempestuous North Atlantic route or the longer Canaries-West Indies route, was hazardous. Mortality rates as high as 50 per cent for a voyage are matters of record. Having arrived in America, the English encountered a climate subject to extremes, a seemingly impenetrable forest barrier and a strange, often hostile, native population. The new environment imposed harsh conditions and the arriving settlers suffered much from hunger, exposure, and epidemic disease. Though the first comers labored under great disabilities, they learned fast. Within a generation, the coastal frontier produced that essentially new man, the competent, self-reliant American pioneer. The quality of the experience of the first settlers is reported directly by William Bradford, and in retrospect by Jeremiah Dummer in his *A Defence of the New-England Charters.*

The original American settlements were private, rather than public, enterprizes. Undoubtedly the early Stuart kings wished it otherwise, but their perpetually straitened finances prevented them from undertaking the costly overseas ventures. The kings turned to individuals and groups, who, for assuming the risk, received magnificent grants of land and power through the colonial charters, which were either corporate or proprietary in form. The charter of Maryland, which was proprietary, has been included in this collection. In its tenurial and governmental aspects, it was medieval in character. Its grants of land and privilege were sweeping. Though perhaps the most liberal of the grants, the Maryland Charter is representative of the principle of colonial beginnings that were rooted in private property and privately exercised political power.

The private origins of the English colonies created both the American opportunity and the imperial dilemma. Under the auspices of corporations and proprietors the colonies began their life without the standardizing restraints of an external authority. Their growth was vigorous and was accompanied by a conviction that Englishmen in America were competent to manage their own affairs. From such a conviction a commitment to liberty, and ultimately to independence, developed. Before the seventeenth century had run its course, the American dominions had assumed a large significance in the imperial scheme. After 1660, English authorities attempted to force the colonies into a standard and uniform pattern of empire. The imperial idea collided head on with private rights, generating Edward Randolph's attacks on the private colonies and their spirited defense as exemplified in Jeremiah Dummer's pamphlet.

Political Concepts

The emigrating seventeenth century Englishman left a nation that was constantly agitated by vigorous and sometimes violent political strife. The central theme of English constitutional development was the successive attempts to establish a balance of power between the community of England and the executive power of the Crown. The Tudors had tipped the balance definitely toward royal power and this imbalance was projected into the seventeenth century. The constitutional crises of the Stuart era had as a common denominator the desire to limit the power of the King and to define the rights of the subject. The limitation of executive power and definition of individual rights were also the major themes of colonial politics.

The concept of constitution as written, fundamental, and superior law is a basic fact of American political systems, with deep colonial roots. The simplest and most primitive expression of this view is the idea that men should have a known law to live by, an idea well illustrated in the person of Thomas Hooker and in the colony of Connecticut. The original magistrates of Massachusetts Bay enforced a law compounded of the Mosaic code and their own inclinations. Though Hooker and his New Town parishioners moved into the Connecticut Valley primarily for economic reasons, there can be no doubt that Hooker was also displeased with the indefinite state of the law in the Bay Colony. His letter to John Winthrop is a vigorous protest against the unilateral use of executive power by the magistrates. Unfortunately his election sermon of 1638 has come down to us only in a shorthand note, but the essence is there: "The foundation of gov't is in the free consent of the people." Hooker's concepts had been given definite expression in the Fundamental Orders of Connecticut, which is an example of a formal and fundamental law—in fact, a constitution.

A second source of American constitutionalism was the colonial charter. At law the charters were not constitutions because they were revocable by legal processes instituted by the writs *quo warranto* or *scire facias*. Yet, the charters contained many features of constitutions and in practice the colonists regarded them as fundamental law. This collection reprints the charter of Maryland. Like other charters, the grant to the Baron Baltimore established a political society by grants of power. It also protected the rights of the subject. The entire document has an air of permanence created by the repeated condition that what is given, is given "forever." The importance that the colonists attached to charters is indicated in the Cambridge Agreement. The charter of Massachusetts Bay created an ordinary joint stock corporation. The emigrating East Anglian Puritans, led by John Winthrop, intended to transform the corporate charter into a constitution. By the Agreement they contracted one with another to come out to New England, provided that the charter come with them. Subsequently they did just that and the charter became the jealously guarded base upon which they erected the Puritan commonwealth.

Through the seventeenth century, the Crown moved intermittently against the charters. The drive to extinguish private rights culminated in parliamentary efforts to vacate all the charters in the early eighteenth century. The Reunification Bill of 1701 was but the first of a series of such attempts. Jeremiah Dummer, an agent of several New England colonies, made the most comprehensive statement for the permanence of the grants in his pamphlet, *A Defence of the New-England Charters.*

The third major source of the concept of constitution was the covenant or compact. Since the English Separatist communities existed outside the law, they established their churches using the covenant, a written contract that stated the rules by which congregations would live. The Leyden or Plymouth Separatists had come out to America to settle on the lands of the Virginia Company of London. By craft or accident the captain who brought them over landed on the territory of the Council for New England. Without authorization to be where they were, the Pilgrims turned naturally enough to the covenant and used it to create a body politic. The simple, brief Mayflower Compact established a political process and demanded the allegiance of the subscribers. It was, in fact, a constitution. This use of voluntary association to create a public authority would be repeated on each successive frontier. The Mayflower covenant, like all such frontier compacts, expressed the idea that the people were competent to create a government without reference to external authority.

Within the colonial jurisdictions, however established, the people strove successfully to install the representative principle and legislative supremacy. The commitment to these principles did not come automatically. In some of the colonies, Virginia, for example, the rigorous conditions imposed by the first effort to subdue the wilderness dictated that power be concentrated in a few hands. In others, such as Massachusetts Bay, the leaders feared that representative government would threaten the special purposes of the province. In yet others, like Maryland and New York, the proprietors regarded legislatures as menaces to their authority. But in every colony the obstacles were overcome.

Wherever the representative principle was excluded or limited, the people protested vigorously. In time, each colony won the right to make law through an elected legislature. The first legislature to be created, the Virginia House of Burgesses, convened originally in 1619. In Massachusetts Bay the magistrates yielded reluctantly to the demand for a representative assembly, and in 1632 they levied a tax without the consent of the General Court. The residents of Watertown protested the tax as a subversion of their basic rights as Englishmen. Though the magistrates carried the day and levied the tax, within two years they had yielded the right of legislation to the General Court. A half century later James, the Duke of York, attempted to govern his colony of New York without a legislature. Opposed in principle to representative government, he refused numerous requests from the province for an assembly. Ultimately he yielded and the first New York legislature immediately passed its famous Charter of Liberties which was, among other things, a strong affirmation of the principle of representative legislatures.

Though the acts of most colonial legislatures were subject to review and veto, the legislatures acted as if they were microparliaments. Consistently, and on the whole, successfully, the assemblies claimed and exercised the privileges for which the English Parliament contended during the seventeenth century. Like Parliament, the American assemblies developed as bicameral legislatures. Since there was no hereditary nobility, the appointed executive council generally served also as the upper legis-

lative house. The function of the upper house is well-illustrated
by events in Massachusetts Bay. Originally the Massachusetts
general court sat as a unicameral legislature. Within it, the
magistrates or councilors demanded the right of the "negative
voice," which meant that in addition to a simple majority of
all members, the consent of a concurrent majority of the magistrates was necessary before legislation could pass. The right of
the negative voice was debated vehemently on several occasions,
and found its resolution in the case of *Sherman* v. *Keayne*, which
is included in this collection. As a result of that case the magistrates began to sit as a separate house. The case illustrates the
role of the upper house of a bicameral legislature as a defender
of property rights.

Within all the jurisdictions the colonists claimed the rights of
Englishmen, by which they primarily meant the procedural rights
of the common law. Yet, clearly and for substantial reasons, the
common law was not available to the Englishman in the dominions. The jurisdiction of the common law courts was limited to
the realm, that is, to England, Wales, and Berwick-on-Tweed.
The courts regarded the overseas dominions as peculiarly and
especially the property of the king. The judges had ruled further
that if the common law was introduced in the dominions then
the law could only be changed by Parliament. In order to protect
their prerogative in the dominions, the kings carefully avoided
any formal introduction of the common law. On the other hand,
it was certainly in the royal interest to have colonial law and
practice reasonably uniform and reasonably consistent with
English law. To further this end, the royally granted charters
contained two restrictions: colonial law was not to be repugnant to English law, and the exercise of charter given power was
not to violate the colonists' rights as Englishmen.

The colonists consistently took the position that they abandoned no right by the act of emigration. They set up a system
of courts that administered a law that was at least a rough
facsimile of the common law. When they found opportunities to
define their rights they looked back to the English constitution
with the result that the colonial claim of right was profoundly
conservative. This is clearly illustrated in the New York Charter
of Liberties of 1683. There is not a novel provision in the docu-

ment and it is an interesting exercise to find the English source of each right claimed by the provincials.

In the seventeenth century, questions of religion necessarily became political issues. With virtually no exception, the European states pursued policies of religious uniformity. Whatever the established religion might be, it was regarded by statesmen as a main bulwark of the state. In a majority of the American colonies the rule of religious uniformity prevailed. The Anglican Church was established in several colonies and Congregationalism dominated most of New England.

For special and practical reasons the Baltimores practiced religious toleration in Maryland. They desired to establish a refuge for their fellow Roman Catholics, but knew that their proprietary holdings would not be profitable unless Protestants also settled there. In 1649 they formalized their policy of toleration in the Statute of Religious Liberty. A negatively stated law, it applied criminal sanctions to acts that denied toleration to Christians professing a belief in the Trinity.

Roger Williams of Rhode Island made a positive statement of religious freedom, which subsequently became a part of the mainstream of American constitutional practice. For Williams, religious freedom was not limited to mere toleration, it went further by advocating the absolute separation of church and state. Exiled from Massachusetts Bay for his heterodox religious and political ideas, Williams practiced toleration at Providence from the beginning. He made the most thorough statement of his view while in England where he had gone in the 1640s to get a patent for Rhode Island. While there he had entered the raging controversy between Independent and Presbyterian and had published his powerful polemic, *The Bloody Tenent of Persecution for Cause of Conscience*. The pamphlet is long and thorny; its brief preface, which states Williams' basic assumptions, is reprinted in this book. Also included is his vigorous letter to John Endecott protesting the Massachusetts governor's persecution of several Baptists.

For Williams, religious liberty had definite limits. The parable of the ship, contained in his letter to the town of Providence, suggests the obedience that all, regardless of their religious beliefs, owed to legally constituted authority. The early Quakers who appeared in New England were agitators who disturbed the public peace and invited persecution. Their views and practices were anathema to Williams and his outspoken challenge to George Fox indicates the depth of his feeling. In a sense Williams anticipated the clear and present danger doctrine of later constitutional law, in stating that liberty was to be restrained when it threatened social order.

In the area of political ideas, the provincial Americans did not develop any native theory. Statements of political theory tended to be made in the heat of some conflict to further some very practical cause. Though the weight of political belief was heavily on the conservative or authoritarian side, the whole record was one of diversity. John Winthrop, the great first governor of Massachusetts Bay, represents the colonial conservative. He believed that the power in government should be in the hands of the magistrates. To a degree he emphasized executive authority, but essentially he exalted the magistrate as judge. His attitude to a popular base for government was that of a doctrinaire conservative. In a letter to Thomas Hooker he states flatly that "the best is always the least, & of that best part the wiser part is always the lesser." In his famous "Little Speech," which is reprinted here, he advances what might be called the "divine right of magistrates."

Whether any colonial leader was democratic in a modern sense remains a subject of debate. Roger Williams' letter to Winthrop reveals a desire to create a simple government for a small community that would reflect the wishes of the inhabitants. Hooker argued that the foundation of political power was in the consent of the people. But the most thorough theoretical statement of a democratic position was made by John Wise, the pastor of Ipswich. Wise was a practicing democrat who had stood out against the arbitrary government of Sir Edmund Andros during Dominion of New England. Later he published two substantial pamphlets, both written in the context of specific disputes about the degree of centralized authority in the New England churches. Wise came out strongly for the authority of the individual, decentralized Congregational Church. In *A Vindication of the Government of New-England Churches* he developed his argument by deriving his principles of just church government from political theory and practice. Having advanced a contract theory, he analyzed the three traditional forms of government—monarchical, aristocratic, and democratic. He concluded that democracy "is a form of government, which the light of nature does highly value, and often directs to as most agreeable to the just and natural prerogatives of human beings."

The Colonial Mind and a Note on Colonial Life

Early American writers aimed to instruct rather than to please, and this purpose established the main boundaries of the colonial literary effort. The first motive for writing, and an enduring one, was a desire to leave a record of their efforts: a very substantial proportion of the early literature consists of diaries, journals, and histories. The literature left by a people mirrors their values and our early literature is dominated by theology. Sermons, tracts, and defenses of polity poured from the presses. Only the poets occupied that large area of literature commonly called *belles lettres.* Most of the poetry was religious or occasional or both. Native drama and fiction did not exist. The great vehicle of popular literature was the almanac, which was crammed with practical advice and moral aphorisms.

A first excursion into early American writing is apt to resemble a walk through a thicket of briars. The pages bristle with italics and bizarre capitalization. The syntax is strange, the punctuation casual, and the spelling erratic. Yet, it is worth the effort to overcome these technical difficulties. Whoever is not moved by William Bradford's story of the landing of the Pilgrims is an insensitive person. Hugh Jones' *The Present State of Virginia* is a model of concise description. In *A Vindication of the Government of New-England Churches,* John Wise sets out a complex argument logically and efficiently. Indeed, except for the official documents, which in all ages seem to be written in jargon, the selections in this volume are examples of direct and forceful prose.

It is hazardous to generalize about the ideas and values of a people, to attempt, for example, a description of the "colonial mind." Given the physical situation, it is remarkable that there was a colonial mind. The two outstanding facts about that mind were its early, tenacious commitment to intellectual standards and the insistence that it not be isolated from the thought of the European world.

The intellectual quality of a society is always created by a minority. In early America, the ministers dominated the world of ideas. It follows that an understanding of clerical thought will take one a long way down the road to an understanding of the colonial mind. The first, giant step toward the maintenance of American intellectual standards resulted from the Puritan desire to perpetuate a learned ministry. The founding of Harvard was symbolic of the commitment to intellectual standards; the question follows, What were those standards? In outlining the course of study at Harvard, *New England's First Fruits* makes it clear that the standards were high, liberal, and European. The setting may have been rustic, but the ideas were not.

After a first foray into the literature produced by the colonial ministry, one is apt to conclude that they were a combative, cantankerous lot and that every point was in dispute. The strong-mindedness of the ministry tends to conceal the fact that they were in agreement about the major tenets of Protestantism. We are indebted to Professors Morison and Miller for making this clear. For example, Miller argues convincingly that the area of agreement between Puritan and Anglican covered 90 per cent of the whole field of their belief.

Societies and individuals have intellectual choices which range from rabid evangelical credulity to cynical skepticism. Though conflicts over values are inevitable, there is ground for compatibility between faith and reason, as the education and works of the seventeenth century clergy evidence. The clergy were at once the heirs and purveyors of two great traditions. The tradition of faith had come down to them from medieval Christianity through the leaders of the Reformation. The tradition of rationalism derived from classical antiquity through the scholars of the Renaissance. The curriculum of Harvard College as early as the 1630s is evidence of this dual obligation.

Most societies have a vision of their ideal man and they often qualify him by describing his ideal education. Cotton Mather, a complex and in some ways self-contradictory man, set out such an ideal. His advice to young ministers is tendered to an elite. It

begins with the need for faith in the face of death. After a long
section dealing with the spiritual aspects of education, it sets
out an extended course of studies in the classics. Though not
without its prejudices, for example, his hostility to scholasticism
as expressed in his contempt for Aristotle and his preference
for Ramean logic, his advice is impressive testimony to the
weight given to humanism in defining the ideal. Nor does
Mather exclude from his ideal the theories that seventeenth-
century science had created. He encourages the young minister
to master mathematics and to learn Copernican astronomy. The
experimental scientists are recommended and Sir Isaac Newton
is held up as "our *Perpetual Dictator.*"

In the eighteenth century, the explicit compromise that accommodated faith, reason, and science and thus produced a model
for a colonial mind tended to fragment. Rationalism led down
the road to deism and liberalism; faith took the bend toward
enthusiasm and fundamentalism.

A description of the colonial economy and society is impossible here, for an outstanding fact of life in early America was
its diversity. In the collection I have tried to illustrate this
diversity with documents drawn from three places and times:
early seventeenth-century New England, early eighteenth-century
Virginia, and mid eighteenth-century Philadelphia. The documents speak for themselves. William Bradford's *Of Plymouth
Plantation* is a chronicle of the trial and triumphs of a godly
people. In *The Present State of Virginia,* Hugh Jones lines out
a concise panorama of life in a plantation colony. Three of the
Franklin documents show an early urban community striving by
various means to solve its problems of security, health, and education. The other, *Poor Richard,* is an example of colonial popular reading material.

The Colonies in the Empire

The first British Empire provides a classic example for the
study of the problems of federalism. Within the empire there
existed a very large variety of special or local interests. Over
and above these specific interests stood the interests of the empire as a whole. Though subject to considerable variation, the

local units wanted some combination of the following: a right to develop their economies along lines that seemed naturally profitable; control of political processes; no external interference in religious matters; and personal and provincial security from hostile Indians and Europeans. Imperial interest demanded an economy regulated according to the tenets of mercantilism with the aim of securing advantage for England; centralized regulation of political processes; provincial conformity to English religious policy; a plan of diplomacy and war that would advance English economic interests and guarantee national security. These two sets of interests were generally in a state of conflict and they often collided. The story of the empire is one of unsuccessful attempts to compromise these issues. At bottom the central problem of the empire was one of law enforcement.

Though their poverty forced the first Stuarts to turn to private agencies to begin the work of colonization, they attempted to maintain a measure of royal control. Prevailing legal theory assigned the basic imperial power to the King and Privy Council. In the Council, policy had its origins and colonial actions found their review. The many pressures on the Council early suggested the wisdom of special committees to direct provincial affairs. The first charter to the Virginia companies had provided for a royal council resident in England, but it was never effective. Charles I appointed several special committees for the plantations and Charles II (1660-85) revived this practice after 1660. In 1675 an enduring body, the Lords of Trade, assumed the responsibilities. By the 1690s that body had atrophied and, as a part of the reform movement of that decade, the King created the Board of Trade. It remained the central agency chiefly concerned with colonial matters down to the American Revolution.

In practice, many other agencies of the central government shared the responsibilities of imperial control; the Secretary of State for the Southern Department was politically responsible for policy. In the later colonial period, the Admiralty, largely through its system of courts, had a stake in American affairs. The Treasury, through the commissioners of customs, was responsible for the enforcement of the laws of trade. After the passage of the Plantation Act of 1673, which levied the first imperial tax in America, the agents of the commissioners appeared in the colonies in substantial numbers. Within the colonies, the Crown pinned its main hope of effective law enforcement on the royal governor. An administrative chart of the empire is very confusing and reveals overlapping authority and a general lack of effective organization.

Before 1660, the Crown moved twice to exercise its authority directly in America. On the first occasion it was successful and the result was the quashing of the Virginia Charter by legal process. After 1624, styling itself the Old Dominion, Virginia furnished the model of the royal colony. The royal power was frustrated when, during the 1630s, private interests combined with the high church policy of Archbishop William Laud to produce an attack on the charter of Massachusetts Bay, but the Puritans made a successful defense.

Immediately after the Stuart restoration of 1660, Parliament moved to give mercantilism its statutory form. The major principles of the navigation system were that shipping should be a national monopoly, that certain valuable products should be shipped only to England, and that the colonial market should be reserved for the English manufacturer. In effect, the mercantile policy dictated that substantial portions of the import and export trade of the colonies should flow through England. After the passage of the acts, the central imperial problem became to force the Americans to trade within the statutory pattern.

Evidence of American nonconformity to imperial plans soon began arriving at London. England's most active agent was Edward Randolph, a man who literally became a transatlantic commuter in the last quarter of the seventeenth century. His first target and always his favorite one was Massachusetts Bay. His original charges tended to emphasize the heterodox political and religious practices of the Bay Colony. Though he never abandoned this theme, he gradually came to stress the failure, first of New England and then of all the colonies, to obey the laws of navigation and trade. Though Randolph proposed many specific reforms, his ultimate answer to the imperial problem was the extinction of the private colonies and consolidation of colonial units.

The first major attempt to implement the policy of consolidation came during the reign of James II (1685-88). To his own colony of New York, James added all of the New England colonies. He appointed Sir Edmund Andros governor of this Dominion of New England. Andros ruled his vast domain with the aid of men like Randolph and Joseph Dudley and he did so without a representative assembly. A vestige of the legislature remained in the appointed council but Andros completely dominated that body and, in effect, governed as an autocrat. Andros governed effectively. In short order he suppressed the town meetings, collected taxes by executive decree, introduced the Anglican Church at Boston, invalidated New England land titles, and clamped down on illegal traders. Had Andros' government survived for any number of years it would have furnished a model for other large colonial units and American history might well have run in another course. But his government did not endure. The flight from England of James II, the invasion by William of Orange (who reigned jointly with Mary II as William III, 1689-1702), and the Glorious Revolution signaled an American revolt that brought down the Dominion of New England as if it were a house of sand.

With the collapse of the Dominion, Randolph and like-minded imperialists turned to other methods of control, which resulted in the changes of the 1690s. In 1695, the new Board of Trade assumed responsibility for the policies and administration of the empire. The following year, Parliament passed a navigation act, largely an administrative measure, which imposed standard rules on royal officials in America. Before 1700, a series of vice-admiralty courts had been created in the colonies. Then, in the first years of the eighteenth century, the policy of colonial consolidation was revived. It took the form of a series of attempts to pass statutes in Parliament that would have wiped out all of the private colonies. The reasons for the failure of these Reunification Bills were multiple. To a degree, circumstances created by crowded legislative calendars defeated them. The colonies employed effective agents who commanded considerable political power as they lobbied against the bills. Perhaps most important was the fact that the bills were overt attacks on private property rights, which invoked the conservatism of many members of Parliament. Dummer's *A Defense of the New-England*

Charters summarized the American arguments. With the failure of the Reunification Bills the period of "salutary neglect" properly may be said to have begun.

The first British Empire had external as well as internal problems. The empire had been conceived in international conflict. It grew and expanded as a result of war, and, in a sense, it expired in that context. By the middle of the sixteenth century the Iberian powers, Portugal and Spain, had pre-empted the imperial opportunities. England had some claims based on voyages of discovery, but was largely excluded from the new trading opportunities. Yet, a little more than two centuries later, Great Britain had put together the greatest empire the world had seen. The concern here is to examine how English foreign policy accomplished the expansion of commercial and colonial opportunity.

Beginning with Elizabeth, the aims of English foreign policy were essentially two: to maintain the European power balance, and to expand the English trading area. Usually these aims were in harmony. For example, when Spain in the sixteenth century under Philip II (1556-98) and France in the seventeenth and eighteenth century under Louis XIV (1643-1715) threatened to dominate Europe, those nations were either already in a strong imperial position or were thrusting in that direction. Under these circumstances vigorous anti-Spanish or anti-French policies served the power balance and mercantile aims of English diplomacy. The Dutch rivalry of the latter half of the seventeenth century was an exception to this coincidence of interest in national foreign policy. In that conflict, the English statesmen had to face hard choices. They chose, in the three Dutch wars, to risk upsetting the balance of power in order to extend the imperial interests.

The aims of English policy created a dilemma in regard to the strategy by which policy would be implemented. The maintenance of the European power balance seemed to point toward the direct intervention of English troops in continental wars. The desire for trade supremacy clearly dictated the aggressive use of sea power. In most instances statesmen chose to rely primarily on sea power and in every case they did so to a considerable degree. Generally England concentrated on her maritime effort and supported her European allies with subsidies. She made her most conspicuous departure from this plan of action in the War of the Spanish Succession (1702-13). The war leader, the Duke of Marlborough, conducted a series of masterful campaigns in the Germanies and the Low Countries. He used sea power primarily in the Mediterranean as an adjunct of his continental operations, but he did not neglect the maritime aims. Under the circumstances, he thought that victories over the armies of Louis XIV would be rewarded with commercial and colonial concessions. The Treaty of Utrecht of 1713 proved him right.

Though British maritime ambitions were world-wide, this analysis is concerned primarily with her American aims and in an ancillary way with her African interests. English interest focused in the Caribbean and her American and North African stakes became valuable largely in that context. The West Indies had the potential to produce subtropical items that were much valued in Europe. Africa furnished the West Indian labor in the form of Negro slaves. During the seventeenth century the island holdings became so highly specialized that the planters imported their food and many other basic supplies. The North American colonies assumed their major significance as suppliers of the West Indian plantations.

From the time of Elizabeth I, England persistently pursued an anti-Spanish policy, aimed at the Caribbean heart of Spain's American empire. The conflict began there, with the raids of John Hawkins and Francis Drake. The War of the Spanish Armada, ended by the Treaty of London of 1604, fixed the northern perimeter of the Spanish empire and opened North America to English colonization. Oliver Cromwell (Lord Protector of the Commonwealth, 1653-58) revived the policy with his "Western Design," which made Jamaica an English possession. During the 1670s the north European nations fought a series of disorderly battles in the Caribbean. Those were the days of the buccaneer, when there was "no peace beyond the [demarcation] line." The Treaties of Madrid and Breda confirmed English possession of a half a dozen islands. The push into the Spanish trading area appeared again at Utrecht where Great Britain was awarded the *assiento*, the contract to supply the Spanish American plantations with African slaves. After 1721, Robert Walpole diverted English policy from overt action against Spain for twenty years, but the desire and the hostility persisted. The maltreatment of English traders by the Spanish coast guard created a series of incidents that wrecked Walpole's policy of peace with the outbreak, in 1739, of the War of Jenkins' Ear. Walpole made a last effort at negotiation in the Convention of Pardo. Among the documents reprinted here is William Pitt's powerful indictment of the Convention as an abandonment of vital English maritime interests. Spain was drawn into the last war of the colonial era, the Seven Years' War (1754-63), as an ally of France, and as a result she lost the Floridas to England by the Treaty of Paris of 1763.

When England started on the road to empire in the late sixteenth century, her interests coincided with those of the Dutch and French. Sea Beggar and Huguenot Corsair raided into the Spanish empire along with Elizabeth's Sea Dogs. As Spanish and Portuguese power shrank, the Dutch, French, and English fell out among themselves. The Anglo-Dutch rivalry was essentially commercial, and reached the point of decision in the Second Dutch War after the Stuart Restoration of 1660. The two nations assumed that the seas of the world were not large enough for them both. With hostile reports pouring in from George Downing, the English ambassador at the Hague, James, the Duke of York, launched a two-pronged aggression that drove the Dutch from New Netherlands and gave the English a substantial stake in the African trade. The anti-Dutch policy is illustrated in the collection by documents written by George Downing.

The climactic struggle with France came in the wake of the Glorious Revolution of 1689. In two wars, Louis XIV had put himself in a dominant European position with aggressive northward moves. William III brought England into the War of the League of Augsburg (1689-97). That war, the War of the Spanish Succession (1702-13), and the War of the Austrian Succession (1744-48), were primarily European. The first two fixed the limits of French ambition; the third turned on the distribution of power in the Germanies. Each of these conflicts had its colonial counterpart—King William's, Queen Anne's, and King

George's War—but these were mere side shows. The most deci-
sive of the first three wars of the Anglo-French conflict was that
of the Spanish Succession. Under Marlborough, English armies
triumphed in Europe and breached the frontiers of France.
England measured her success at Utrecht where she acquired
Gibraltar, Minorca, Hudson's Bay, Nova Scotia, Newfoundland,
and the *assiento* rights.

By 1750 it was clear that Great Britain and France were
engaged in a world-wide race for imperial pre-eminence. The
new conflict, the Seven Years', or French and Indian War, came
on after the two nations collided in the Ohio River Valley. The
war began badly for Britain and the first years were a chronicle of catastrophe. In 1757, William Pitt came to power; he
appointed new commanders and employed them to concentrate
effort in North America. Pitt saw control of the continent as the
key to all. Who controlled it, controlled the Caribbean and an
important part of world trade. In 1758, the tide turned and in
the following two years the British rush to victory became a
torrent. In 1760 Spain entered the contest as an ally of France.
Pitt lost office on the issue of the conduct of the war. The next
year, the new king, George III (1760-1820), began the negotiations that led to the Treaty of Paris of 1763. Though Pitt
condemned the peace as an abandonment of English interests,
the nation made great gains. At Paris, England won Canada,
the Spanish Floridas, and a dominant role in India.

By 1763, British foreign policy had realized its aims. The
nation had acted as the arbiter of European affairs and no
nation threatened her security. In commerce and empire England
stood in an absolutely pre-eminent position. So circumstanced,
British statesmen turned to the job of reorganizing the expanded
empire. The result of those efforts was the American Revolution
and the end of the first British Empire.

1

Richard Hakluyt

Discourse Concerning Westerne Planting (1584-1585)[1]

Richard Hakluyt (1552?-1616) was a graduate of Oxford. Though
he continuously held a variety of ecclesiastical positions, the dominant theme of his life was an intense interest in maritime affairs,
especially the voyages of exploration and discovery. His collected
works are a main primary source of the maritime expansion of Europe.
His first published volume, *Divers Voyages touching the Discovery of
America*, appeared in 1582, bringing him to the attention of highly
placed English officials, including the lord high admiral. The year after
the publication of *Divers Voyages* he went to Paris as the chaplain to
the English ambassador. There he gathered additional materials concerning European maritime activity and he also wrote the *Discourse
Concerning Westerne Planting*. In 1589 he published *The Principall
Navigations, Voaiges, and Discoveries of the English Nation;* ten years
later a vastly expanded version was printed. This was Hakluyt's great
work, epic in theme and treatment and a classic of vigorous Elizabethan prose.

His interest in the sea quite naturally led Hakluyt to an interest in
colonization. The *Discourse Concerning Westerne Planting* argues the
advantages that would accrue to England if she established colonies
overseas. In it, Hakluyt appears as a prophet of a theory of economic
action that would later be called mercantilism. The *Discourse* was not
published in Hakluyt's day but it did circulate in manuscript and we
know that Elizabeth possessed a copy.

Wallace Notestein, *The English People on the Eve of Colonization,
1603-1630* (New York: Harper & Row, 1954) is a good recent account
of the prevailing social and economic conditions. Alfred L. Rowse,
The Expansion of Elizabethan England (New York: St. Martin's Press,

1. Charles Deane (ed.), *Documentary History of the State of Maine*
(Cambridge: John Wilson & Son, 1877), II, 1-161 [in Collections of the
Maine Historical Society.]

1955) is vigorously written. The most comprehensive scholarly account of the mercantile system is Ephraim Lipson, *The Economic History of England* (London: Adam & Charles Black, 1948). Volumes II, III are entitled "The Age of Mercantilism." Also excellent on mercantilism is Lawrence A. Harper, *The English Navigation Laws; a Seventeenth-Century Experiment in Social Engineering* (New York: Columbia University Press, 1939). In reading the *Discourse*, note (1) what religious objectives Hakluyt thought might be advanced by overseas expansion; (2) how he thought England's demographic problems might be relieved; (3) the contemplated effects of colonization upon trade; (4) the ways in which expansion would aid England's contest with Spain; (5) what Hakluyt considered would be the effect of colonization upon the royal revenues; (6) the expected impact of colonization upon English sea power; and (7) Hakluyt's summary of reasons why England should colonize America.

[Note on spelling: To a large degree, original spelling has been retained in all the documents. Changes have been made in a few instances to clarify meaning.]

Cap. I. That this Western discovery will be greatly for the enlargement of the gospel of Christ, whereunto the princes of the reformed religion are chiefly bound, amongst whom her majesty is principal.

. . . Even so wee, whiles wee have soughte to goe into other countries (I woulde I might say to preache the gospell), God by the frustratinge of our actions semeth to forbydd us to followe those courses, and the people of AMERICA crye oute unto us, their nexte neighboures, to come and helpe them, and bring unto them the gladd tidinges of the gospell. Unto the prince and people that shalbe the occasion of this worthie worke, and shall open their cofers to the furtheraunce of this most godly enterprise, God shall open the bottomles treasures of his riches, and fill them with aboundaunce of his hidden blessinges; as he did to the goodd Queene Isabella, which beinge in extreme necessitie, laied her owne jewells to gage for money to furnishe out Columbus for the firste discovery of the West Indies.

And this enterprise the princes of the relligion (amonge whome her Majestie is principall) oughte the rather to take in hande, because the papistes confirme themselves and drawe other to theire side, shewinge that they are the true Catholicke churche because they have bene the onely converters of many millions of infidells to Christianitie. Yea, I myselfe have bene demaunded of them, how many infidells have been by us converted? Whereunto, albeit I alleaged the example of the mynisters which were sente from Geneva with Villegagnon into Bresill, and those that wente with John Ribault into Florida, as also those of our nation that went with Ffrobisher, Sir Fraunces Drake, and Ffenton; yet in very deede I was not able to name any one infidell by them converted. But God, quoth I, hath his tyme for all men, whoe calleth some at the nynthe, and some at the eleventh houer. And if it please him to move the harte of her Majestie to put her helpinge hande to this godly action, she shall finde as willinge subjectes of all sortes as any other prince in all Christendome. And as for the boastinge of your conversion of such multitudes of infidells, it may justly be compted rather a perversion, seeinge you have drawen them as it were oute of Sylla into Charibdis, that is to say, from one error into another. Nowe therefore I truste the time is at hande when by her Majesties forwardnes in this enterprise, not only this objection and suche like shalbe aunswered by our frutefull labor in Godds harvest amonge the infidells, but also many inconveniences and strifes amongest ourselves at home, in matters of ceremonies, shalbe ended. For those of the clergye which by reason of idlenes here at home are now alwayes coyninge of newe opynions, havinge by this voyadge to set themselves on worke in reducinge the savages to the chefe principles of our faith, will become lesse contentious, and be contented with the truthe in relligion alreadie established by authoritie. So they that shall beare the name of Christians shall shewe themselves worthye of their vocation, so shall the mouthe of the adversarie be stopped, so shall contention amongest brethren be avoyded, so shal the gospell amonge infidells be published.

Cap. IV. That this enterprize will be for the manifolde employment of nombers of idle men, and for bredinge of many sufficient, and for utteraunce of the greate quantitie of the comodities of our realme.

It is well worthe the observation to see and consider what the like voyadges of discoverye and plantinge in the Easte and Weste Indies hath wroughte in the kingdomes of Portingale and Spayne; bothe which realmes, beinge of themselves poore

and barren and hardly able to susteine their inhabitaunts, by
their discoveries have founde suche occasion of employmente,
that these many yeres we have not herde scarcely of any pirate
of those twoo nations; whereas wee and the Frenche are moste
infamous for our outeragious, common, and daily piracies.
Againe, when hearde wee almoste of one theefe amongest them?
The reason is, that by these, their newe discoveries, they have
so many honest wayes to set them on worke, as they rather wante
men then meanes to employe them. But wee, for all the statutes
that hitherto can be devised, and the sharpe execution of the
same in poonishinge idle and lazye persons, for wante of sufficient occasion of honest employmente, cannot deliver our
commonwealthe from multitudes of loyterers and idle vaga-
bondes. Truthe it is, that throughe our longe peace and seldome
sicknes (twoo singuler blessinges of Almightie God) wee are
growen more populous than ever heretofore; so that nowe there
are of every arte and science so many, that they can hardly lyve
one by another, nay rather they are readie to eate upp one
another; yea many thousandes of idle persons are within this
realme, which, havinge no way to be sett on works, be either
mutinous and seeke alteration in the state, or at leaste very
burdensome to the commonwealthe, and often fall to pilferinge
and thevinge and other lewdnes, whereby all the prisons of the
lande are daily pestred and stuffed full of them, where either
they pitifully pyne awaye, or els at lengthe are miserably
hanged, even xx^{ti}. at a clappe oute of some one jayle. Whereas
if this voyadge were put in execution, these pety theves mighte
be condempned for certen yeres in the westerne partes, especially in Newefounde lande, in sawinge and fellinge of tymber
for mastes of shippes, and deale boordes; in burninge of the
firres and pine trees to make pitche, tarr, rosen, and sope ashes;
in beatinge and workinge of hempe for cordage; and, in the
more southerne partes, in settinge them to worke in mynes of
golde, silver, copper, leade, and iron; in dragginge for perles
and currall; in plantinge of suger canes, as the Portingales have
done in Madera; in mainenteinaunce and increasinge of silke
wormes for silke, and in dressinge the same; in gatheringe of
cotten whereof there is plentie; in tillinge of the soile there for
graine; in dressinge of vines whereof there is great aboundaunce

for wine; olives, whereof the soile is capable, for oyle; trees for oranges, lymons, almondes, figges, and other frutes, all which are founde to growe there already; in sowinge of woade and madder for diers, as the Portingales have don in the Azores; in dressinge of raw hides of divers kindes of beastes; in makinge and gatheringe of salte, as in Rochel and Bayon, which may serve for the newe lande fisshinge; in killinge the whale, seale, porpose, and whirlepoole for trayne oile; in fisshinge, saltinge, and dryenge of linge, codde, salmon, herringe; in makinge and gatheringe of hony, waxe, turpentine; in hewinge and shapinge of stone, as marble, jeate, christall, freestone, which will be goodd balaste for our shippes homewardes, and after serve for noble buildinges; in makinge of caske, oares, and all other manner of staves; in buildinge of fortes, townes, churches; in powdringe and barrellinge of fishe, fowles, and fleshe, which will be notable provision for sea and lande; in dryenge, sortinge, and packinge of fethers, whereof may be had there marvelous greate quantitie.

Besides this, such as by any kinde of infirmitie cannot passe the seas thither, and now are chardgeable to the realme at home, by this voyadge shal be made profitable members, by employinge them in England in makinge of a thousande triflinge thinges, which will be very goodd marchandize for those countries where wee shall have moste ample vente thereof.

And seinge the savages of the Graunde Bay, and all alonge the mightie ryver that ronneth upp to Canada and Hochelaga, are greately delighted with any cappe or garment made of course wollen clothe, their contrie beinge colde and sharpe in the winter, it is manifeste wee shall finde greate utteraunce of our clothes, especially of our coursest and basest northerne doosens, and our Irishe and Welshe frizes and rugges; whereby all occupations belonginge to clothinge and knittinge shalbe freshly sett on worke, as cappers, knitters, clothiers, wollmen, carders, spynners, weavers, fullers, sheremen, dyers, drapers, hatters, and such like, whereby many decayed townes may be repaired.

In somme, this enterprice will mynister matter for all sortes and states of men to worke upon; namely, all severall kindes of artificers, husbandmen, seamen, marchauntes, souldiers, capitaines, phisitions, lawyers, devines, cosmographers, hidrographers, astronomers, historiographers; yea, olde folkes, lame persons, women, and younge children, by many meanes which hereby shall still be mynistred unto them, shalbe kepte from idlenes, and be made able by their owne honest and easie labour to finde themselves, withoute surchardginge others.

Nowe if her Majestie take these westerne discoveries in hande, and plante there, it is like that in shorte time wee shall vente as greate a masse of clothe in those partes as ever wee did in the Netherlandes, and in tyme moche more; which was the opinion of that excellent man, Mr. Roberte Thorne, extante in printe in the laste leafe savinge one of his discourse to Doctor Lea, embassador for King Henry the Eighte, in Spaine, with Charles the Emperour, whose wordes are these: And althoughe (saieth he) wee wente not into the said ilandes of spicerye, for that they are the Emperours or Kinges of Portingale, wee shoulde by the way, and comynge once to the lyne equinoctiall, finde landes no lesse riche of golde and spicerie, as all other landes are under the said lyne equinocticall; and also shoulde, if wee may passe under the northe, enjoye the navigation of all Tartarye, which should be no lesse profitable to our comodities of clothe, then those spiceries to the Emperour and Kinge of Portingale.

This beinge soe, it cometh to passe, that whatsoever clothe wee shall vente on the tracte of that firme, or in the ilandes of the same, or in other landes, ilandes, and territories beyonde, be they within the circle articke or withoute, all these clothes, I say, are to passe oute of this realme full wroughte by our naturall subjectes in all degrees of labour. And if it come aboute in tyme that wee shall vente that masse there that wee vented in the Base Contries, which is hoped by greate reason, then shall all that clothe passe oute of this realme in all degrees of labour full wroughte by the poore naturall subjectes of this realme, like as the quantitie of our clothe dothe passe that goeth hence to Russia, Barbarie, Turkye, Persia, &c. . . .

And on the other side wee are to note, that all the comodities wee shall bringe thence, wee shall not bringe them wroughte, as wee bringe now the comodities of Fraunce and Flaunders, &c., but shall receave them all substaunces unwroughte, to the employmente of a wonderfull multitude of the poore subjectes of this realme in returne. And so to conclude, what in the nomber of thinges to goe oute wroughte, and to come in unwroughte, there nede not one poore creature to steale, to starve, or to begge as they doe.

And to answer objections; where fooles for the swarminge of beggers alleage that the realme is too populous, Salomon saieth, that the honour and strengthe of a prince consisteth in the multitude of the people. And if this come aboute, that worke may be had for the multitude, where the realme hath nowe one thousande for the defence thereof, the same may have five thousande. For when people knowe howe to live, and howe to mayneteyne and feede their wives and children, they will not abstaine from mariage as nowe they doe. And the soile thus aboundinge with corne, fleshe, milke, butter, cheese, herbes, rootes, and frutes, &c., and the seas that environ the same so infinitely aboundinge in fishe, I dare truly affirme, that if the nomber in this realme were as greate as all Spaine and Ffraunce have, the people beinge industrious, I say, there shoulde be founde victualls enoughe at the full in all bounty to suffice them all. And takinge order to cary hence thither our clothes made in hose, coates, clokes, whoodes, &c., and to returne thither hides of their owne beastes, tanned and turned into shoes and bootes, and other skinnes of goates, whereof they have store, into gloves, &c., no doubte but wee shall sett on worke in this realme, besides sailers and suche as shalbe seated there in those westerne discovered contries, at the leaste C. M. subjectes, to the greate abatings of the goodd estate of subjectes of forreine princes, enemies, or doubtfull frendes, and this *absque injuria,* as the lawyers say, albeit not *sine dammo.* And havinge a vente of lynnen, as the Spaniardes have in the rest of that firme, wee may sett our people, in making the same, infinitely on worke, and in many other thinges besides; which time will bringe aboute, thoughe nowe, for wante of knowledge and full experience of this trade, wee cannot enter into juste accompte of all particulers.

Cap. VII. What speciall meanes may bringe Kinge Phillippe from his highe throne, and make him equall to the princes his neighboures; wherewithall is shewed his weakeness in the West Indies.

Firste, it is to be considered that his domynions and territories oute of Spaine lye farr distant from Spaine, his chefest force; and farr distante one from another; and are kepte by greate tyrannie; and *quos metuunt oderunt* [whom they fear they hate]. And the people kepte in subjection desire nothinge more than freedome. And like as a little passage given to water, it maketh his owne way; so give but a small meane to suche kepte in tyranie, they will make their owne way to libertie; which way may easely be made. And entringe into the consideration of the way how this Phillippe may be abased, I meane firste to begynne with the West Indies, as there to laye a chefe foundation for his overthrowe. And like as the foundation of the strongest holde undermyned and removed, the mightiest and strongest walles fall flatt to the earthe; so this prince, spoiled or intercepted for a while of his treasure, occasion by lacke of the same is geven that all his territories in Europe oute of Spaine slide from him, and the Moores enter into Spaine it selfe, and the people revolte in every forrein territorie of his, and cutt the throates of the proude hatefull Spaniardes, their governours. For this Phillippe already owinge many millions, and of late yeres empaired in credite, bothe by lacke of abilitie of longe tyme to pay the same, and by his shameful losse of his Spaniardes and dishonors in the Lowe Contries, and by lacke of the yerely renewe of his revenewe, he shall not be able to wage his severall garrisons kepte in his severall frontiers, territories, and places, nor to corrupte in princes courtes, nor to doe many feates. And this weyed, wee are to knowe what Phillip is in the West Indies; and that wee be not abused with Spanish braggs, and made to beleve what he is not; and so, drawen into vain feare, suffer fondly and childishly our owne utter spoile. And therefore wee are to understande that Phillippe rather governeth in the West Indies by opinion, then by mighte; ffor the small manred of Spaine, of itself beinge alwayes at the best slenderly peopled, was never able to rule so many regions, or to kepe in subjection such worldes of people as be there, were it not for the error of the Indian people, that thincke he is that he is not, and that doe imagine that Phillippe hath a thousande Spaniardes for every single naturall subjecte that he hath there. And like as the Romaynes, allured hither into Britaine, perced the Iland, and planted here and there in the mouthes of rivers and upon straites, and kepte colonies, as at Westchester upon the River of Dee, at York upon the River of Owse, and upon the Rivers of Thames and Severne, and yet in truthe never enioyed more of the contries rounde aboute then the Englishe, planted at Bulloine and Calice, did of the French soile adjoyninge, nor in effecte had the Brittishe nation at comaundement; even so hath the Spaniarde perced the Indies, and planted here and there very thinlye and slenderlye, withoute havinge the Indian multitude in subjection, or in their townes and fortes any nomber to holde any of them againste the meanest force of a prince; so as in truthe the Spaniarde is very weake there. And it is knowen to Sir Fraunces Drake, and to Mr. Hawkins, and Miles Phillipps (which Miles lyved xiiij. yeres in Nova Spania), and to dyvers others of her Majesties subjectes besides that have been there, that the ilandes there abounde with people and nations that rejecte the proude and bluddy government of the Spaniarde, and that doe mortally hate the Spaniarde. And they also knowe that the Moores, and suche as the Spaniardes have broughte thither for the mynes and for slavery, have fledd from them into the inlandes, and of them selves maineteine in many places frontier warres againste the Spaniarde, and many tymes so prevaile, and especially of late, that the Spaniardes have bene inforced to sende the Spanishe marchauntes them selves into the warres, althoughe it be againste the special privledges graunted by Charles, the late Emperour, to the marchauntes, as may plainely appere by Spanishe marchauntes letters taken by Sir Fraunces Drake passinge in the sea of Sur towarde Panama, to be conveyed into Spaine. And it is thoughte that Sir Fraunces Drake and some other Englishe are of so great credite with the Symerons and with those that mayneteyne those frontier warrs, that he mighte, bringinge thither a fewe capitaines and some of our meaner souldiers late trayned in the Base Contries, with archers and lighte furniture, &c., bringe to passe that, joyninge with those inland people, Kinge Phillippe mighte either be deprived of his governemente there, or at the leaste of the takinge of his yerely benefite of the mynes. Thus with small chardge and fewe men, nowe and then renewinge this matter by a few sailes to be sent thither for the comforte of suche as shalbe there resident, and for the incouragemente of the Symerons, greater effecte may followe then by meetinge with his golden flete, or by takinge of his treasures once or twise at the sea; for by this meanes, or by a platforme well to be sett downe, England may enjoye the benefite of the Indian mynes, or at the leaste kepe Phillippe from possessinge the same.

Hereunto if wee adde our purposed westerne discoveries, and there plante and people really, and fortifie strongly, and there builde shippes and maineteine a navy in special porte or portes, wee may by the same either encounter the Indian fleete, or be at hande as it were to yelde freshe supplye, courage, and comforte, by men or munition, to the Chichimici and the Symerons and suche other as shalbe incited to the spoile of the mynes; which in tyme will, if it be not looked to, bringe all princes to weake estate, that Phillippe, either for relligion or other cause, dothe hate; as the aforesaide Monsieur de Aldegond, in his pithie and moste earneste exhortation to all Christian kinges, princes, and potentates to beware of Kinge Phillipps ambitious growinge, dothe wisely and moste providently forwarne.

To this may be added (the realme swarming with lustie youthes that be turned to no profitable use), there may be sente bandes of them into the Base Contries in more rounde nombers then are sente as yet. Ffor if he presently prevaile there, at our doors, farewell the traficque that els wee may have there (whereof wise men can say moche). And if he settle there, then let the realme saye adewe to her quiet state and safetie.

If these enter into the due consideration of wise men, and if platformes of these thinges be sett downe and executed duelye and with spede and effecte, no doubte but the Spanishe empire falles to the grounde, and the Spanishe kings shall be lefte bare as Aesops proude crowe; the peacocke, the perot, the pye, and the popingey, and every other birde havinge taken home from him his gorgeous fethers, he will, in shorte space, become a laughinge stocke for all the worlde; with such a mayme to the Pope and to that side, as never hapned to the sea of Rome by the practise of the late Kinge of famous memory, her Majesties father, or by all the former practises of all the Protestant princes of Germanie, or by any other advise layde downe by Monsieur de Aldegond, here after by them to be put in execution. If you touche him in the Indies, you touche the apple of his eye; for take away his treasure, which is *neruus belli*, [sinews of war], and which he hath almoste oute of his West Indies, his olde bandes of souldiers will soone be dissolved, his purposes defeated, his power and strengthe diminished, his pride abated, and his tyranie utterly suppressed.

Cap. XII. That the passage in this voyadge is easie and shorte, that it cutteth not nere the trade of any other mightie princes, or nere their contries, that it is to be perfourmed at all times of the yere, and nedeth but one kinde of winde; that Ireland, beinge full of goodd havens on the southe and weste side, is the nerest parte of Europe to it, which by this trade shalbe in more securitie, and the sooner drawen to more civilitie.

In this voyadge wee may see by the globe that wee are not to passe the burnte zone, nor to passe throughe the frozen seas, but in a temperate climate unto a contrie muche like to those partes of Gascoigne and Guyen, where heretofore our nation for a longe tyme have inhabited. And it requireth not, as longe voyadges doe, the takinge in of freshe water by the way in divers places, by reason it may be sailed in five or sixe weekes. Whereby the marchante nede (not) to expecte twoo or three yeres for one returne, as in the voyadge of Sir Fraunces Drake, of Fenton and William Hawkins; but may receave twoo returnes every yere in the selfe same shippes, I saye, and well repose themselves at their arryvalls; which thinge I myselfe have seene and understoode in Ffraunce this presente yere don by the Frenchemen; whoe, settinge furthe in January, broughte their banke fishe which they tooke on the Bancke, forty or three-score leagues from Newfoundelande, to Roan, in greate quantitie, by the ende of May, and afterwarde returned this yere againe to the fisshinge, and are looked for at home towardes the fifte of November. To the spedy perfourmaunce of which voyadge this is a speciall furtheraunce: that whereas moste of our other voyadges of like lengthe require twoo or three sortes of windes at the leaste, one onely winde suffiseth to make this; which was no doubte the cause of the quicke returne of my frende Stephen Bellinger of Roan, whoe departed from Newhaven in January was twelve monethes, arryved at Cape Briton in xx^{ti}. daies space, and from thence discouered very diligently CC. leagues towardes Norumbega, and had traficque with the people in tenne or twelue places; founde a towne conteyninge fourescore houses, and returned home, with a diligent description of the coaste, in the space of foure monethes, with many comodities of the contrie, which he shewed me.

Moreover this passage is neither by the Straites of Giberaulter, nor on the coastes of Spaine, Portingall, Fraunce, nor Flanders, neither by the Sounde of Denmarke, nor Wardhouse in Norwey; so as in takinge our course on the highe seas wee shall not be in daunger of the corsaries in the Levant, nor of the gallies of Barbarie, nor of the Turke, nor of any state of Italie, neither of the Spaniarde, the Frenche, nor the Dane, nor of any other prince nor potentate within the Sounde in the northe, or in the northeaste partes of the worlde.

Wee may also travell thither and perfourme the same at all times of the yere, with the like facilitie as our marchantes of Bristowe, Weymouthe, and other partes of the West Contries travell for woade to the iles of St. Mighell and Tercera (which are halfe the way thither) all the yere longe. For this coaste is never subjecte to the ise, which is never lightly seene to the southe of Cape Razo in Newfounde lande.

Besides this, in our way as wee passe to and froe, wee shall have in tempestes and other necessities the portes of Ireland to our aide, and no nerer coaste of any enemye. Moreover by the ordinary entercourse wee may annoye the enemyes to Ireland, and succour the Queens Majesties faithfull subjects, and drawe the Irishe by little and little to more civilitie; and in shorte tyme wee may yelde them from the coastes of America whatsoever comodities they nowe receave at the handes of the Spaniardes. So the Spaniardes shall wante the ordynarye vitualls they receave every yere from thence, whereby they cannot contynue traficque, nor fall so aptly to practize againste our governemente there as heretofore by their trade thither they have don and doe daily, to the greate expences of her Majestie, and no small indaungeringe and troublinge of our state.

And to conclude: in tradinge to these contries wee shall not nede, for feare of the Spanishe bloudy Inquisition, to throwe our bibles and prayer bookes over boorde into the sea before

our arryvall at their portes, as these many yeres wee have don
and yet doe, nor take suche horrible oathes as are exacted of
our men by the Spanishe searchers, to suche dayly wilfull and
highe offence of Almightie God, as we are driven to continually
in followinge our ordinary trafficque into the Kinge of Spaines
domynions; whereof at large wee have spoken before in the
seconde chapiter.

Cap. XIII. That hereby the revenewes and customes of her Majestie,
both outewarde and inwarde, shall mightely be inlarged by the toll,
excises, and other dueties which withoute oppression may be raysed.

The manifolde testimonies, verbatim alleaged by me in the
thirde chapiter, of John Ribault, John Verarsanus, Stephen
Gomes, Vasques de Coronado, Jacques Cartier, Gasper Corterialis,
and others, which all were the discoverers of the coaste and
inland of America betwene 30 and 63 degrees, prove infallibly
unto us that golde, silver, copper, perles, pretious stones, and
turqueses, and emraldes, and many other commodities, have
bene by them founde in those regions. To which testimonies I
shoulde have added many more if I had not feared to be tedious.
Nowe the fifte parte of all these aforenamed comodities cannot
choose but amounte to a greate matter, beinge yerely reserved
unto her Majestie, accordinge to the tenor of the patent graunted
by King Henry the Seaventh in the xjth. yere of his raigne to
John Gabote and his three sonnes, Lewes, Sebastian, and
Sancius. . . .

What gaines this imposition may turne unto the Crowne of
England in shorte tyme wee may more then gesse, havinge but
an eye to the Kinge of Spaines revenewes, which he nowe hath
oute of all his domynions in all the West Indies.

The like in all respectes may be saied of the revenewes of
the Crowne of Portingale, which, beinge of itselfe one of the
smallest and poorest kingdomes of all Christendome, became in
shorte space so riche and honourable soone after their entringe
into their southesterne discoveries, traficques, and conquestes,
that, before the deathe of their late younge kinge Sebastian,
their embassadors woulde strive and challenge for the chefest
place with the embassadores of the greatest kinges of Christen-

dome; as I have hearde it dyvers tymes spoken at Paris at my lordes table by men of greate honour and experience, in which cities moste princes and states of Christendome have their embassadors commonly resident.

To leave them and to come to our nation, I say that amonge other meanes to encrease her Majesties customes this shalbe one, especially that by plantinge and fortifieinge nere Cape Briton, what by the strengthe of our shipps beinge harde at hande, and bearinge the sway already amongst all nations that fishe at Newfoundelande, and what by the fortes that there may be erected and helde by our people, wee shall be able to inforce them, havinge no place els to repaire unto so convenient, to pay us suche a contynual custome as shall please us to lay upon them; which imposition of twoo or three hundred shippes laden yerely with sondry sortes of fishe, trane oyle, and many kyndes of furres and hides, cannot choose but amounte to a greate matter, beinge all to be levied upon straungers. And this not onely wee may exacte of the Spaniardes and Portingales, but also of the Frenche men, our olde and auncient enemyes. What shoulde I speake of the customes of the greate multitudes of course clothes, welshe frise, and Irishe ruggs, that may be uttered in the more northerly partes of the lande amonge the Esquimawes of the Grande Bay, and amonge them of Canada, Saguynay, and Hochelaga, which are subjecte to sharpe and nippinge winters, albeit their somers be hotter moche then oures. Againe, the multitudes of small iron and copper workes, wherewith they are exceedingly delighted, will not a little encrease the customes, beinge transported oute of the lande. I omitt the rehersall of a thousande other triflinge wares, which, besides they may sett many women, children, and impotent persons on worke in makinge of them, woulde also helpe to the encreasinge of the customes. Lastly, whatsoever kind of commodyties shoulde be broughte from thence by her Majesties subjectes into the realme, or be thither transported oute of the realme, cannot choose but inlarge the revenewes of the Crowne very mightely, and inriche all sortes of subjectes in generally.

Cap. XIV. That this action will be for the greate increase, mayneteynaunce, and safetie of our navie, and especially of great shippinge, which is the strengthe of our realme, and for the supportation of all those occupations that depende upon the same.

In the Statutes moste providently ordeyned for increase and maineteynaunce of our navigation in the raignes of Kinge Richarde the Seconde, Kinge Henry the Eighth, and her Majestie that nowe is, thoughe many and sondry rewardes were proposed to incourage our people unto the sea, yet still I fynde complaintes of decaye of the navye, notwithstandinge so many goodly priviledges to mayneteine fisshermen, the ordeyninge of Wendisday to be a newe fishe day for the better utteraunce of their fishe that they shoulde take at sea, yea, albeit there hath bene graunted a certen proportionable allowaunce oute of the exchequer to suche as woulde builde any shippes of burden to serve the prince in tyme of warr, yet very little hath bene done in that behalfe. For, setting the Citie of London aparte, goe your way into the west parte of England and Wales, and searche howe many shippes of CC. tonnes and upwardes those partes can afforde, and you shall finde (God wotteth) no such nomber as at the firste you did imagine. At this day I am assured there are scarce twoo of CC. tonnes belonginge to the whole citie of Bristowe, and very fewe or none of the like burden alonge the channell of Severne from Glocester to the Landes Ende on the one side, and Milforde Haven on the other. Nowe, to remedie this greate and unknowen wante, no enterprise possibly can be devised more fitt to increase our greate shippinge then this Westerne fortifienge and planting. For in this action wee are not to cutt over the narrowe seas, in a day or a nighte, betwene Flaunders, Fraunce, or Ireland, in small barkes of xx. or xxx^{ti}. tonnes; but we are to passe over the breste of the maine ocean, and to lye at sea a moneth or six weekes together, whereby wee shall be constrayned of our selves, withoute chardginge of the Prince, to builde greate shippes, as well to avoide the daunger of tempest as also for the commoditie of portage, whereunto the greater shippes in longe voyadges are moste conveniente, which the Portingales and Spaniardes have founde oute by longe experience, whoe for that cause builde shippes of v. vj. vij. viij. C. and a M. tonnes, to sende into their Easterne and Westerne Indies.

The like whereof wee shalbe the rather invited to doe, since by this voyadge wee shall have many thinges for little or nothinge, that are necessarie for the furniture of greate shippinge. For beinge possessed of Newfounde lande, which the laste yere was seazed upon in her Majesties name, wee may have tarr, rosen, mastes, and cordage for the very workenmanshippe of the same. All which comodities cannot choose but wonderfully invite our men to the buildinge of greate shippinge, especially havinge store of the best shipwrights of the worlde, whereof some, for wante of employmente at home, have bene driven to flye into forren partes, as into Denmarke. Moreover, in the judgemente of those that are experte in sea causes, it will breede more skilfull, connynge, and stowte pilotts and maryners then other belonginge to this lande. For it is the longe voyadges (so they be not to excessive longe, nor throughe intemperate clymates, as those of the Portingales into their West Indies) that harden seamen, and open unto them the secretes of navigation; the natures of the windes; the currentes and settinge of the sea; the ebbinge and flowinge of the mayne ocean; the influence of the sonne, the moone, and of the rest of the celestiall planetts, and force which they have at sondry seasons upon that mightie body. . . .

Cap. XX. A brefe collection of certaine reasons to induce her Majestie and the state to take in hande the westerne voyadge and the plantinge there.

1. The soyle yeldeth, and may be made to yelde, all the severall comodities of Europe, and of all kingdomes, domynions, and territories that England tradeth withe, that by trade of marchandize cometh into this realme.

2. The passage thither and home is neither to longe nor to shorte, but easie, and to be made twise in the yere.

3. The passage cutteth not nere the trade of any prince, nor nere any of their contries or territories, and is a safe passage, and not easie to be annoyed by prince or potentate whatsoever.

4. The passage is to be perfourmed at all times of the yere, and in that respecte passeth our trades in the Levant Seas within the Straites of Juberalter, and the trades in the seas within the Kinge of Denmarkes Straite, and the trades to the portes of

Norwey and of Russia, &c.; for as in the south weste Straite
there is no passage in somer by lacke of windes, so within the
other places there is no passage in winter by ise and extreme
colde.

5. And where England nowe for certen hundreth yeres last
passed, by the peculiar comoditie of wolles, and of later yeres
by clothinge of the same, hath raised it selfe from meaner state
to greater wealthe and moche higher honour, mighte, and power
then before, to the equallinge of the princes of the same to the
greatest potentates of this parte of the world; it cometh nowe so
to passe, that by the greate endevour of the increase of the
trade of wolles in Spaine and in the West Indies, nowe daily
more and more multiplienge, that the wolles of England, and
the clothe made of the same, will become base, and every day
more base then other; which prudently weyed, it behoveth this
realme, if it meane not to returne to former olde meanes and
basenes, but to stande in present and late former honour, glorye,
and force, and not negligently and sleepingly to slyde into
beggery, to foresee and to plante at Norumbega or some like
place, were it not for any thing els but for the hope of the vent
of our woll indraped, the principall and in effecte the onely
enrichinge contynueinge naturall comoditie of this realme. And
effectually pursueinge that course, wee shall not onely finde on
that tracte of lande, and especially in that firme northwarde (to
whom warme clothe shalbe righte wellcome), an ample vente,
but also shall, from the north side of that firme, finde oute
knowen and unknowen ilandes and domynions replenished with
people that may fully vent the aboundaunce of that our comoditie, that els will in fewe yeres waxe of none or of small value
by forreine aboundaunce, &c.; so as by this enterprice wee shall
shonne the imminent mischefe hanginge over our heades, that
els muste nedes fall upon the realme, without breache of peace
or sworde drawen againste this realme by any forreine state;
and not offer our auncient riches to scornefull neighboures at
home, nor sell the same in effecte for nothinge, as wee shall
shortly, if presently it be not provaided for. The increase of
the wolles of Spaine and America is of highe pollicie, with
greate desire of our overthrowe, endevoured; and the goodnes
of the forren wolles our people will not enter into the considera-

tion of, nor will not beleve aughte, they be so sotted with opinion of their owne; and, if it be not foresene and some such place of vent provided, farewell the goodd state of all degrees in this realme.

6. This enterprise may staye the Spanishe Kinge from flowinge over all the face of that waste firme of America, if wee seate and plante there in time, in tyme I say, and wee by plantinge shall lett him from makinge more shorte and more safe returnes oute of the noble portes of the purposed places of our plantinge, then by any possibilitie he can from the parte of the firme that nowe his navies by ordinary courses come from, in this that there is no comparison betwene the portes of the coastes that the Kinge of Spaine dothe nowe possesse and use, and the portes of the coastes that our nation is to possesse by plantinge at Norumbega, and on that tracte faste by, more to the northe and northeaste, and in that there is from thence a moche shorter course, and a course of more temperature, and a course that possesseth more contynuaunce of ordinary windes, then the present course of the Spanishe Indian navies nowe dothe. And England possessinge the purposed place of plantinge, her Majestie may, by the benefete of the seate, havinge wonne goodd and royall havens, have plentie of excellent trees for mastes, of goodly timber to builde shippes and to make greate navies, of pitche, tarr, hempe, and all thinges incident for a navie royall, and that for no price, and withoute money or request. Howe easie a matter may it be to this realme, swarminge at this day with valiant youthes, rustinge and hurtfull by lacke of employment, and havinge goodd makers of cable and of all sortes of cordage, and the best and moste connynge shipwrights of the worlde, to be lordes of all those sees, and to spoile Phillipps Indian navye, and to deprive him of yerely passage of his treasure into Europe, and consequently to abate the pride of Spaine and of the supporter of the greate Antechriste of Rome, and to pull him downe in equallitie to his neighbour princes, and consequently to cutt of the common mischefes that come to all Europe by the peculiar aboundaunce of his Indian treasure, and thiss withoute difficultie.

7. This voyadge, albeit it may be accomplished by barke or smallest pynnesse for advise or for a necessitie, yet for the

distaunce, for burden and gaine in trade, the marchant will not for profitts sake use it but by shippes of greate burden; so as this realme shall have by that meane shippes of greate burden and of greate strengthe for the defence of this realme, and for the defence of that newe seate, as nede shall require, and withall greate increase of perfecte seamen, which greate princes in time of warres wante, and which kinde of men are neither nourished in fewe daies nor in fewe yeres.

8. This newe navie of mightie newe stronge shippes, so in trade to that Norumbega and to the coastes there, shall never be subjecte to arreste of any prince or potentate, as the navie of this realme from time to time hath bene in the portes of the empire, in the portes of the Base Contries, in Spaine, Fraunce, Portingale, &c., in the tymes of Charles the Emperour, Fraunces the Frenche kinge, and others; but shall be alwayes free from that bitter mischeefe, withoute grefe or hazarde to the marchaunte or to the state, and so alwaies readie at the comaundement of the prince with mariners, artillory, armor, and munition, ready to offende and defende as shalbe required.

9. The greate masse of wealthe of the realme imbarqued in the marchantes shippes, caried oute in this newe course, shall not lightly, in so farr distant a course from the coaste of Europe, be driven by windes and tempestes into portes of any forren princes, as the Spanishe shippes of late yeres have bene into our portes of the Weste Contries, &c.; and so our marchantes in respecte of private state, and of the realme in respecte of a generall safetie from venture of losse, are by this voyadge oute of one greate mischefe.

10. No forren commoditie that comes into England comes withoute payment of custome once, twise, or thrise, before it come into the realme, and so all forren comodities becrme derer to the subjectes of this realme; and by this course to Norumbega forren princes customes are avoided; and the forren comodities cheapely purchased, they become cheape to the subjectes of England, to the common benefite of the people, and to the savinge of greate treasure in the realme; whereas nowe the realme becomethe poore by the purchasinge of forreine comodities in so greate a masse at so excessive prices.

11. At the firste traficque with the people of those partes,

the subjectes of this realme for many yeres shall chaunge many cheape comodities of these partes for thinges of highe valor there not estemed; and this to the greate inrichinge of the realme, if common use faile not.

12. By the greate plentie of those regions the marchantes and their factors shall lye there cheape, buye and repaire their shippes cheape, and shall returne at pleasure withoute staye or restrainte of forreine prince; whereas upon staies and restraintes the marchaunte raiseth his chardge in sale over of his ware; and, buyenge his wares cheape, he may mainteine trade with smalle stocke, and withoute takinge upp money upon interest; and so he shalbe riche and not subjecte to many hazardes, but shalbe able to afforde the comodities for cheape prices to all subjectes of the realme.

13. By makinge of shippes and by preparinge of thinges for the same, by makinge of cables and cordage, by plantinge of vines and olive trees, and by making of wyne and oyle, by husbandrie, and by thousandes of thinges there to be done, infinite nombers of the Englishe nation may be set on worke, to the unburdenynge of the realme with many that nowe lyve chardgeable to the state at home.

14. If the sea coste serve for makinge of salte, and the inland for wine, oiles, oranges, lymons, figges, &c., and for makinge of iron, all which with moche more is hoped, withoute sworde drawen, wee shall cutt the combe of the Frenche, of the Spanishe, of the Portingale, and of enemies, and of doubtfull frendes, to the abatinge of their wealthe and force, and to the greater savinge of the wealthe of the realme.

15. The substaunces servinge, wee may oute of those partes receave the masse of wrought wares that now wee receave out of Fraunce, Flaunders, Germanye, &c.; and so wee may daunte the pride of some enemies of this realme, or at the leaste in parte purchase those wares, that nowe wee buye derely of the Frenche and Flemynge, better cheape; and in the ende, for the parte that this realme was wonte to receave, dryve them oute of trade to idlenes for the settinge of our people on worke.

16. Wee shall by plantinge there inlarge the glory of the gospell, and from England plante sincere relligion, and provide a safe and a sure place to receave people from all partes of the

worlde that are forced to flee for the truthe of Gods worde.

17. If frontier warres there chaunce to aryse, and if thereupon wee shall fortifie, it will occasion the trayninge upp of our youthe in the discipline of warr, and make a nomber fitt for the service of the warres and for the defence of our people there and at home.

18. The Spaniardes governe in the Indies with all pride and tyranie; and like as when people of contrarie nature at the sea enter into gallies, where men are tied as slaves, all yell and crye with one voice, Liberta, liberta, as desirous of libertie and freedome, so no doubte whensoever the Queene of England, a prince of such clemencie, shall seate upon that firme of America, and shalbe reported throughe oute all that tracte to use the naturall people there with all humanitie, curtesie, and freedome, they will yelde themselves to her governement, and revolte cleane from the Spaniarde, and specially when they shall understande that she hathe a noble navie, and that she aboundeth with a people moste valiaunte for theyr defence. And her Majestie havinge Sir Fraunces Drake and other subjectes already in credite with the Symerons, a people or greate multitude alreadye revolted from the Spanishe governemente, she may with them and a fewe hundrethes of this nation, trayned upp in the late warres of Fraunce and Flaunders, bringe greate thinges to passe, and that with greate ease; and this broughte so aboute, her Majestie and her subjectes may bothe enjoye the treasure of the mynes of golde and silver, and the whole trade and all the gaine of the trade of marchandize, that nowe passeth thither by the Spaniardes onely hande, of all the comodities of Europe; which trade of marchandize onely were of it selfe suffycient (withoute the benefite of the riche myne) to inriche the subjectes, and by customes to fill her Majesties coffers to the full. And if it be highe pollicie to mayneteyne the poore people of this realme in worke, I dare affirme that if the poore people of England were five times so many as they be, yet all mighte be sett on worke in and by workinge lynnen, and suche other thinges of marchandize as the trade into the Indies dothe require.

19. The present shorte trades causeth the maryner to be cast of, and ofte to be idle, and so by povertie to fall to piracie. But this course to Norumbega beinge longer, and a contynu-

aunce of the employmente of the maryner, dothe kepe the maryner from idlenes and from necessitie; and so it cutteth of the principal actions of piracie, and the rather because no riche praye for them to take cometh directly in their course or any thing nere their course.

20. Many men of excellent wittes and of divers singular giftes, overthrowen by suertishippe, by sea, or by some folly of youthe, that are not able to live in England, may there be raised againe, and doe their contrie goodd service; and many nedefull uses there may (to greate purpose) require the savinge of greate nombers, that for trifles may otherwise be devoured by the gallowes.

21. Many souldiers and servitours, in the ende of the warres, that mighte be hurtfull to this realme, may there be unladen, to the common profite and quiet of this realme, and to our forreine benefite there, as they may be employed.

22. The frye of the wandringe beggars of England, that growe upp idly, and hurtefull and burdenous to this realme, may there be unladen, better bredd upp, and may people waste contries to the home and forreine benefite, and to their owne more happy state.

23. If Englande crie oute and affirme, that there is so many in all trades that one cannot live for another, as in all places they doe, this Norumbega (if it be thoughte so goodd) offreth the remedie.

2

William Bradford

Of Plymouth Plantation[1]

In the first decade of the seventeenth century, a Separatist or Independent community gathered around the squire William Brewster and the ministers Richard Clifton and John Robinson. In his seventeenth or eighteenth year, William Bradford (1590-1657) joined the congregation. By so doing, he associated himself with a group that based its religion on Calvinism, voluntary association, and a belief in the separation of Church and state, the Scrooby congregation. In the view of James I and the Anglican bishops, each of these tenets was religiously unsound and outright illegal. Officers of Church and state sporadically moved against the Separatist communities and all such groups lived in fear of persecution. This fear caused the congregation to move to the Netherlands in 1608. An eleven year sojourn there proved unsatisfactory and in 1619 these Leyden separatists began negotiations with the London Company of Virginia that ultimately put them aboard the *Mayflower* in the late autumn of 1620.

At Plymouth, the Pilgrims formed a simple, agrarian community. The government provided by the famous compact was a direct democracy of the freemen. In practice, the governor had considerable power. When the first governor, John Carver, died in 1621, Bradford replaced him and served as governor for thirty of the remaining thirty-five years of his life. Through these years "Bradford was the 'government' and the arbiter of the destinies of the colony."

The best single work dealing with the settlement of the colonies is Charles M. Andrews, *The Colonial Period of American History* (4 vols.; New Haven: Yale University Press, 1934-38). For Plymouth, see Vol. I, ch. 13, 14. A modern biography of the founder is Brad-

---

1. William Bradford, *Bradford's History "Of Plymouth Plantation." From the Original Manuscript* (Boston: Wright & Potter, 1898), pp. 6-9, 14-15, 29-33, 94-97, 111, 114, 121, 134-35, 162-63, 200-201.

ford Smith, *Bradford of Plymouth* (Philadelphia: Lippincott, 1951).
Thomas J. Wertenbaker, *The First Americans, 1607-1690* (New York:
Macmillan, 1927) is a social history of the first cycle of settlement.

In reading the following selection note (1) the form and style
employed by the author; (2) what religious views distinguished the
Separatists from the Anglicans; (3) the explanation advanced for the
persecutions of Elizabeth I; (4) why the congregation wanted to
leave Holland; (5) what impact the American environment made
upon the first settlers; (6) what adjustments to the demands of the
wilderness the newcomers made; (7) by what means the colonists
shifted from company to private ownership of property; and (8) the
reasons advanced for building a compact community in New England.

THE ONE SIDE LABOURED TO HAVE THE RIGHT WORSHIP
of God & discipline of Christ established in the
church, according to the simplicitie of the gospell, without
the mixture of mens inventions, and to have & to be ruled by the
laws of Gods word, dispensed in those offices, & by those
officers of Pastors, Teachers, & Elders, &c. according to the
Scripturs. The other partie, though under many colours & pretences, endevored to have the Epicopall dignitie (affter the
popish maner) with their large power & jurisdiction still retained; with all those courts, cannons, & ceremonies, togeather
with all such livings, revenues, & subordinate officers, with other
such means as formerly upheld their antichristian greatness, and
enabled them with lordly & tyranous power to persecute the
poore servants of God. . . .

And this conte[n]tion dyed not with queene Mary, nor was
left beyonde the seas, but at her death these people returning
into England under gracious queene Elizabeth, many of them
being preferred to bishopricks & other promotions, according to
their aimes and desires, that inveterate hatered against the holy
discipline of Christ in his church hath continued to this day.
In somuch that for fear it should preveile, all plotts & devices
have been used to keepe it out, incensing the queene & state
against it as dangerous for the comon wealth; and that it was
most needfull that the fundamentall poynts of Religion should
be preached in those ignorante & superstitious times; and to win

the weake & ignorante, they might retaine diverse harmles cermoneis; and though it were to be wished that diverse things were reformed, yet this was not a season for it. And many the like, to stop the mouthes of the more godly, to bring them over to yeeld to one ceremoney after another, and one corruption after another; by these wyles begyleing some & corrupting others till at length they begane to persecute all the zealous professors in the land (though they knew little what this discipline mente) both by word & deed, if they would not submitte to their ceremonies, & become slaves to them & their popish trash, which have no ground in the word of God, but are relikes of that man of sine. And the more the light of the gospell grew, the more they urged their subscriptions to these corruptions. So as (notwithstanding all their former pretences & fair colures) they whose eyes God had not justly blinded might easily see whereto these things tended. And to cast contempte the more upon the sincere servants of God, they opprobriously & most injuriously gave unto, & imposed upon them, that name of Puritans which is said the Novatians out of pride did assume & take unto themselves. And lamentable it is to see the effects which have followed. Religion hath been disgraced, the godly greeved, afflicted, persecuted, and many exiled, sundrie have lost their lives in prisones & otherways. On the other hand, sin hath been countenanced, ignorance, profannes, & atheisme increased, & the papists encouraged to hope againe for a day. . . .

But . . . they could not long continue in any peacable condition, but were hunted & persecuted on every side, so as their former afflictions were but as flea-bitings in comparison of these which now came upon them. For some were taken & clapt up in prison, others had their houses besett & watcht night and day, & hardly escaped their hands; and the most were faine to flie & leave their howses & habitations, and the means of their livelihood. Yet these & many other sharper things which afterward befell them, were no other then they looked for, and therefore were the better prepared to bear them by the assistance of Gods grace & spirite. Yet seeing them selves thus molested, and that ther was no hope of their continuance ther, by a joynte consente they resolved to goe into the Low-Countries, wher they heard was freedome of Religion for all men. . . .

Showing the reasons & causes of their remoovall [from Leyden] In the agitation of their thoughts, and much discours of things hear aboute, at length they began to incline to this conclusion, of remooval to some other place. Not out any newfangledness, or other such like giddie humor, by which men are oftentimes transported to their great hurt & danger, but for sundrie weightie & solid reasons. . . .

As necessitie was a taskmaster over them, so they were forced to be such, not only to their servants, but in a sorte, to their dearest children, they which as it did not a litle wound the tender harts of many a loving father & mother, so it produced likwise sundrie sad & sorowful effects. For many of their children, that were of best dispositions and gracious inclinations, haveing learned to bear the yoake in their youth, and willing to bear parte of their parents burden, were, often times, so oppressed with their hevie labours, that though their minds were free and willing, yet their bodies bowed under the weight of the same, and became decreped in their early youth; the vigor of nature being consumed in the very budd as it were. But that which was more lamentable, and of all sorowes most heavie to be borne, was that many of their children, by these occasions, and the great licentiousnes of youth in that countrie, and the manifold temptations of the place, were drawne away by evill examples into extravagante & dangerous courses, getting the reines off their neks, & departing from their parents. Some became souldiers, others tooke upon them farr viages by sea, and others some worse courses, tending to dissolutnes & danger of their soules, to the great greefe of their parents and dishonour of God. So that they saw their posterities would be in danger to degenerate & be corrupted.

Lastly, (and which was not least,) a great hope & inward zeall they had of laying some good foundation, or at least to make some way therunto, for the propagating & advancing the gospell of the kingdom of Christ in those remote parts of the world; yea, though they should be but even as stepping-stones unto others for the performing of so great a work. . . .

The place they had thoughts on was some of those vast & unpeopled countries of America, which are frutfull & fitt for habitation, being devoyd of all civill inhabitants, wher ther are only salvage & brutish men, which range up and downe. . . .

Being thus arived in a good harbor and brought safe to land, they fell upon their knees & blessed the God of Heaven, who had brought them over the vast and furious ocean, and delivered them from all the periles & miseries thereof, againe to set their feete on the firme and stable earth, their proper elemente. . . .

But hear I cannot but stay & make a pause, and stand half amased at this poore peoples presente condition; and so I thinke will the reader too, when he well considers the same. Being thus passed the vast ocean, and a sea of troubles before in their preparation (as may be remembred by that which wente before), they had now no freinds to wellcome them, nor inns to entertaine or refresh their weatherbeaten bodys, no houses or much less townes to repaire too, to seeke for succoure. It is recorded in scripture as a mercie to the apostle and his shipwraked company, that the barbarians shewed them no smale kindness in refreshing them, but these savage barbarians, when they mette with them (as after will appeare) were readier to fill their sids with arrows then otherwise. And for the season it was winter, and they that know the winters of that cuntrie know them to be sharp & violent, & subjecte to cruell & feirce stormes, deangerous to travill to known places, much more to serch an unknown coast. Besids, what could they see but a hidious & desolate wildernes, full of wild beasts & willd men? and what multituds ther might be of them they knew not. . . . For sumer being done, all things stand upon them with a wetherbeaten face; and the whole countrie, full of woods & thickets, represented a wild & savage heiw. If they looked behind them, ther was the mighty ocean which they had passed, and was now as a maine barr & goulfe to separate them from all the civill parts of the world. If it be said they had a ship to sucour them, it is trew; but what heard they daly from the master and company? but that with speede they should looke out a place with their shallop, wher they would be at some near distance; for the season was shuch as he would not stirr from thence till a safe harbor was discovered by them wher they would be, and he might goe without danger; and that victells consumed apace, but he must & would keepe sufficient for them selves & their returne. Yes, it was muttered by some, that if they gott not a place in time, they would turne them & their goods ashore & leave them. Let it also be considered what weake hopes of supply & succoure they left behinde them, that might bear up their minds in this sade condition and trialls they were under; and they could not but be very smale. . . . What could now sustaine them but the spirite of God & his grace? May not & ought not the children of these fathers rightly say: *Our fathers were Englishmen which came over this great ocean, and were ready to perish in this willderness; but they cried unto the Lord, and he heard their voyce, and looked on their adversitie, &c. Let them therefore praise the Lord because he is good, & his mercies endure for ever. Yea, let them which have been redeemed of the Lord, shew how he hath delivered them from the hand of the oppressour. When they wandered in the deserte willderness out of the way, and found no citie to dwell in, both hungrie, & thirstie, their sowle was overwhelmed in them. Let them confess before the Lord his loving kindness, and his wonderfull works before the sons of men.* . . .

In these hard & difficulte beginings they found some discontents & murmurings arise amongst some, and mutinous speeches & carriags in other; but they were soone quelled & overcome by the wisdome, patience, and just & equall carrage of things by the Governor and better part, which clave faithfully togeather in the maine. But that which was most sadd & lamentable was, that in 2. or 3. moneths time halfe of their company dyed, espetialy in Jan: & February, being the depth of winter, and wanting houses & other comforts; being infected with the scurvie & other diseases, which this long vioage & their inacomodate condition had brought upon them; so as ther dyed some times 2. or 3. of a day, in the foresaid time; that of 100. & odd persons, scarce 50. remained. And of these in the time of most distres, ther was but 6. or 7. sound persons, who , to their great commendations be it spoken, spared no pains, night or day, but with abundance of toyl and hazard of their own health, fetched them woode, made them fires, drest them meat, made their beds, washed their lothsome cloaths, cloathed &

uncloathed them; in a word, did all the homly & necessarie
offices for them which dainty & quesie stomacks cannot endure
to be named; and all this willingly & cherfully, without any
grudging in the least, shewing herein their true love unto their
freinds & brethren. . . .

All this while the Indians came skulking about them. . . .

Afterwards they (as many as were able) began to plant ther
corne, in which servise Squanto stood them in great stead, showing them both the manner how to set it, and after how to dress
& tend it. Also he tould them excepte they gott fish & set with
it (in these old grounds) it would come to nothing, and he
showed them that in the middle of Aprill they should have store
enough come up the brooke, by which they begane to build,
and taught them how to take it, and wher to get other provis-
sions necessary for them; àll which they found true by triall
& experience. Some English seed they sew, as wheat & pease,
but it came not to good, eather by the badnes of the seed, or
latenes of the season, or both, or some other defecte. . . .

They begane now to gather in the small harvest they had,
and to fitte up their houses and dwellings against winter, being
all well recovered in health & strength, and had all things in
good plenty; for as some were thus imployed in affairs abroad,
otheres were exercised in fishing, aboute codd, & bass, & other
fish, of which they tooke good store, of which every family had
their portion. All the somer there was no wante. And now begane to come in store of foule, as winter approached, of which
this place did abound when they came first (but afterward decreased by degrees). And besids water foule, ther was great
store of wild Turkies, of which they tooke many, besids venison,
&c. Besids they had aboute a peck a meale a weeke to a person,
or now since harvest, Indean corne to that proportion. Which
made many afterwards write so largely of their plenty here to
their freinds in England, which were not fained, but true
reports. . . .

Only I shall remember one passage more, rather of mirth
then of waight. On the day called Christmasday, the Governor
caled them out to worke, (as was used,) but the most of this
new-company excused them selves and said it wente against
their consciences to work on that day. So the Governor tould

them that if they made it a mater of conscience, he would spare them till they were better informed. So he led-away the rest and left them; but when they came home at noone from their worke, he found them in the streete at play, openly; some pitching the barr, some at stoole-ball, and shuch like sports. So he went to them, and tooke away their implements, and tould them that was against his conscience, that they should play & others worke. If they made the keeping of it mater of devotion, let them kepe their houses, but ther should be no gaming or revelling in the streets. Since which time nothing hath been atempted that way, at least openly. . . .

All this whille no supply was heard of, neither knew they when they might expecte any. So they begane to thinke how they might raise as much corne as they could, and obtaine a beter crope then they had done, that they might not still thus languish in miserie. At length, after much debate of things, the Governor (with the advise of the cheefest amongest them) gave way that they should set corne every man for his owne perticuler, and in that regard trust to them selves; in all other things to goe on in the generall way as before. And so assigned to every family a parcell of land according to the proportion of their number for that end, only for present use (but made no devission for inheritance), and ranged all boys & youth under some familie. This had very good success; for it made all hands very industrious, so as much more corne was planted then other waise would have bene by any means the Governor or any other could use, and saved him a great deall of trouble, and gave farr better contente. The women now wente willingly into the feild, and tooke their litle-ons with them to set corne, which before would aledg weaknes, and inabilitie; whom to have compelled would have bene thought great tiranie and oppression.

The experience that was had in this comone course and condition, tried sundrie years, and that amongst godly and sober men, may well evince the vanities of that conceite of Platos & other ancients, applauded by some of later times;—that the taking away of propertie, and bringing in comunitie into a comone wealth, would make them happy and florishing; as if they were wiser then God. For this comunitie (so farr as it was) was found to breed much confusion & discontent, and retard much

imploymet that would have been to their benefite and comforte. . . .

And before I come to other things I must speak a word of
their planting this year; they having found the benefite of their
last years harvest, and setting corne for their particuler, having
therby with a great deale of patience overcome hunger & famine.
Which maks me remember a saing of Senecas, *Epis:* 123. *That
a great parte of libertie is a well governed belly, and to be
patiente in all wants.* They begane now highly to prise corn as
more pretious then silver, and those that had some to spare
begane to trade on with another for smale things, by the quarte,
potle, & peck, &c.; for money they had none, and if any had,
corne was prefered before it. That they might therefore encrease their tillage to better advantage, they made suite to the
Governor to have some portion of land given them for continuance, and not by yearly lotte, for by that means, that which the
more industrious had brought into good culture (by much
pains) one year, came to leave it the nexte, and often another
might injoye it; so as the dressing of their lands were the more
sleighted over, & to lese profite. Which being well considered,
their request was granted. And to every person was given only
one accre of land, to them & theirs, as nere to the towne as
might be, and they had no more till the 7. years were expired.
The reason was, that they might be kept close together both
for more saftie and defence, and the better improvement of
the generall imployments.

3

The Charter of Maryland (1632)[1]

First as a member of Parliament and then as one of the principal secretaries of state, George Calvert (*c.* 1580-1632) served the first two Stuart Kings for a quarter of a century. In the 1620s, he advocated the marriage of the heir apparent, Charles, to the Spanish infanta, and in the course of negotiating the match, Calvert became a Roman Catholic. Abortive marriage diplomacy ignited latent English anti-Catholicism and forced Calvert's resignation, but Charles I rewarded his service by making him an Irish peer, the first Baron Baltimore.

Calvert had been interested in colonization before his conversion to Catholicism: he was a stockholder in the Virginia Company of London and a member of the Council for New England. It is impossible to determine the precise time when Calvert conceived the idea of a colony for religious minorities. We know that several Jesuit priests with whom he had contact were interested in a Catholic mission in America. He first attempted a settlement in Newfoundland, but discouraged by the bleak climate, he abandoned "Avalon" and attempted to settle in Virginia. He was unwelcome there because of his religion.

Calvert next turned his attention to the possibility of settlement in the Virginia area. A proposal to found a colony in what was to be Carolina was defeated by the Virginia interests. Finally, the Calverts obtained a patent for a colony north of Virginia. By the time it passed the seals, George Calvert was dead, and the work was taken up by his son, Cecilius.

Two sound histories of the colonial South that contain substantial sections on Maryland are Wesley F. Craven, *The Southern Colonies in the Seventeenth Century, 1607-1689* (Baton Rouge: Louisiana

1. Francis N. Thorpe (ed.), *The Federal and State Constitutions, Colonial Charters, and Other Organic Laws of the States, Territories, and Colonies Now or Heretofore forming the United States of America* (7 vols.; Washington: Government Printing Office, 1907) III, pp. 1669-86.

State University Press, 1949) and Thomas J. Wertenbaker, *The Old South: the Founding of American Civilization* (New York: Scribners, 1942). For a brilliant essay on the medieval institutional roots of the new empire see Julius Goebel, Jr., "Matrix of Empire," which is an introduction to Joseph H. Smith, *Appeals to the Privy Council from the American Plantations* (New York: Columbia University Press, 1950). The grant to Baltimore bestowed more extensive rights than any other proprietary charter. In reading it (1) look for evidence of its essentially feudal character; (2) determine the significance of the waiving of the statute Quia Emptores; (3) note the form of government provided; and (4) note what substantial rights are guaranteed to the individual settler coming out to Maryland and what they might imply concerning problems of recruitment of colonists.

CHARLES, BY THE GRACE OF GOD, OF ENGLAND, SCOT-
land, France, and Ireland, king, Defender of the Faith, &c. To all to whom these Presents come, Greeting.

II. Whereas our well beloved and right trusty Subject Caecilius Calvert, Baron of Baltimore, in our Kingdom of Ireland, Son and Heir of George Calvert, Knight, late Baron of Baltimore, in our said Kingdom of Ireland, treading in the steps of his Father, being animated with a laudable, and pious Zeal for extending the Christian Religion, and also the Territories of our Empire, hath humbly besought Leave of us, that he may transport, by his own Industry, and Expense, a numerous Colony of the English Nation, to a certain Region, herein after described, in a Country hitherto uncultivated, in the Parts of America, and partly occupied by Savages, having no knowledge of the Divine Being, and that all that Region, with some certain Privileges, and Jurisdiction, appertaining unto the wholesome Government, and State of his Colony and Region aforesaid, may by our Royal Highness be given, granted and confirmed unto him, and his Heirs.

III. Know Ye therefore, that We, encouraging with our Royal Favour, the pious and noble purpose of the aforesaid Barons of Baltimore, of our special Grace, certain knowledge, and mere Motion, have Given, Granted and Confirmed, and by this our present Charter, for Us our Heirs, and Successors, do Give,

Grant and Confirm, unto the aforesaid Caecilius, now Baron of
Baltimore, his Heirs, and Assigns, all that Part of the Peninsula,
or Chersonese, lying in the Parts of America, between the Ocean
on the East and the Bay of Chesapeake on the West, divided
from the Residue thereof by a Right Line drawn from the
Promontory, or Head-Land, called Watkin's Point, situate upon
the Bay aforesaid, near the river Wigloo, on the West, unto the
main Ocean on the East; and between that Boundary on the
South, unto that Part of the Bay of Delaware on the North,
which lieth under the Fortieth Degree of North Latitude from
the Equinoctial, where New England is terminated; And all
that Tract of Land within the Metes underwritten (that is to
say) passing from the said Bay, called Delaware Bay, in a right
Line, by the Degree aforesaid, unto the true meridian of the
first Fountain of the River of Pattowmack, thence verging toward the South, unto the further Bank of the said River, and
following the same on the West and South, unto a certain Place,
called Cinquack, situate near the mouth of the said River, where
it disembogues into the aforesaid Bay of Chesapeake, and thence
by the shortest Line unto the aforesaid Promontory or Place,
called Watkin's Point; so that the whole tract of land, divided
by the Line aforesaid, between the main Ocean and Watkin's
Point, unto the Promontory called Cape Charles. and every the
Appendages thereof, may entirely remain excepted for ever to
Us, our Heirs and Successors.

IV. Also We do grant and likewise Confirm unto the said
Baron of Baltimore, his Heirs, and Assigns, all Islands and Inlets
within the Limits aforesaid, all and singular the Islands, and
Islets from the Eastern Shore of the aforesaid Region, towards
the East, which had been, or shall be formed in the Sea, situate
within Ten marine Leagues from the said shore; with all and
singular the Ports, Harbours, Bays, Rivers, and Straits belonging
to the Region or Islands aforesaid, and all the Soil, Plains,
Woods, Marshes, Lakes, Rivers, Bays, and Straits, situate, or
being within the Metes, Bounds, and Limits aforesaid, with the
Fishings of every kind of Fish, as well of Whales, Sturgeons,
and other royal Fish, as of other Fish, in the Sea, Bays, Straits,
or Rivers, within the Premises, and the fish there taken; And
moreover all Veins, Mines, and Quarries, as well opened as hid-

den, already found, or that shall be found within the Region, Islands, or Limits aforesaid, of Gold, Silver, Gems, and precious Stones, and any other whatsoever, whether they be of Stones, or Metals, or of any other Thing, or Matter whatsoever; And furthermore the Patronages, and Advowsons of all Churches which (with the increasing Worship and Religion of Christ) within the said Region, Islands, Islets, and Limits aforesaid, hereafter shall happen to be built, together with License and Faculty of erecting and founding Churches, Chapels, and Places of Worship, in convenient and suitable places, within the Premises, and of causing the same to be dedicated and consecrated according to the Ecclesiastical Laws of our Kingdom of England, with all, and singular such, and as ample Rights, Jurisdictions, Privileges, Prerogatives, Royalties, Liberties, Immunities, and royal Rights, and temporal Franchises whatsoever, as well by Sea as by Land, within the Region, Islands, Islets, and Limits aforesaid, to be had, exercised, used, and enjoyed, as any Bishop of Durham, within the Bishoprick or County Palatine of Durham, in our Kingdom of England, ever heretofore hath had, held, used, or enjoyed, or of right could, or ought to have, hold, use, or enjoy.

V. And we do by these Presents, for us, our Heirs, and Successors, Make, Create, and Constitute Him, the now Baron of Baltimore, and his Heirs, the true and absolute Lords and Proprietaries of the Region aforesaid, and of all other Premises (except the before excepted) saving always the Faith and Allegiance and Sovereign Dominion due to Us, our Heirs, and Successors; to have, hold, possess, and enjoy the aforesaid Region, Islands, Islets, and other the Premises, unto the aforesaid now Baron of Baltimore, and to his Heirs and Assigns, to the sole and proper Behoof and Use of him, the now Baron of Baltimore, his Heirs and Assigns, forever. To Hold of Us, our Heirs and Successors, Kings of England, as of our Castle of Windsor, in our County of Berks, in free and common Soccage, by Fealty only for all Services, and not in Capite, nor by Knight's Service, Yielding therefore unto Us, our Heirs and Successors Two Indian Arrows of these Parts, to be delivered at the said Castle of Windsor, every Year, on Tuesday in Easter Week: And also the fifth Part of all Gold and Silver Ore, which shall happen from Time to Time, to be found within the aforesaid Limits.

VI. Now, That the aforesaid Region, thus by us granted and described, may be eminently distinguished above all other Regions of that Territory, and decorated with more ample Titles, Know Ye, that We, of our more especial Grace, certain knowledge, and mere Motion, have thought fit that the said Region and Islands be erected into a Province, as out of the Plenitude of our royal Power and Prerogative, We do, for Us, our Heirs and Successors, erect and incorporate the same into a Province, and nominate the same Maryland, by which Name We will that it shall from henceforth be called.

VII. And forasmuch as We have above made and ordained the aforesaid now Baron of Baltimore, the true Lord and Proprietary of the whole Province aforesaid, Know Ye therefore further, that We, for Us, our Heirs and Successors, do grant unto the said now Baron, (in whose Fidelity, Prudence, Justice, and provident Circumspection of Mind, We repose the greatest Confidence) and to his Heirs, for the good and happy Government of the said Province, free, full, and absolute Power, by the Tenor of these Presents, to Ordain, Make, and Enact Laws, of what Kind soever, according to their sound Discretions, whether relating to the Public State of the said Province, or the private Utility of Individuals, of and with the Advice, Assent, and Approbation of the Free-Men of the same Province, or the greater Part of them, or of their Delegates or Deputies, whom We will shall be called together for the framing of Laws, when, and as often as Need shall require, by the aforesaid now Baron of Baltimore, and his Heirs, and in the Form which shall seem best to him or them, and the same to publish under the Seal of the aforesaid now Baron of Baltimore, and his Heirs, and duly to execute the same upon all Persons, for the time being, within the aforesaid Province, and the Limits thereof, or under his or their Government and Power, in Sailing towards Maryland, or thence Returning, Outward-bound, either to England, or elsewhere, whether to any other Part of Our, or of any foreign Dominions, wheresoever established, by the Imposition of Fines, Imprisonment, and other Punishment whatsoever; even if it be necessary, and the Quality of the Offence require it, by Privation of Member, or Life, by him the aforesaid now Baron of Baltimore and his Heirs, or by his or their Deputy, Lieutenant, Judges, Justices, Magistrates, Officers, and Ministers, to be constituted and appointed according to the Tenor and true Intent of these Presents, and to constitute and ordain Judges, Justices, Magistrates and Officers of what kind, for what Cause, and with what Power soever, within that Land, and the Sea of those Parts, and in such form as to the said now Baron of Baltimore, or his Heirs, shall seem most fitting; And also to Remit, Release, Pardon, and Abolish, all Crimes and Offences whatsoever against such Laws, whether before, or after Judgment passed; and to do all and singular other Things belonging to the Completion of Justice, and to Courts, Praetorian Judicatories, and Tribunals, Judicial Forms and Modes of Proceeding, although express Mention thereof in these Presents be not made; and, by Judges by them delegated, to award Process, hold Pleas, and determine in those Courts, Praetorian Judicatories, and Tribunals, in all Actions, Suits, Causes, and Matters whatsoever, as well Criminal as Personal, Real and Mixed, and Praetorian: Which said Laws, so to be published as abovesaid, We will enjoin, charge and command, to be most absolute and firm in Law, and to be Kept in those Parts by all the Subjects and Liege-Men of Us, our Heirs, and Successors, so far as they concern them, and to be inviolably observed under the Penalties therein expressed, or to be expressed. So, nevertheless, that the Laws aforesaid to be consonant to Reason, and be not repugnant or contrary, but (so far as conveniently may be) agreeable to the Laws, Statutes, Customs, and Rights of this Our Kingdom of England.

VIII. And forasmuch as, in the Government of so great a Province, sudden accidents may frequently happen, to which it will be necessary to apply a Remedy, before the Freeholders of the said Province, their Delegates, or Deputies, can be called together for the framing of Laws; neither will it be fit that so great a Number of People should immediately, on such emergent Occasion, be called together, We therefore, for the better Government of so great a Province, do Will and Ordain, and by these Presents, for Us, our Heirs and Successors, do grant unto the said now Baron of Baltimore, and to his Heirs, that the aforesaid now Baron of Baltimore, and his Heirs, by themselves, or by their Magistrates and Officers, thereunto duly to be constituted as aforesaid, may, and can make and constitute fit and Wholesome Ordinances from Time to Time, to be Kept and observed within the Province aforesaid, as well for the Conservation of the Peace, as for the better Government of the People inhabiting therein, and publicly to notify the same to all Persons whom the same in any wise do or may affect. Which Ordinances We will to be inviolably observed within the said Province, under the Pains to be expressed in the same. So that the said Ordinances be consonant to Reason and be not repugnant nor contrary, but (so far as conveniently may be done) agreeable to the Laws, Statutes, or Rights of our Kingdom of England: And so that the same Ordinances do not, in any Sort, extend to oblige, bind, charge, or take away the Right or Interest of any Person or Persons, of, or in Member, Life, Freehold, Goods or Chattels.

IX. Furthermore, that the New Colony may more happily increase by a Multitude of People resorting thither, and at the same Time may be more firmly secured from the Incursions of Savages, or of other Enemies, Pirates, and Ravagers: We therefore, for Us, our Heirs and Successors, do by these Presents give and grant Power, License and Liberty, to all the Liege-Men and Subjects, present and future, of Us, our Heirs and Successors, except such to whom it shall be expressly forbidden, to transport themselves and their Families to the said Province, with fitting Vessels, and suitable Provisions, and therein to settle, dwell and inhabit; and to build and fortify Castles, Forts, and other Places of Strength, at the Appointment of the aforesaid now Baron of Baltimore, and his Heirs, for the Public and their own Defence; the Statute of Fugitives, or any other whatsoever to the contrary of the Premises in any wise notwithstanding.

X. We will also, and of our more abundant Grace, for Us, our Heirs and Successors, do firmly charge, constitute, ordain, and command, that the said Province be of our Allegiance; and that all and singular the Subjects and Liege-Men of Us, our Heirs and Successors, transplanted, or hereafter to be transplanted into the Province aforesaid, and the Children of them, and of others their Descendants, whether already born there, or hereafter to be born, be and shall be Natives and Liege-Men of Us, our Heirs and Successors, of our Kingdom of England and Ireland; and in all Things shall be held, treated, reputed, and esteemed as the faithful Liege-Men of Us, and our Heirs and Successors, born within our Kingdom of England; also Lands, Tenements, Revenues, Services, and other Hereditaments whatsoever, within our Kingdom of England, and other our Dominions, to inherit, or otherwise purchase, receive, take, have, hold, buy, and possess, and the same to use and enjoy, and the same to give, sell, alien and bequeath; and likewise all Privileges, Franchises and Liberties of this our Kingdom of England, freely, quietly, and peaceably to have and possess, and the same may use and enjoy in the same manner as our Liege-Men born, or to be born within our said Kingdom of England, without Impediment, Molestation, Vexation, Impeachment, or Grievance of Us, or any of our Heirs or Successors; any Statute, Act, Ordinance, or Provision to the contrary thereof, notwithstanding.

XI. Furthermore, That our Subjects may be incited to undertake this Expedition with a ready and cheerful mind: Know Ye, that We, of our especial Grace, certain Knowledge, and mere Motion, do, by the Tenor of these Presents, give and grant, as well as to the aforesaid Baron of Baltimore, and to his Heirs, as to all other Persons who shall from Time to Time repair to the said Province, either for the Sake of Inhabiting, or of Trading with the Inhabitants of the Province aforesaid, full License to Ship and Lade in any the Ports of Us, our Heirs and Successors, all and singular their Goods, as well movable, as immovable, Wares and Merchandizes, likewise Grain of what Sort soever, and other Things whatsoever necessary for Food and Clothing, by the Laws and Statutes of our Kingdoms and Dominions, not prohibited to be transported out of the said Kingdoms; and the same to transport, by themselves, or their Servants or Assigns, into the said Province, without the Impediment or Molestation of Us, our Heirs or Successors, or any Officers of Us, our Heirs or Successors, (Saving unto Us, our Heirs and Successors, the Impositions, Subsidies, Customs, and other Dues payable for the same Goods and Merchandizes) any Statute, Act, Ordinance, or other Thing whatsoever to the contrary notwithstanding.

XII. But because, that in so remote a Region, placed among so many barbarous Nations, the Incursions as well of the Barbarians themselves, as of other Enemies, Pirates and Ravagers, probably will be feared. Therefore We have Given, and for Us, our Heirs, and Successors, do Give by these Presents, as full and unrestrained Power, as any Captain-General of an Army ever hath had, unto the aforesaid now Baron of Baltimore, and to his Heirs and Assigns, by themselves, or by their Captains, or other Officers to summon to their Standards, and to array all men, of whatsoever Condition, or wheresoever born, for the Time being, in the said Province of Maryland, to wage War, and to pursue, even beyond the Limits of their Province, the Enemies and Ravagers aforesaid, infesting those Parts by Land and by Sea, and (if God shall grant it) to vanquish and captivate them, and the Captives to put to Death, or according to their Discretion, to save, and to do all other and singular the Things which appertain, or have been accustomed to appertain unto the Authority and Office of a Captain-General of an Army.

XIII. We also will, and by this our Charter, do give unto the aforesaid now Baron of Baltimore, and to his Heirs and Assigns, Power, Liberty, and Authority, that, in Case of Rebellion, sudden Tumult, or Sedition, if any (which God forbid) should happen to arise, whether upon Land within the Province aforesaid, or upon the High Sea in making a Voyage to the said Province of Maryland, or in returning thence, they may, by themselves, or by their Captains, or other Officers, thereunto deputed under their Seals (to whom We, for Us, our Heirs and Successors, by these Presents, do Give and Grant the fullest Power and Authority) exercise Martial Law as freely, and in as ample Manner and Form, as any Captain-General of an Army by virtue of his Office may, or hath accustomed to use the same, against the seditious Authors of Innovations in those Parts, withdrawing themselves from the Government of him or them, refusing to serve in War, flying over to the Enemy, exceeding their Leave of Absence, Deserters, or otherwise howsoever offending against the Rule, Law, or Discipline of War.

XIV. Moreover, left in so remote and far distant a Region, every Access to Honors and Dignities may seem to be precluded, and utterly barred, to Men well born, who are preparing to engage in the present Expedition, and desirous of deserving well, both in Peace and War, of Us, and our Kingdom; for this

Cause, We, for Us, our Heirs and Successors, do give free and plenary Power to the aforesaid now Baron of Baltimore, and to his Heirs and Assigns, to confer Favors, Rewards and Honors, upon such Subjects, inhabiting within the Province aforesaid, as shall be well deserving, and to adorn them with whatsoever Titles and Dignities they shall appoint; (so that they be not such as are now used in England) also to erect and incorporate Towns into Boroughs, and Boroughs into Cities, with suitable Privileges and Immunities, according to the Merits of the Inhabitants, and Convenience of the Places; and to do all and singular other Things in the Premises, which to him or them shall seem fitting and convenient; even although they shall be such as, in their own Nature, require a more special Commandment and Warrant than in these Presents may be expressed.

XV. We will also, and by these Presents do, for Us, our Heirs and Successors, give and grant License by this our Charter, unto the aforesaid now Baron of Baltimore, his Heirs and Assigns, and to all Persons whatsoever, who are, or shall be Residents and Inhabitants of the Province aforesaid, freely to import and unlade, by themselves, their Servants, Factors or Assigns, all Wares and Merchandizes whatsoever, which shall be collected out of the Fruits and Commodities of the said Province, whether the Product of the Land or the Sea, into any the Ports whatsoever of Us, our Heirs and Successors, of England or Ireland, or otherwise to dispose of the same there; and, if Need be, within One Year, to be computed immediately from the Time of unlading thereof, to lade the same Merchandizes again, in the same, or other Ships, and to export the same to any other Countries they shall think proper, whether belonging to Us, or any foreign Power which shall be in Amity with Us, our Heirs or Successors: Provided always, that they be bound to pay for the same to Us, our Heirs and Successors, such Customs and Impositions, Subsidies and Taxes, as our other Subjects of our Kingdom of England, for the Time being, shall be bound to pay, beyond which We will that the Inhabitants of the aforesaid Province of the said Land, called Maryland, shall not be burdened.

XVI. And furthermore, of our more ample special Grace, and of our certain Knowledge, and mere Motion, We do, for Us, our

Heirs and Successors, grant unto the aforesaid now Baron of
Baltimore, his Heirs and Assigns, full and absolute Power and
Authority to make, erect, and constitute, within the Province
of Maryland, and the Islands and Islets aforesaid, such, and so
many Sea-Ports, Harbors, Creeks, and other Places of Unlading
and Discharge of Goods and Merchandizes out of Ships, Boats, and
other Vessels, and of Lading in the same, and in so many,
and such Places, and with such Rights, Jurisdictions, Liberties,
and Privileges, unto such Parts respecting, as to him or them
shall seem most expedient: And, that all and every the Ships,
Boats, and other Vessels whatsoever, coming to, or going from
the Province aforesaid, for the Sake of Merchandizing, shall be
laden and unladen at such Ports only as shall be so erected and
constituted by the said now Baron of Baltimore, his Heirs and
Assigns, any Usage, Custom, or other Thing whatsoever to the
contrary notwithstanding, Saving always to Us, our Heirs and
Successors, and to all the Subjects of our Kingdoms of England
and Ireland, of Us, our Heirs and Successors, the Liberty of
Fishing for Sea-Fish, as well in the Sea, Bays, Straits, and
navigable Rivers, as in the Harbors, Bays, and Creeks of the
Province aforesaid; and the Privilege of Salting and Drying
Fish on the Shores of the same Province; and, for that Cause, to
cut down and take Hedging-Wood and Twigs there growing,
and to build Huts and Cabins, necessary in this Behalf, in the
same Manner, as heretofore they reasonably might, or have used
to do. Which Liberties and Privileges, the said Subjects of Us,
our Heirs and Successors, shall enjoy, without notable Damage
or Injury in any wise to be done to the aforesaid now Baron
of Baltimore, his Heirs or Assigns, or to the Residents and
Inhabitants of the same Province in the Ports, Creeks, and
Shores aforesaid, and especially in the Woods and Trees there
growing. And if any Person shall do Damage or Injury of this
Kind, he shall incur the Peril and Pain of the heavy Displeasure
of Us, our Heirs and Successors, and of the due Chastisement of
the Laws, besides making Satisfaction.

XVII. Moreover, We will, appoint, and ordain, and by these
Presents, for Us, our Heirs and Successors, do grant unto the
aforesaid now Baron of Baltimore, his Heirs and Assigns, that
the same Baron of Baltimore, his Heirs and Assigns, from Time to

Time, forever, shall have, and enjoy the Taxes and Subsidies payable, or arising within the Ports, Harbors, and other Creeks and Places aforesaid, within the Province aforesaid, for Wares bought and sold, and Things there to be laden, or unladen, to be reasonably assessed by them, and the People there as aforesaid, on emergent Occasion; to whom We grant Power by these Presents, for Us, our Heirs and Successors, to assess and impose the said Taxes and Subsidies there, upon just Cause and in due Proportion.

XVIII. And furthermore, of our special Grace, and certain Knowledge, and mere Motion, We have given, granted, and confirmed, and by these Presents, for Us, our Heirs and Successors, do give, grant and confirm, unto the said now Baron of Baltimore, his Heirs and Assigns, full and absolute License, Power, and Authority, that he, the aforesaid now Baron of Baltimore, his Heirs and Assigns, from Time to Time hereafter, forever, may and can, at his or their Will and Pleasure, assign, alien, grant, demise, or enfeoff so many, such, and proportionate Parts and Parcels of the Premises, to any Person or Persons willing to purchase the same, as they shall think convenient, to have and to hold to the same Person or Persons willing to take or purchase the same, and his and their Heirs and Assigns, in Fee-simple, or Fee-tail, or for Term of Life, Lives or Years; to hold of the aforesaid now Baron of Baltimore, his Heirs and Assigns, by so many, such, and so great Services, Customs and Rents of this Kind, as to the same now Baron of Baltimore, his Heirs, and Assigns, shall seem fit and agreeable, and not immediately of Us, our Heirs and Successors. And We do give, and by these Presents, for Us, our Heirs and Successors, do grant to the same Person and Persons, and to each and every of them, License, Authority and Power, that such Person and Persons may take the Premises, or any Parcel thereof, of the aforesaid now Baron of Baltimore, his Heirs and Assigns, and hold the same to them and their Assigns, or Heirs, of the aforesaid Baron of Baltimore, his Heirs and Assigns, of what Estate of Inheritance soever, in Fee Simple or Fee-tail, or otherwise, as to them and the now Baron of Baltimore, his Heirs and Assigns, shall seem expedient; the Statute made in the Parliament of Lord Edward, Son of King Henry, late King of England, our Progenitor, commonly called the "Statute Quia Emptores Terrarum," heretofore published in our Kingdom of England, or any other Statute, Act, Ordinance, Usage, Law, or Custom, or any other Thing, Cause, or Matter, to the contrary thereof, heretofore had, done, published, ordained or provided to the contrary thereof notwithstanding.

XIX. We also, by these Presents, do give and grant License to the same Baron of Baltimore, and to his Heirs, to erect any Parcels of Land within the Province aforesaid, into Manors, and in every of those Manors, to have and to hold a Court-Baron, and all Things which to a Court Baron do belong; and to have and to Keep View of Frank-Pledge, for the Conservation of the Peace and better Government of those Parts, by themselves and their Stewards, or by the Lords, for the Time being to be deputed, or other of those Manors when they shall be constituted, and in the same to exercise all Things to the View of Frank Pledge belong.

XX. And further We will, and do, by these Presents, for Us, our Heirs and Successors, covenant and grant to, and with the aforesaid now Baron of Baltimore, His Heirs and Assigns, that We, our Heirs, and Successors, at no Time hereafter, will impose, or make or cause to be imposed, any Impositions, Customs, or other Taxations, Quotas, or Contributions whatsoever, in or upon the Residents or Inhabitants of the Province aforesaid for their Goods, Lands, or Tenements within the same Province, or upon any Tenements, Lands, Goods or Chattels within the Province aforesaid, or in or upon any Goods or Merchandizes within the Province aforesaid, or within the Ports or Harbors of the said Province, to be laden or unladen; And We will and do, for Us, our Heirs and Successors, enjoin and command that this our Declaration shall, from Time to Time, be received and allowed in all our Courts and Praetorian Judicatories, and before all the Judges whatsoever of Us, our Heirs and Successors, for a sufficient and lawful Discharge, Payment, and Acquittance thereof, charging all and singular the Officers and Ministers of Us, our Heirs and Successors, and enjoining them under our heavy Displeasure, that they do not at any Time presume to attempt any Thing to the contrary of the Premises, or that may in any wise contravene the same, but that they, at all Times, as is fitting, do aid and assist the aforesaid now Baron of Baltimore, and his Heirs, and the aforesaid Inhabitants and Merchants of the Province of Maryland aforesaid, and their Servants and Ministers, Factors and Assigns, in the fullest Use and Enjoyment of the Charter.

XXI. And furthermore We will, and by these Presents, for Us, our Heirs and Successors, do grant unto the aforesaid now Baron of Baltimore, his Heirs and Assigns, and to the Freeholders and Inhabitants of the said Province, both Present and to come, and to every of them, that the said Province, and the Freeholders or Inhabitants of the said Colony or Country, shall not henceforth be held or reputed a Member or Part of the Land of Virginia, or of any other Colony already transported, or hereafter to be transported, or be dependent on the same, or subordinate in any kind of Government, from which We do separate both the said Province, and Inhabitants thereof, and by these Presents do will to be distinct, and that they may be immediately subject to our Crown of England, and dependent on the same forever.

XXII. And if, peradventure, hereafter it may happen, that any Doubts or Questions should arise concerning the true Sense and Meaning of any Word, Clause, or Sentence, contained in this our present Charter, We will charge and command, That Interpretation to be applied always, and in all Things, and in all Courts and Judicatories whatsoever, to obtain which shall be judged to be the more beneficial, profitable, and favorable to the aforesaid now Baron of Baltimore, his Heirs and Assigns: Provided always, that no Interpretation thereof be made, whereby God's holy and true Christian Religion, or the Allegiance due to Us, our Heirs and Successors, may in any wise suffer by Change, Prejudice, or Diminution; although express Mention be not made in these Presents of the true yearly Value or Certainty of the Premises, or of any Part thereof; or of other Gifts and Grants made by Us, our Heirs and Successors, unto the said now Lord Baltimore, or any Statute, Act, Ordinance, Provision, Proclamation or Restraint, heretofore had, made, published, ordained or provided, or any other Thing, Cause, or Matter whatsoever, to the contrary thereof in any wise notwithstanding.

XXIII. In Witness Whereof We have caused these our Letters to be made Patent. Witness Ourself at Westminster, the Twentieth Day of June, in the Eighth Year of our Reign.

4

New England Political Documents (1620-1672)

It is impossible to find common denominators in the pattern of political action in early New England. The documents selected represent a variety of emerging political concepts.

Of greatest significance is the idea that men should have a known law to live by and that the fundamental rules of government should be set out in a constitution. Theoretically, at least, the constitution is produced by a voluntary association for political purposes, with the terms of the association stated in a compact or contract. The Mayflower Compact, which is the covenant of a separatist church adapted to civil society, is such an association. The Cambridge Agreement is the mutual pledge of the leading Puritans within the Massachusetts Bay Company to come out to America, if the charter of the company came with them. When executed, the Agreement made possible the transformation of the charter into the constitution of a self-governing commonwealth. The Fundamental Orders of Connecticut represents the first deliberate attempt to set out rules of government in a formal document.

Within the newly constituted governments, the people strove to establish legislative control. In Massachusetts Bay, Winthrop and the magistrates grudgingly yielded until the freemen of the colony were represented in the general court. Then the issue arose of the power of the majority of those enfranchised relative to that of the propertied minority. The case of *Sherman* v. *Keayne* highlighted that conflict and led to a bicameral legislature.

Thomas Hooker (1586-1647), the founder of Connecticut, and John Winthrop (1588-1649), the governor of Massachusetts, set out opposite views of the nature and necessity of popular consent to public decisions. Hooker preferred a government rooted in a broad base of consent, which delivered judgment in accordance with known public law. Winthrop distrusted the people and would have limited them to electing the magistrates. By that choice they ratified the rectitude of the magistrates and installed them as moral, but fallible executors and judges.

In the seventeenth century, the question of religious freedom was necessarily political. In New England the rule of religious uniformity prevailed, with the outstanding exception, of course, of Roger Williams. Expelled from Massachusetts Bay for a variety of heterodox opinions, Williams established practical religious freedom in Rhode Island. In the 1640s, he returned to England to obtain a charter for the colony, and while there, he entered the raging controversy between Independents and Presbyterians. His contribution was the potent polemic, *The Bloody Tenent of Persecution for Cause of Conscience*. The preface sets out his basic views. His letter to the town of Providence and his challenge to George Fox show that even for Williams, religious freedom had its limits.

In *Seedtime of the Republic, The Origin of the American Tradition of Political Liberty* (New York: Harcourt, Brace, 1953), Clinton Rossiter surveys the general factors causing "the Rise of Liberty." Part two contains essays about colonial leaders, among them, Thomas Hooker and Roger Williams. Samuel E. Morison, *Builders of the Bay Colony* (Boston: Houghton Mifflin, 1930) contains perceptive short biographies of nine Puritan leaders. The most recent and probably the most objective biography of Williams is Ola E. Winslow, *Master Roger Williams, A Biography* (New York: Macmillan, 1957). In reading the Mayflower Compact note (1) the implied aims of colonization; (2) what institution was formed by the compact; and (3) what its objectives were. In reading the Cambridge Agreement note (1) the terms of the agreement; and (2) what provisos were established. In reading The Fundamental Orders of Connecticut note (1) the expressed reasons for founding a government; (2) what framework of government was adopted; (3) what electoral provisions were included; (4) what protection against inexperience, moral incompetence, and tyranny were written into the agreement; and (5) in whose hands sovereignty was lodged. In reading the selections from Thomas Hooker's writings note (1) Hooker's view of the relative reliability of judges vis-à-vis the law; (2) the bases of his judgment; and (3) how he established the claim of the people to a voice in their own government. In reading the selections from Roger Williams note (1) the content of his announcement to Winthrop; (2) the point on which he sought Winthrop's advice; (3) the theses Williams presented in the Preface to *The Bloody Tenent;* (4) what Williams had to say about conscience and the need for preserving its freedom from coercion; (5) the character and quality of his arguments and rhetoric; and (6) what limitations upon the free exercise of conscience he allowed. In reading the selection from Winthrop's report of *Sherman* v. *Keayne* note (1) what occasioned the dispute; (2) what basic principle of government emerged during the dispute; (3) what fears the magistrates displayed over the possible loss of their veto power; and (4) what accommodation was forced upon the magistrates as a result of the case. In reading John Winthrop's "Little Speech on Liberty" note (1) what occasioned his little speech; (2) what he thought was the cause of the troubles agitating the country; (3) why he thought the people should exercise forebearance with their magistrates; (4) how he distinguished between the two kinds of liberty; and (5) how he sought to harmonize or synthesize the claims of authority and liberty.

A. The Mayflower Compact (1620)[1]

IN THE NAME OF GOD, AMEN. WE, WHOSE NAMES are underwritten, the Loyal Subjects of our dread Sovereign Lord King *James,* by the Grace of God, of *Great Britain, France,* and *Ireland,* King, *Defender of the Faith,* &c. Having undertaken for the Glory of God, and Advancement of the Christian Faith, and Honour of our King and Country, a Voyage to plant the first Colony in the northern Parts of *Virginia;* Do by these Presents, solemnly and mutually, in the Presence of God and one another, covenant and combine ourselves together into a civil Body Politick, for our better Ordering and Preservation, and Furtherance of the Ends aforesaid: And by Virtue hereof do enact, constitute, and frame, such just and equal Laws, Ordinances, Acts, Constitutions, and Officers, from time to time, as shall be thought most meet and convenient for the general Good of the Colony; unto which we promise all due Submission and Obedience. IN WITNESS whereof we have hereunto subscribed our names at *Cape-Cod* the eleventh of *November,* in the Reign of our Sovereign Lord King *James,* of *England, France,* and *Ireland,* the eighteenth, and of *Scotland,* the fifty-fourth, *Anno Domini,* 1620.

---

1. Francis N. Thorpe, (ed.), *The Federal and State Constitutions, Colonial Charters, and Other Organic Laws of the States, Territories, and Colonies Now or Heretofore forming the United States of America* (7 vols.; Washington: Government Printing Office, 1907) III, 1841.

B. The Cambridge Agreement (1629)[1]

Upon due consideracion of the state of the plantacion now in hand for new England, wherein wee (whose names are hereunto subscribed) have ingaged ourselves: and having weighed the greatnes of the worke in regard of the consequence, Gods glory and the churches good: As also in regard of the difficultyes and discouragements which in all probabilityes must be forcast upon the prosecution of this businesse: Considering whithall that this whole adventure growes upon the joynt confidence we have in each others fidelity and resolucion herein, so as no man of us would have adventured it without assurance of the rest: Now for the better encourragement of ourselves and others that shall joyne with us in this action, and to the end that every man may without scruple dispose ,of his estate and afayres as may best fitt his preparacion for this voyage, It is fully and faithfully agreed amongst us, and every of us doth hereby freely and sincerely promise and bynd himselfe in the word of a Christian and in the presence of God who is the searcher of all hearts, that we will be ready in our persons, and with such of our severall familyes as are to go with us and such provisions as we are able conveniently to furnish ourselves withall, to embark for the said plantacion by the first of march next, at such port or ports of this land as shall be agreed upon by the Company, to the end to passe the Seas (under Gods protection) to inhabite and continue in new England. Provided alwayes that before the last of September next the whole government together with the Patent for the said plantacion bee first by an order of Court legally transferred and established to remayne with us and others which shall inhabite upon the said plantacion. And provided also that if any shall be hindered by such just and inevitable Lett or other cause to be allowed by 3 parts of foure of these whose names are hereunto subscribed, then such persons for such tymes and during such letts to be dischardged of this bond. And we do further promise every one for himselfe that

---

1. *Winthrop Papers* (3 vols.; Boston: The Massachusetts Historical Society, 1929-43), II, 151-52. Original in the library of The Massachusetts Historical Society. Reprinted by permission.

shall fayle to be ready through his own default by the day appointed, to pay for every dayes default by the summe of *li.* to the use of the Company who shall be ready by the same day and tyme.

This was done by order of Court the 29th of August. 1629.

C. The Fundamental Orders of Connecticut (1638-39)[1]

Forasmuch as it hath pleased the Allmighty God by the wise disposition of his diuyne pruidence so to Order and dispose of things that we the Inhabitants and Residents of Windsor, Harteford and Wethersfield are now cohabiting and dwelling in and vppon the River of Conectecotte and the Lands thereunto adioyneing; And well knowing where a people are gathered togather the word of God requires that to mayntayne the peace and vnion of such a people there should be an orderly and decent Gouerment established according to God, to order and dispose of there affayres of the people at all seasons as occation shall require; doe therefore assotiate and conioyne our selues to be as one Publike State or Comonwelth; and doe, for our selues and our Successors and such as shall be adioyned to vs att any tyme hereafter, enter into Combination and Confederation togather, to mayntayne and preserve the liberty and purity of the gospell of our Lord Jesus wch we now prfesse, as also there disciplyne of the Churches, wch according to the truth of the said gospell is now practised amongst vs; As also in our Ciuell Affaires to be guided and gouerned according to such Lawes, Rules, Orders and decrees as shall be made, ordered & decreed, as followeth:

1. It is Ordered, sentenced and decreed, that ther shall be yerely two generall Assemblies or Courts, the one the second thursday in Aprill, the other the second thursday in September, following; the first shall be called the Courte of Election, wherein shall be yerely Chosen from tyme to tyme soe many Magestrats and other publike Officers as shall be found requisitte: Whereof one to be chosen Gouernour for the yeare ensueing and vntill another be chosen, and noe other Mages-

---

1. Thorpe, *The Federal and State Constitutions, I,* 519-22.

trate to be chosen for more then one yeare; pruided allwayes there be sixe chosen besids the Gouernour; wch being chosen and sworne according to an Oath recorded for that purpose shall haue power to administer justice according to the Lawes here established, and for want thereof according to the rule of the word of God; wch choise shall be made by all that are admitted freemen and haue taken the Oath of Fidelity, and doe cohabitte wthin this Jurisdiction, (hauing beene admitted Inhabitants by the maior prt of the Towne wherein they liue) or the mayor prte of such as shall be then prsent.

2. It is Ordered, sentensed and decreed, that the Election of the aforesaid Magestrats shall be on this manner: euery prson prsent and quallified for choyse shall bring in (to the prsons deputed to receaue the) one single papr wth the name of him written in yt whom he desires to haue Gouernour, and he that hath the greatest number of papers shall be Gouernor for that yeare. And the rest of the Magestrats or publike Officers to be chosen in this manner: The Secretary for the tyme being shall first read the names of all that are to be put to choise and then shall seuerally nominate them distinctly, and euery one that would haue the prson nominated to be chosen shall bring in one single paper written vppon, and he that would not haue him chosen shall bring in a blanke: and euery one that hath more written papers than blanks shall be a Magistrat for that yeare; wch papers shall be receaued and told by one or more that shall be then chosen by the court and sworne to be faythfull therein; but in case there should not be sixe chosen as aforesaid, besids the Gouernor, out of those wch are nominated, then he or they wch haue the most written paprs shall be a Magestrate or Magestrats for the ensueing yeare, to make vp the aforesaid nuber.

3. It is Ordered, sentenced and decreed, that the Secretary shall not nominate any prson, nor shall any prson be chosen newly into the Magestracy wch was not prpownded in some Generall Courte before, to be nominated the next Election; and to that end yt shall be lawfull for ech of the Townes aforesaid by their deputyes to nominate any two who they conceaue fitte to be put to election; and the Courte may ad so many more as they judge requisitt.

4. It is Ordered, sentenced and decreed that noe prson be chosen Gouernor aboue once in two yeares, and that the Gouernor be always a meber of some approved congregation, and formerly of the Magestracy wthin this Jurisdiction; and all the Magestrats Freemen of this Comonwelth: and that no Magestrate or other publike officer shall execute any prte of his or their Office before they are seuerally sworne, wch shall be done in the face of the Courte if they be prsent, and in case of absence by some deputed for that purpose.

5. It is Ordered, sentenced and decreed, that to the aforesaid Courte of Election the seurall Townes shall send their deputyes, and when the Elections are ended they may prceed in any publike searuice as at other Courts. Also the other Generall Courte in September shall be for makeing of lawes, and any other publike occation, wch conserns the good of the Comonwelth.

6. It is Ordered, sentenced and decreed, that the Gournor shall, ether by himselfe or by the secretary, send out sumons to the Constables of eur Towne for the cauleing of these two standing Courts, on month at lest before their seurall tymes: And also if the Gournor and the gretest prte of the Magestrats see cause vppon any spetiall occation to call a generall Courte, they may giue order to the secretary soe to doe wthin fowerteene dayes warneing; and if vrgent necessity so require, vppon a shorter notice, giueing sufficient grownds for yt to the deputyes when they meete, or els be questioned for the same; And if the Gournor and Major prte of Magestrats shall ether neglect or refuse to call the two Generall standing Courts or ether of them, as also at other tymes when the occations of the Comonwelth require, the Freemen thereof, or the Major prte of them, shall petition to them soe to doe: if then yt be ether denyed or neglected the said Freemen or the Major prte of them shall haue power to giue order to the Constables of the seuerall Townes to doe the same, and so may meete togather, and chuse to themselues a Moderator, and may prceed to do any Acte of power, wch any other Generall Courte may.

7. It is Ordered, sentenced and decreed that after there are warrants giuen out for any of the said Generall Courts, the Constable or Constables of ech Towne shall forthwth give notice

distinctly to the inhabitants of the same, in some Publike Assembly or by goeing or sending fro howse to howse, that at a place and tyme by him or them lymited and sett, they meet and assemble themselues togather to elect and chuse certen deputyes to be att the Generall Courte then following to agitate the afayres of the comonwelth; wch said Deputyes shall be chosen by all that are admitted Inhabitants in the seurall Townes and haue taken the oath of fidellity; pruided that non be chosen a Deputy for any Generall Courte wch is not a Freeman of this Comonwelth.

The a-foresaid deputyes shall be chosen in manner following: euery prson that is prsent and quallified as before exprssed, shall bring the names of such, written in seurrall papers. as they desire to haue chosen for that Imployment, and these 3 or 4, more or lesse, being the nuber agreed on to be chosen for that tyme, that haue greatest nuber of papers written for them shall be deputyes for that Courte; whose names shall be endorsed on the backe side of the warrant and returned into the Courte, wth the Constable or Constables hand vnto the same.

8. It is Ordered, sentenced and decreed, that Wyndsor, Hartford and Wethersfield shall haue power, ech Towne, to send fower of their freemen as deputyes to euery Generall Courte; and whatsoeuer other Townes shall be hereafter added to this Jurisdiction, they shall send so many deputyes as the Courte shall judge meete, a resonable prportion to the nuber of Freemen that are in the said Townes being to be attended therein; wch deputyes shall have the power of the whole Towne to giue their voats and alowance to all such lawes and orders as may be for the publike good, and unto wch the said Townes are to be bownd.

9. It is ordered and decreed, that the deputyes thus chosen shall haue power and liberty to appoynt a tyme and a place of meeting togather before any Generall Courte to aduise and consult of all such things as may concerne the good of the publike, as also to examine their owne Elections, whether according to the order, and if they or the gretest prte of them find any election to be illegall they may seclud such for prsent fro their meeting, and returne the same and their resons to the Courte; and if yt prou true, the Courte may fyne the prty or prtyes so

intruding and the Towne, if they see cause, and giue out a warrant to goe to a newe election in a legall way, either *in whole or in prte.* Also the said deputyes shall haue power to fyne any that shall be disorderly at their meetings, or for not coming in due tyme or place according to appoyntment; and they may returne the said fynes into the Courte if yt be refused to be paid, and the tresurer to take notice of yt, and to estreete or levy the same as he doth other fynes.

10. It is Ordered, sentenced and decreed, that euery Generall Courte, except such as through neglecte of the Gournor and the greatest prte of Magestrats the Freemen themselves doe call, shall consist of the Gouernor, or some one chosen to moderate the Court, and 4 other Magestrats at lest, wth the major prte of the deputyes of the seuerall Townes legally chosen; and in case the Freemen or major prte of them through neglect or refusall of the Gouernor and major prte of the magestrats, shall call a Courte, that yt shall consist of the major prte of Freemen that are prsent or thier deputyes, wth a Moderator chosen by them: *In wch said Generall Courts shall consist the supreme power of the Comonwelth,* and they only shall haue power to make laws or repeale them, to graunt leuyes, to admitt of Freemen, dispose of lands vndisposed of, to seuerall Townes or prsons, and also shall haue power to call ether Courte or Magestrate or any other prson whatsoeuer into question for any misdemeanour, and may for just causes displace or deale otherwise according to the nature of the offence; and also may deale in any other matter that concerns the good of this comonwelth, excepte election of Magestrats, wch shall be done by the whole boddy of Freemen: In wch Courte the Gouernour or Moderator shall haue power to order the Courte to giue liberty of spech, and silence vnceasonable and disorderly speakings, to put all things to voate, and in case the vote be equall to haue the casting voice. But non of these Courts shall be adiorned or dissolued wthout the consent of the major prte of the Court.

11. It is ordered, sentenced and decreed, that when any Generall Courte vppon the occasions of the Comonwelth haue agreed vppon any sum or somes of mony to be leuyed vppon the seuerall Townes wthin this Jurisdiction, that a Comittee be chosen to sett out and appoynt wt shall be the prportion of

euery Towne to pay of the said leuy, prvided the Comittees be made vp of an equall nuber out of each Towne.

14th January, 1638 the 11 Orders abouesaid are voted.

D. From the Writings of Thomas Hooker (1637-38)[1]

Thomas Hooker to John Winthrop (1637)

. . . From this seeming miscarriage in these particulars, you lead us to look unto the fountain from whence these and many other inconveniences will easily follow: namely, "to refer the decision of a civil question or controversy to whole churches, cannot be safe, nor warranted by any rule," as you conceive. I confess, you are now launched into a depth, and I have little to draw withal; and as far as I can either see or observe, there be few disputes, that ever came to my view, that find any bottom here. An answer, I suppose, must issue from the right judgment of the principles of state and church, as they are combined one with another. Something I have sometimes thought of the point, but the full debate of it would be too large for an ordinary letter. I shall attend only those things which you seasonably and pregnantly express in the cause. And here, I fully assent to those staple principles which you set down; to wit, that the people should choose some from amongst them—that they should refer matter of counsel to their counsellors, matter of judicature to their judges: only, the question here grows— what rule the judge must have to judge by; secondly, who those counsellors must be.

That in the matter which is referred to the judge, the sentence should lie in his breast, or be left to his discretion, according to which he should go, I am afraid it is a course which wants both safety and warrant: I must confess, I ever looked at it as a way which leads directly to tyranny, and so to confusion, and must plainly profess, if it was in my liberty, I should choose neither to live nor leave my posterity under such a government. Sit liber judex as the lawyers speak. 17 Deut., 10, 11—Thou shalt observe to do according to all that they inform,

---

1. *Collections of the Connecticut Historical Society* (30 vols.; Hartford: published for the Society, 1860-1957), I, 1-15, 20-21.

according to the *sentence of the Law*. Thou shalt seek the Law at his mouth: not ask what his discretion allows, but what the Law requires. . . .

And we know in other countries, had not the law overruled the lusts of men and the crooked ends of judges, many times, both places and people had been, in all reason, past all relief, in many cases of difficulty. You will know what the Heathen man said, by the candle-light of common sense: The law is not subject to passion, nor to be taken aside with self-seeking ends, and therefore ought to have chief rule over rulers themselves.

It's also a truth, that counsel should be sought from counsellors; but the question yet is, who those should be. Reserving smaller matters, which fall in occasionally in common course, to a lower counsel, in matters of greater consequence, which concern the common good, a general counsel, chosen by all, to transact businesses which concern all, I conceive, under favour, most suitable to rule and most safe for relief of the whole. This was the practice of the Jewish church, directed by God, Deut. 17: 10, 11; 2 Chron., 19; and the approved experience of the best ordered States give in evidence this way. Salomons' one wise man, and the one wise woman in Abel that delivered the city, shows the excellency of wisdom and of counsel where it is, but doth not conclude that one or few should be counsellors, since in the multitude of counsellors there is safety.

Thomas Hooker, Sermon to the General Court (1638)

Text: Deut. i:13. "Take you wise men, and understanding, and known among your tribes, and I will make them rulers over you." Captains over thousands, and captains over hundreds— over fifties—over tens, &c.

Doctrine. I. That the choice of public magistrates belongs unto the people, by God's own allowance.

II. The privilege of election, which belongs to the people, therefore must not be exercised according to their humours, but according to the blessed will and law of God.

III. They who have power to appoint officers and magistrates, it is in their power, also, to set the bounds and limitations of the power and place unto which they call them.

Reasons. 1. Because the foundation of authority is laid, firstly, in the free consent of the people.

2. Because, by a free choice, the hearts of the people will be more inclined to the love of the persons [chosen] and more ready to yield [obedience].

3. Because, of that duty and engagement of the people.

Uses. The lesson taught is threefold:

1st. There is matter of thankful acknowledgment, in the [appreciation] of God's faithfulness toward us, and the permission of these measures that God doth command and vouchsafe.

2dly. Of reproof—to dash the conceits of all those that shall oppose it.

3dly. Of exhortation—to persuade us, as God hath given us liberty, to take it.

And lastly—as God hath spared our lives, and given us them in liberty, so to seek the guidance of God, and to choose in God and for God."

E. From the Writings of Roger Williams (1636-72)[1]

Roger Williams to John Winthrop (c. 1636)

MUCH HONORED SIR—The frequent experience of your loving ear, ready and open toward me (in what your conscience hath permitted) as also of that excellent spirit of wisdom and prudence wherewith the Father of Lights hath endued you, embolden me to request a word of private advise with the soonest convenience, if it may be, by this messenger.

The condition of myself and those few families here planting with me, you know full well: we have no Patent: nor doth the face of Magistracy suit with our present condition. Hitherto, the masters of families have ordinarily met once a fortnight and consulted about our common peace, watch, and planting; and mutual consent have finished all matters with speed and peace.

Now of late some young men, single persons (of whom we

---

1. *The Complete Writings of Roger Williams,* ed. with an Introduction by Perry Miller (7 vols.; New York: Russell & Russell, Inc., 1963), III, 3-4; VI, 3-7, 219-28, 278-79, 357-60. Reprinted by permission.

had much need) being admitted to freedom of inhabitation, and promising to be subject to the orders made by the consent of the householders, are discontented with their estate, and seek the freedom of vote also, and equality, &c.

Beside, our dangers (in the midst of these dens of lions) now especially, call upon us to be compact in a civil way and power.

I have therefore had thoughts of propounding to my neighbors a double subscription, concerning which I shall humbly crave your help.

The first concerning ourselves, the matters of families: thus,

We whose names are hereunder written, late inhabitants of the Massachusetts, (upon occasion of some difference of conscience,) being permitted to depart from the limits of that Patent, under the which we came over into these parts, and being cast by the Providence of the God of Heaven, remote from others of our countrymen amongst the barbarians in this town of New Providence, do with free and joint consent promise each unto other, that, for our common peace and welfare (until we hear further of the King's royal pleasure concerning ourselves) we will from time to time subject ourselves in active or passive obedience to such orders and agreements, as shall be made by the greater number of the present householders, and such as shall be hereafter admitted by their consent into the same privilege and covenant in our ordinary meeting. In witness whereof we hereunto subscribe, &c.

Concerning those few young men, and any who shall hereafter (by your favorable connivance) desire to plant with us, this,—

We whose names are hereunder written, being desirous to inhabit in this Town of New Providence, do promise to subject ourselves in active or passive obedience to such orders and agreements as shall be made from time to time, by the greater number of the present householders of this Town, and such whom they shall admit into the same fellowship and privilege. In witness whereof, &c.

Hitherto we choose one, (named the officer,) to call the meeting at the appointed time: now it is desired by some of us that the householders by course perform that work, as also gather votes and see the watch go on, &c.

I have not yet mentioned these things to my neighbors, but shall as I see cause upon your loving counsel.

As also since the place I have purchased, secondly, at mine own charge and engagements, the inhabitants paying (by consent thirty shillings a piece as they come, until my charge be out for their particular lots: and thirdly, that I never made any other covenant with any person, but that if I got a place he should plant there with me: my query is this,—

Whither I may not lawfully desire this of my neighbors, that as I freely subject myself to common consent, and shall not bring in any person into the town without their consent: so also that against my consent no person be violently brought in and received.

I desire not to sleep in security and dream of a nest which no hand can reach. I cannot but expect changes, and the change of the last enemy death, yet dare I not despise a liberty, which the Lord seemeth to offer me, if for mine own or other peace: and therefore have I been thus bold to present my thoughts unto you. . . .

Preface to The Bloody Tenent of Persecution
for Cause of Conscience (1644)

First, That the blood of so many hundred thousand soules of Protestants and Papists, spilt in the Wars of present and former Ages, for their respective Consciences, is not required nor accepted by Jesus Christ the Prince of Peace.

Secondly, Pregnant Scripturs and Arguments are throughout the Worke proposed against the Doctrine of persecution for cause of Conscience.

Thirdly, Satisfactorie Answers are given to Scriptures, and objections produced by Mr. Calvin, Beza, Mr. Cotton, and the Ministers of the New English Churches and others former and later, tending to prove the Doctrine of persecution for cause of Conscience.

Fourthly, The Doctrine of persecution for cause of Conscience, is proved guilty of all the blood of the Soules crying for vengeance under the Altar.

Fifthly, All Civill States with their Officers of justice in their respective constitutions and administrations are proved essentially Civill, and therefore not Judges, Governours or Defendours of the Spirituall or Christian state and Worship.

Sixtly, It is the will and command of God, that (since the comming of his Sonne the Lord Jesus) a permission of the most Paganish, Jewish, Turkish, or Antichristian consciences and worships, bee granted to all men in all Nations and Countries: and they are onely to bee fought against with that Sword which is only (in Soule matters) able to conquer, to wit, the Sword of Gods Spirit, the Word of God.

Seventhly, The state of the Land of Israel, the Kings and people thereof in Peace & War, is proved figurative and ceremoniall, and no patterne nor president for any Kingdome or civill state in the world to follow.

Eightly, God requireth not an uniformity of Religion to be inacted and inforced in any civill state; which inforced uniformity (sooner or later) is the greatest occasion of civill Warre, ravishing of conscience, persecution of Christ Jesus in his servants, and of the hypocrisie and destruction of millions of souls.

Ninthly, In holding an inforced uniformity of Religion in a civill state, wee must necessarily disclaime our desires and hopes of the Jewes conversion to Christ.

Tenthly, An inforced uniformity of Religion throughout a Nation or civill state, confounds the Civill and Religious, denies the principles of Christianity and civility, and that Jesus Christ is come in the Flesh.

Eleventhly, The permission of other consciences and worships then a state professeth, only can (according to God) procure a firme and lasting peace, (good assurance being taken according to the wisedome of the civill state for uniformity of civill obedience from all sorts.)

Twelfthly, lastly, true civility and Christianity may both flourish in a state or Kingdome, notwithstanding the permission of divers and contrary consciences, either of Jew or Gentile.

Roger Williams to John Endecott (1651)

. . . Be pleased then (honored Sir) to remember that, that

thing which we call Conscience is of such a nature, (especially in Englishmen) as once a Pope of Rome at the suffering of an Englishman in Rome, himself observed) that although it be groundless, false, and deluded, yet it is not by any arguments or torments easily removed.

I speak not of the stream of the multitude of all nations, which have their ebbings and flowings in religion, (as the longest sword, and strongest arm of flesh carries it.) But I speak of Conscience, a persuasion fixed in the mind and heart of a man, which enforceth him to judge (as Paul said of himself a persecutor) and to do so and so, with respect to God, his worship, &c.

This Conscience is found in all mankind, more or less, in Jews, Turks, Papists, Protestants, Pagans, &c. And to this purpose let me freely without offence remember you (as I did Mr. Clarke newly come up from his sufferings amongst you) I say, remember you of the same story I did him, 'twas that of William Hartley, in Queen Elizabeth her days, who receiving the sentence of hanging, drawing, &c., spake confidently (as afterward he suffered) what tell you me of hanging, &c. If I had ten thousand millions of lives, I would spend them all for the Faith of Rome, &c.

Sir, I am far from glancing the least countenance on the Consciences of Papists, yea or on some Scotch and English Protestants too, who turn up all roots, and lay all level and in blood, for exaltation of their own way and Conscience. All that I observe is, that boldness and confidence, zeal and resolution, as it is commendable in a kind when it seriously respects a Deity, so also, the greatest confidence hath sometimes need of the greatest search and examination.

I confess, that for confidence no Romish Priest, hath ever exceeded the martyrs or witnesses of Jesus: Witness (amongst so many) that holy English woman, who cried out, that if every hair of her head were a life or man, they should burn for the name of the Lord Jesus: But Sir, your principles and conscience, not to respect Romish or English, saints or sinners: William Hartley, and that Woman, with all their lives, you are bound by your Conscience to punish (and it may be) to hang or burn, if they transgress against your Conscience, and that because

(according to Mr. Cotton's monstrous distinction (as some of
his chief brethren to my knowledge hath called it) not because
they sin in matters of Conscience, (which he denies the Magistrate to deal in,) but because they sin against their Conscience.

Secondly, It is so notoriously known, that the Consciences of
the most holy men, zealous for God and his Christ to death
and admiration, yea, even in our own country, and in Queen
Mary's days especially, have been so grossly mislead by mistaken
Consciences in matters concerning the worship of God, the
coming out of the Antichristian Babel, and the rebuilding of
the spiritual Jerusalem that I need but hint who were they that
penned the Common Prayer (in its time, as glorious an idol,
and as much adored by Godly persons, as any invention now
extant.) I say who they were that lived and died (five in the
flames) zealous for their Bishopricks, yea and some too too
zealous for their Popish ceremonies, against the doubting Consciences of their Brethren: At which and more, we that now
have risen in our Father's stead, wonder and admire how such
piercing eyes could be deceived, such Watchmen blinded and
deluded. But

Thirdly, We shall not so much wonder when we lift up our
trembling eyes to Heaven, and remember ourselves (poor dust)
that our thoughts are not as the thoughts of our Maker, that,
that which in the eyes of man (as the Lord Jesus tells us, Luc.
16.) is of high and sweet esteem, it stinks and is abomination
with God: Hence such Worships, such Churches, such glorious
professions and practices may be, as may ravish themselves and
the beholders, when with the piercing eyes of the most High,
they may look counterfeit and ugly, and be found but (spiritu-
ally) Whores and Abominations.

Fourthly, Wise men used to enquire, what Motives, what
Occasions, what Snares, what Temptations were there, which
moved, which drew, which allured, &c. This is the Apology
which the five Apologists (Mr. Goodwin, Mr. Nye, &c.,) made
to the Parliament, to wit, That they were not tempted with the
moulding of New Commonwealths, after which they might be
moved to frame their religion, &c.

Surely, Sir, the baits, the temptations, the snares laid to catch
you, were not few, nor common, nor laid to every foot. Saul

pretended zeal to the name of God, and love to Israel in per-
secuting the poor Gibeonites to death, but honor me before
the people, was the main engine that turned the wheels of all
his actions and devotions. What set Jeroboam's brains to consult and plot the invention of a new Religion, Worship, Priests,
&c., but honor, and the fear of the loss of his gained honor?
What moved Jehu to be false and halting with God after so
much glorious zeal in the Reformation? Yea, I had almost said,
what moved David to stab Uriah (the fire of God) with his
pen, but the fear of dishonor in the discovery of his sin, though
doubtless there was some mixtures of the fear of his God's
displeasure and dishonor, also?

Sir, it is no small offer, the choice and applause and rule over
so many towns, so many holy, of many wise, in such a holy way
as you believe you are in: To say nothing of strong drinks and
wines, the fat and sweet of this and other lands: These and
others are snares which without abundant strength from God
will catch and hold the strongest feet: Sir, I have known you
strong, in repelling strong temptations, but I cannot but fear
and lament, that some of these and others have been too strong
and potent for you.

Fifthly, We not only used to say proverbially, but the Spirit
of God expressly tells us, that there is a mind-bewitching, a
bewitching of the very consciences and spirits of men. That as
in witchcraft, a stronger and supernatural power lays hold upon
the powers of Nature, with a suppressing or elevating of those
powers beneath or above themselves: So is it with the very
Spirits and Consciences of the most intelligent and conscientious,
when the Father of Spirits is pleased in his righteous displeasure
and jealously, so to suffer it to be with ours. . . .

. . . Oh remember it is a dangerous combat for the potsheards
of the earth to fight with their dreadful Potter: It is a dismal
battle for poor naked feet to kick against the Pricks; It is a
dreadful voice from the King of Kings, and Lord of Lords:
Endicot, Endicot, why huntest thou me? why huntest thou me?
why imprisonest thou me? why finest, why so bloodily whippest,
why wouldest thou (did not I hold thy bloody hands) hang and
burn me? Yea, Sir, I beseech you remember that it is a dan-

gerous thing to put this to the may be, to the venture or hazard, to the possibility. If it is possible (may you well say) that since I hunt, I hunt not the life of my Saviour, and the blood of the Lamb of God. I have fought against many several sorts of Consciences, is it beyond all possibility and hazard, that I have not fought against God, that I have not persecuted Jesus in some of them?

Sir, I must be humbly bold to say, that 'tis impossible for any man or men to maintain their Christ by their sword, and to worship a true Christ! to fight against all Consciences opposite to theirs, and not to fight against God in some of them, and to hunt after the precious life of the true Lord Jesus Christ. Oh remember whether your Principles and Consciences must in time and opportunity force you. 'Tis but worldly policy and compliance with men and times (God's mercy overruling) that holds your hands from murdering of thousands and ten thousands were your power and command as great as once the bloody Roman Emperors was.

The truth is (and yourself and others have said it) by your principles such whom you count Heretics, Blasphemers, Seducers, to be put to death; you cannot be faithful to your principles and Consciences, if you satisfy them with but imprisonment, fining, whipping and banishing the Heretics, and by saying that banishing is a kind of death, as some chief with you (in my case formerly) have said it.

Sir, 'Tis like you knew or have heard of the man that said he would never conform publicly, although he did subscribe in private for his liberty sake of Preaching: That, although he did conform in some things, yet in all he never would: That, although he did himself yield, yet he would not molest and enforce others: That although he yielded that others did molest them, yet himself would never persecute, and yet did all.

But oh poor dust and ashes, like stones once rolling down the Alps, like the Indian canoes or English boats loose and adrift, where stop we until infinite mercy stop us, especially when a false fire of zeal and Confidence drives us, though against the most Holy and eternal himself?

Oh remember the black Catalogues it hath pleased the most jealous and righteous God to make of his fiery Judgments and most dreadful strokes on eminent and remarkable persecutors even in this life. It hath been his way and course in all countries, in Germany, France and England, (especially) whatever their pretences have been against Heretics, Rebels, Schismatics, Blasphemers, Seducers, &c. How hath he left them to be their own Accusers, Judges, Executioners, some by hanging, some by stabbing, some by drowning and poisoning themselves, some by running mad, and some by drinking in the very same cup which they had filled to others?

Some may say, such persecutors hunted God and Christ, but I, but we, &c. I answer, the Lord Jesus Christ foretold how wonderfully the wisest of the world, should be mistaken in the things of Christ, and a true visible Christ Jesus! When did we see thee naked, hungry, thirsty, sick, in prison, &c. How easy, how common, how dreadful these mistakes?

Oh remember once again (as I began) and I humbly desire to remember with you, that every gray hair now on both our heads, is a Boanerges, a son of Thunder, and a warning piece to prepare us, for the weighing of our last anchors, and to be gone from hence, as if we had never been.

'Twas mercy infinite, that stopped provoked Justice from blowing out our Candles in our youths, but now the feeding Substance of the Candles gone, and 'tis impossible without repentance,) to recall our actions! nay with repentance, to recall our minutes past us.

Sir, I know I have much presumed upon your many weighty affairs and thoughts, I end with an humble cry to the Father of mercies, that you may take David's counsel, and silently commune with your own heart upon your bed, reflect upon your own spirit, and believe Him that said it to his over zealous disciples, You know not what spirit you are of: That, no sleep may seize upon your eyes, nor slumber upon your eyelids, until your serious thoughts have seriously, calmly, and unchangeably (through help from Christ Jesus) fixed.

First, On a moderation towards the Spirits and Consciences of all mankind, merely differing from or opposing yours with only Religious and Spiritual opposition.

Secondly, A deep and cordial resolution (in these wonderful searching, disputing and dissenting times) to search, to listen,

to pray, to fast, and more fearfully, more tremblingly to enquire
what the holy pleasure, and the holy mysteries of the most Holy
are; in whom I humbly desire to be

Your poor fellow-servant, unfeignedly,

respective and faithful,

ROGER WILLIAMS.

Roger Williams to the Town of Providence (c. 1654)

That I should ever speak or write a tittle, that tends to such
an infinite liberty of conscience, is a mistake, and which I have
ever disclaimed and abhorred. To prevent such mistakes, I shall
only propose this case: There goes many a ship to sea, with
many hundred souls in one ship, whose weal and woe is common, and is a true picture of a commonwealth, or a human
combination or society. It has fallen out sometimes, that both
papists and protestants, Jews and Turks, may be embarked in
one ship; upon which supposal I affirm, that all the liberty of
conscience, that ever I pleaded for, turns upon these two things
—that none of the papists, protestants, Jews, or Turks, be forced
to come to the ship's prayers or worship, if they practice any.
I further add, that I never denied, that notwithstanding this
liberty, the commander of this ship ought to command the ship's
course, yea, and also command that justice, peace and sobriety,
be kept and practiced, both among the seamen and all the passengers. If any of the seamen refuse to perform their services,
or passengers to pay their freight; if any refuse to help, in person or purse, towards the common charges or defence; if any
refuse to obey the common laws and orders of the ship, concerning their common peace or preservation; if any shall mutiny
and rise up against their commanders and officers; if any should
preach or write that there ought to be no commanders or officers, because all are equal in Christ, therefore no masters nor
officers, no laws nor orders, nor corrections nor punishments;—
I say, I never denied, but in such cases, whatever is pretended,
the commander or commanders may judge, resist, compel and
punish such transgressors, according to their deserts and merits.
This if seriously and honestly minded, may, if it so please the

Father of lights, let in some light to such as willingly shut not their eyes.

I remain studious of your common peace and liberty.

ROGER WILLIAMS

Roger Williams to George Fox or any other of my Countrymen at Newport, who say they are the Apostles and Messengers of Christ Jesus (1672)

In humble confidence of the help of the Most High, I offer to maintain in public, against all comers, these fourteen Propositions following, to wit: the first seven at Newport, and the other seven at Providence. For the time when, I refer it to G. Fox and his friends at Newport.

Only I desire

1. To have three days notice, before the day you fix on.

2. That without interruption (or many speaking at once) the Conference may continue from nine in the morning till about four in the afternoon; and

3. That if either of the seven Propositions be not finished in one day, the Conference may continue and go on some few hours the next day.

4. That either of us disputing, shall have free uninterrupted liberty to speak (in Answers and Replies) as much and as long as we please, and thus give the opposite the same liberty.

That the whole may be managed with that ingenuity and humanity, as such an exercise, by such persons in such conditions, at such a time, ought to be managed and performed, the Propositions are these that follow:

First. That the people called Quakers, are not true Quakers according to the Holy Scriptures.

2. That the Christ they profess is not the true Lord Jesus Christ.

3. That the Spirit by which they are acted, is not the Spirit of God.

4. That they do not own the Holy Scriptures.

5. Their principles and professions, are full of contradictions and hypocrisies.

6. That their religion is not only an heresy in the matters of worship, but also in the doctrines of Repentance, Faith, &c.

7. Their religion is but a confused mixture of Popery, Armineanisme, Socinesanisme, Judaisme, &c.

8. The people called Quakers (in effect) hold no God, no Christ, no Spirit, no Angel, no Devil, no Resurrection, no Judgement, no Heaven, no Hell, but what is in man.

9. All that their Religion requires (external and internal) to make converts and proselites, amounts to no more than what a reprobate may easily attain unto and perform.

10. That the Popes of Rome do not swell with, and exercise a greater pride, then the quakers Spirit have expressed, and doth aspire unto, although many truly humble souls may be in other Religions.

11. The Quakers' Religion is more obstructive and destructive to the conversion and salvation of the souls of people, then most of the Religions this day extant in the world.

12. The sufferings of the Quakers are not true evidence of the Truth of their Religion.

13. That their many books and writings are extremely poor, lame, naked, and swelled up only with high titles and words of boasting and vapor.

14. That the spirit of their Religion tends mainly,

1. To reduce persons from civility to barbarism.

2. To an arbitrary government, and the dictates and decrees of that sudden Spirit that acts them.

3. To a sudden cutting off of people, yea of Kings and Princes opposing them.

4. To as fiery persecutions for matters of religion and Conscience, as hath been or can be practiced by any Hunters or Persecutors in the world.

Under these forementioned heads (if the Spirit of the Quakers dare civilly to argue) will be opened many of the Popish, Protestant, Jewish and Quakers Positions, which cannot here be mentioned, in the Dispute (if God please) they must be alledged, and the examination left to every person's conscience, as they will answer to God, (at their own perils) in the great day approaching.

F.

Sherman v. Keayne (1642-44)[1]

At the same general court there fell out a great business upon
a very small occasion. Anno 1636, there was a stray sow in
Boston, which was brought to Captain Keayne: he had it cried
divers times, and divers came to see it, but none made claim to
it for near a year. He kept it in his yard with a sow of his own.
Afterwards one Sherman's wife, having lost such a sow, laid
claim to it, but came not to see it, till Captain Keayne had killed
his own sow. After being showed the stray sow, and finding it
to have other marks then she had claimed her sow by, she gave
out that he had killed her sow. The noise hereof being spread
about the town, the matter was brought before the elders of
the church as a case of offence; many witnesses were examined,
and Captain Keayne was cleared. She not being satisfied with
this, by the instigation of one George Story, a young merchant
of London, who kept in her house, (her husband being then in
England,) and had been brought before the governor upon
complaint of Captain Keayne as living under suspicion, she
brought the cause to the inferior court at Boston, where, upon a
full hearing, Capt. Keayne was again cleared, and the jury gave
him £3 for his cost, and he bringing his action against Story
and her for reporting about that he had stolen her sow, recovered
£20 damages of either of them. Story upon this searcheth town
and country to find matter against Captain Keayne about this
stray sow, and got one of his witnesses to come into Salem court
and to confess there that he had forsworn himself; and upon this
he petitions in Sherman's name, to this general court, to have the
cause heard again, which was granted, and the best part of seven
days were spent in examining of witnesses and debating of the
cause; and yet it was not determined, for there being nine
magistrates and thirty deputies, no sentence could by law pass
without the greater number of both, which neither plaintiff nor

---

1. James K. Hosmer (ed.), *Winthrop's Journal* (2 vols.; New York: Charles
Scribner's Sons, 1908), II, 64-66, 120-21, 164. Reprinted by permission of
Barnes and Noble, Inc.

defendant had, for there were for the plaintiff two magistrates and fifteen deputies, and for the defendant seven magistrates and eight deputies, the other seven deputies stood doubtful. Much contention and earnestness there was, which indeed did mostly arise from the difficulty of the case, in regard of cross witnesses, and some prejudices (as one professed) against the person, which blinded some men's judgments that they could not attend the true nature and course of the evidence. For all the plaintiff's witnesses amounted to no more but an evidence of probability, so as they might all swear true, and yet the sow in question might not be the plaintiff's. But the defendant's witnesses gave a certain evidence, upon their certain knowledge, and that upon certain grounds, (and these as many and more and of as good credit as the others,) so as if this testimony were true, it was not possible the sow should be the plaintiff's. Besides, whereas the plaintiff's wife was admitted to take her oath for the marks of her sow, the defendant and his wife (being a very godly sober woman) was denied the like, although propounded in the court by Mr. Cotton, upon that rule in the law he shall swear he hath not put his hands to his neighbor's goods. Yet they both in the open court solemnly, as in the presence of God, declared their innocency, etc. Further, if the case had been doubtful, yet the defendant's lawful possession ought to have been preferred to the plaintiff's doubtful title, for in equali jure melior est conditio possidentis. But the defendant being of ill report in the country for a hard dealer in his course of trading, and having been formerly censured in the court and in the church also, by admonition for such offences, carried many weak minds strongly against him. And the truth is, he was very worthy of blame in that kind, as divers others in the country were also in those times, though they were not detected as he was; yet to give every man his due, he was very useful to the country both by his hospitality and otherwise. But one dead fly spoils much good ointment.

There was great expectation in the country, by occasion of Story's clamors against him, that the cause would have passed against the captain, but falling out otherwise, gave occasion to many to speak unreverently of the court, especially of the magistrates, and the report went, that their negative voice had hindered the course of justice, and that these magistrates must be put out, that the power of the negative voice might be taken away. Thereupon it was thought fit by the governor and other of the magistrates to publish a declaration of the true state of the cause, that truth might not be condemned unknown. This was framed before the court brake up; for prevention whereof, the governor tendered a declaration in nature of a pacification, whereby it might have appeared, that, howsoever the members of the court dissented in judgment, yet they were the same in affection, and had a charitable opinion of each other; but this was opposed by some of the plaintiff's part, so it was laid by. And because there was much laboring in the country upon a false supposition, that the magistrate's negative voice stopped the plaintiff in the case of the sow, one of the magistrates published a declaration of the necessity of upholding the same. . . .

The sow business had started another question about the magistrates' negative vote in the general court. The deputies generally were very earnest to have it taken away; whereupon one of the magistrates wrote a small treatise, wherein he laid down the original of it from the patent, and the establishing of it by order of the general court in 1634, showing thereby how it was fundamental to our government, which, if it were taken away, would be a mere democracy. He showed also the necessity and usefulness of it by many arguments from scripture, reason, and common practice, etc. Yet this would not satisfy, but the deputies and common people would have it taken away; and yet it was apparent (as some of the deputies themselves confessed) the most did not understand it. An answer also was written (by one of the magistrates as was conceived) to the said treatise undertaking to avoid all the arguments both from the patent and from the order, etc. This the deputies made great use of in this court, supposing they had now enough to carry the cause clearly with them, so as they pressed earnestly to have it presently determined. But the magistrates told them the matter was of great concernment, even to the very frame of our government; it had been established upon serious consultation and consent of all the elders; it had been continued without any inconvenience or apparent mischief these fourteen years, therefore it would not be safe nor of good report to alter on such a sudden, and without the advice of the elders: offering withal, that if upon such advice and consideration it should appear to be inconvenient, or not warranted by the patent and the said order, etc., they should be ready to join with them in taking it away. Upon these propositions they were stilled, and so an order was drawn up to this effect, that it was desired that every member of the court would take advice, etc., and that it should be no offence for any, either publicly or privately, to declare their opinion in the case, so it were modestly, etc., and that the elders should be desired to give their advice before the next meeting of this court. It was the magistrates' only care to gain time, that so the people's heat might be abated, for then they knew they would hear reason, and that the advice of the elders might be interposed; and that there might be liberty to reply to the answer, which was very long and tedious, which accordingly was done soon after the court, and published to good satisfaction. One of the elders also wrote a small treatise, wherein scholastically and religiously he handled the question, laying down the several forms of government both simple and mixt, and the true form of our government, and the unavoidable change into a democracy, if the negative voice were taken away; and answered all objections, and so concluded for the continuance of it, so as the deputies and the people also, having their heat moderated by time, and their judgments better informed by what they had learned about it, let the cause fall, and he who had written the answer to the first defence, appeared no further in it. . . .

At the same court in the first month, upon the motion of the deputies, it was ordered that the court should be divided in their consultations, the magistrates by themselves, and the deputies by themselves, what the one agreed upon they should send to the other, and if both agreed, then to pass, etc. This order determined the great contention about the negative voice.

G. John Winthrop, "Little Speech on Liberty" (1645)[1]

I suppose something may be expected from me, upon this

---

1. Hosmer, *Winthrop's Journal*, II, 237-39.

charge that is befallen me, which moves me to speak now to you; yet I intend not to intermeddle in the proceedings of the court, or with any of the persons concerned therein. Only I bless God, that I see an issue of this troublesome business. I also acknowledge the justice of the court, and, for mine own part, I am well satisfied, I was publicly charged, and I am publicly and legally acquitted, which is all I did expect or desire. And though this be sufficient for my justification before men, yet not so before the God, who hath seen so much amiss in my dispensations (and even in this affair) as calls me to be humble. For to be publicly and criminally charged in this court, is matter of humiliation, (and I desire to make a right use of it,) notwithstanding I be thus acquitted. If her father had spit in her face, (saith the Lord concerning Miriam,) should she not have been ashamed seven days? Shame had lien upon her, whatever the occasion had been. I am unwilling to stay you from your urgent affairs, yet give me leave (upon this special occasion) to speak a little more to this assembly. It may be of some good use, to inform and rectify the judgments of some of the people, and may prevent such distempers as have arisen amongst us. The great questions that have troubled the country, are about the authority of the magistrates and the liberty of the people. It is yourselves who have called us to this office, and being called by you, we have our authority from God, in way of an ordinance, such as hath the image of God eminently stamped upon it, the contempt and violation whereof hath been vindicated with examples of divine vengeance. I entreat you to consider, that when you choose magistrates, you take them from among yourselves, men subject to like passions as you are. Therefore when you see infirmities in us, you should reflect upon your own, and that would make you bear the more with us, and not be severe censurers of the failings of your magistrates, when you have continual experience of the like infirmities in yourselves and others. We account him a good servant, who breaks not his covenant. The covenant between you and us is the oath you have taken of us, which is to this purpose, that we shall govern you and judge your causes by the rules of God's laws and our own, according to our best skill. When you agree with a workman to build you a ship or house, etc., he undertakes as well for his skill as for his faithfulness, for it is his profession, and you pay him for both. But when you call one to be a magistrate, he doth not profess nor undertake to have sufficient skill for that office, nor can you furnish him with gifts, etc., therefore you must run the hazard of his skill and ability. But if he fail in faithfulness, which by his oath he is bound unto, that he must answer for. If it fall out that the case be clear to common apprehension, and the rule clear also, if he transgress here, the error is not in the skill, but in the evil of the will: it must be required of him. But if the case be doubtful, or the rule doubtful, to men of such understanding and parts as your magistrates are, if your magistrates should err here, yourselves must bear it.

For the other point concerning liberty, I observe a great mistake in the country about that. There is a twofold liberty, natural (I mean as our nature is now corrupt) and civil or federal. The first is common to man with beasts and other creatures. By this, man, as he stands in relation to man simply, hath liberty to do what he lists; it is a liberty to evil as well as to good. This liberty is incompatible and inconsistent with authority, and cannot endure the least restraint of the most just authority. The exercise and maintaining of this liberty makes men grow more evil, and in time to be worse than brute beasts: omnes sumus licentia deteriores. This is that great enemy of truth and peace, that wild beast, which all the ordinances of God are bent against, to restrain and subdue it. The other kind of liberty I call civil or federal, it may also be termed moral, in reference to the covenant between God and man, in the moral law, and the politic covenants and constitutions, amongst men themselves. This liberty is the proper end and object of authority, and cannot subsist without it; and it is a liberty to that only which is good, just, and honest. This liberty you are to stand for, with the hazard (not only of your goods, but) of your lives, if need be. Whatsoever crosseth this, is not authority, but a distemper thereof. This liberty is maintained and exercised in a way of subjection to authority; it is of the same kind of liberty wherewith Christ hath made us free. The woman's own choice makes such a man her husband; yet being so chosen, he is her lord, and she is to be subject to him, yet in a way of liberty, not of bondage; and a true wife accounts her subjection her honor and freedom, and would not think her condition safe and free, but in her subjection to her husband's authority. Such is the liberty of the church under the authority of Christ, her king and husband; his yoke is so easy and sweet to her as a bride's ornaments; and if through frowardness or wantonness, etc., she shake it off, at any time, she is at no rest in her spirit, until she take it up again; and whether her lord smiles upon her, and embraceth her in his arms, or whether he frowns, or rebukes, or smites her, she apprehends the sweetness of his love in all, and is refreshed, supported, and instructed by every such dispensation of his authority over her. On the other side, ye know who they are that complain of this yoke and say, let us break their bands, etc., we will not have this man to rule over us. Even so, brethren, it will be between you and your magistrates. If you stand for your natural corrupt liberties, and will do what is good in your own eyes, you will not endure the least weight of authority, but will murmur, and oppose, and be always striving to shake off that yoke; but if you will be satisfied to enjoy such civil and lawful liberties, such as Christ allows you, then will you quietly and cheerfully submit unto that authority which is set over you, in all the administrations of it, for your good. Wherein, if we fail at any time, we hope we shall be willing (by God's assistance) to hearken to good advice from any of you, or in any other way of God; so shall your liberties be preserved, in upholding the honor and power of authority amongst you.

New England's First Fruits (1643)[1]

This pamphlet was published in London in 1643. The first part, which deals with the Indians, is omitted here; the first section reprinted exhibits the great and justifiable pride of the Puritans in having established a college in the early stages of settlement. The General Court of Massachusetts Bay voted to establish a college in 1636, and two years later, John Harvard bequeathed some £400 and his library to the college. The real beginnings of Harvard College came in 1640 when Henry Dunster was inaugurated president, and he established a curriculum based on the traditional arts and sciences. A Cambridge graduate, the young president would not compromise his idea of what a college should be. He built Harvard on the English collegiate model with tutors and scholars in residence. The first class of nine graduated in 1642 and this event apparently prompted the publication of the pamphlet.

It commonly has been assumed that the educational purposes of the Puritans were controlled exclusively by religious considerations. In *The Puritan Pronaos,* Samuel Eliot Morison takes issue with this view. "The bachelor's course was intended to be, and was, a liberal education for the times, having no practical or professional value, equally suitable for a future divine, physician, or ruler." The second section of the document reprinted here is an example of the extensive promotional literature of the seventeenth century. It emphasizes the economic advantage of New England and attempts to allay the fears of potential colonists.

Samuel E. Morison, *The Intellectual Life of Colonial New England* (New York: New York University Press, 1951) was originally published as *The Puritan Pronaos.* It is especially good in its analysis of New England education. The intellectual base of the orthodox Puritan community is the theme of Perry Miller, *The New England Mind; the Seventeenth Century* (New York: Macmillan, 1939). In reading this selection note (1) what educational purposes Harvard College was

---

1. *Old South Leaflet #51* (Boston: Directors of the Old South Work, n.d.).

expected to serve; (2) how it was organized; (3) the main elements of the curriculum; (4) what rules were provided for the students; (5) what degree requirements were established; (6) what evidences of divine favor in support of the colony the authors discovered; (7) what further evidence of favor the authors hoped for; and (8) what arguments the authors used to popularize the colony in Britain.

AFTER GOD HAD CARRIED US SAFE TO NEW ENGLAND, and wee had builded our houses, provided necessaries for our liveli-hood, rear'd convenient places for Gods worship and setled the Civill Government: One of the next things we longed for, and looked after was to advance *Learning*, and perpetuate it to Posterity, dreading to leave an illiterate Ministery to the Churches, when our present Ministers shall lie in the Dust. And as wee were thinking and consulting how to effect this great Work; it pleased God to stir up the heart of one Mr. *Harvard* (a godly Gentlemen and a lover of Learning, there living amongst us) to give the one halfe of his Estate (it being in all about £700) towards the erecting of a Colledge, and all his Library: after him another gave £300. others after them cast in more, and the publique hand of the State added the rest: the Colledge was, by common consent, appointed to be at *Cambridge*, (a place very pleasant and accommodate and is called (according to the name of the first founder) *Harvard Colledge*.

The Edifice is very faire and comely within and without, having in it a spacious Hall; (where they daily meet at Commons, Lectures, Exercises) and a large Library with some Bookes to it, the gifts of diverse of our friends, their Chambers and studies also fitted for, and possessed by the Students, and all other roomes of Office necessary and convenient, with all needfull Offices thereto belonging: And by the side of the Colledge a faire *Grammar* Schoole, for the training up of young Schollars, and fitting of them for *Academicall Learning*, that still as they are judged ripe, they may be received into the Colledge of this Schoole. Master *Corlet* is the Mr., who hath very well approved himselfe for his abilities, dexterity and painfulnesse in teaching and education of the youth under him.

Over the Colledge is master *Dunster* placed, as President, a learned conscionable and industrious man, who has so trained up his Pupills in the tongues and Arts, and so seasoned them with the principles of Divinity and Christianity that we have to our great comfort, (and in truth) beyond our hopes, beheld their progresse in Learning and godlinesse also; the former of these hath appeared in their publique declamations in *Latine* and *Greeke,* and Disputations Logicall and Philosophicall, which they have beene wonted (besides their ordinary Exercises in the Colledge-Hall) in the audience of the Magistrates, Ministers, and other Schollars, for the probation of their growth in Learning, upon set dayes, constantly once every moneth to make and uphold: The latter hath been manifested in sundry of them by the savoury breathings of their Spirits in their godly conversation. Insomuch that we are confident if these early blossomes may be cherished and warmed with the influence of the friends of Learning, and lovers of this pious worke, they will by the help of God, come to happy maturity in a short time.

Over the Colledge are twelve Overseers chosen by the generall Court, six of them are of the Magistrates, the other six of the Ministers, who are to promote the best good of it, and (having a power of influence into all persons in it are to see that every one be diligent and proficient in his proper place.

2. Rules, and Precepts that are observed in the Colledge

1. When any Schollar is able to understand *Tully,* or such like classicall Latine Author *extempore,* and make and speake true Latine in Verse and Prose, *suo ut aiunt Marte;* And decline perfectly the Paradigim's of *Nounes* and *Verbes* in the *Greek* tongue: Let him then and not before be capable of admission into the Colledge.

2. Let every Student be plainly instructed, and earnestly pressed to consider well, the maine end of his life and studies is, *to know God and Jesus Christ which is eternall life,* Joh. 17. 3. and therefore to lay *Christ* in the bottome, as the only foundation of all sound knowledge and Learning.

And seeing the Lord only giveth wisedome, Let every one

seriously set himselfe by prayer in secret to seeke it of him, *Prov* 2, 3.

3. Every one shall so exercise himselfe in reading the Scriptures twice a day, that he shall be ready to give such an account of his proficiency therein, both in *Theoretticall* observations of the Language, and *Logick,* and in *Practicall* and spirituall truths, as his Tutor shall require, according to his ability; seeing *the entrance of the word giveth light, it giveth understanding to the simple,* Psalm. 119. 130.

4. That they eschewing all profanation of Gods Name, Attributes, Word, Ordinances, and times of Worship, doe studie with good conscience, carefully to retaine God, and the love of his truth in their mindes else let them know, that (notwithstanding their Learning) God may give them up *to strong delusions,* and in the end *to a reprobate minde,* 2 Thes. 2. 11, 12. Rom. 1. 28.

5. That they studiously redeeme the time; observe the generall houres appointed for all the Students, and the speciall houres for their owne *Classis:* and then dilligently attend the Lectures without any disturbance by word or gesture. And if in any thing they doubt, they shall enquire as of their fellowes, so, (in case of *Non satisfaction*) modestly of their Tutors.

6. None shall under any pretence whatsoever, frequent the company and society of such men as lead an unfit, and dissolute life.

Nor shall any without his Tutors leave, or (in his absence) the call of Parents or Guardians, goe abroad to other Townes.

7. Every Schollar shall be present in his Tutors chamber at the 7th. houre in the morning, immediately after the sound of the Bell, at his opening the Scripture and prayer, so also at the 5th. houre at night, and then give account of his owne private reading, as aforesaid in Particular the third, and constantly attend Lectures in the Hall at the houres appointed? But if any (without necessary impediment) shall absent himself from prayer or Lectures, he shall bee lyable to Admonition, if he offend above once a weeke.

8. If any Schollar shall be found to transgresse any of the Lawes of God, or the Schoole, after twice Admonition, he shall be lyable, if not *adultus,* to correction, if *adultus,* his name shall

be given up to the Overseers of the Colledge, that he may bee admonished at the publick monethly Act.

3. The times and order of their Studies, unlesse experience shall show cause to alter

The second and third day of the weeke, read Lectures, as followeth.

To the first yeare at 8th. of the clock in the morning *Logick*, the first three quarters, *Physicks* the last quarter.

To the second yeare at the 9th. houre, *Ethicks* and *Politicks*, at convenient distances of time.

To the third yeare at the 10th. *Arithmetick* and *Geometry*, the three first quarters, *Astronomy* the last.

Afternoone

The first yeare disputes at the second houre.
The 2d. yeare at the 3d. houre.
The 3d. yeare at the 4th. every one in his Art.

The 4th. day reads Greeke

To the first yeare the *Etymologie and Syntax* at the eighth houre.
To the 2d. at the 9th. houre, *Profodia* and *Dialects*.

Afternoone

The first yeare at 2d houre practice the precepts of *Grammar* in such Authors as have variety of words.

The 2d. yeare at 3d. houre practice in *Poesy, Nonnus, Duport*, or the like.

The 3d yeare perfect their *Theory* before noone, and exercise *Style, Composition, Imitation, Epitome*, both in Prose and Verse, afternoone.

The fift day reads Hebrew, and the Easterne Tongues

Grammar to the first yeare houre the 8th.
To the 2d. *Chaldee* at the 9th. houre
To the 3d. *Syriack* at the 10th. houre.

Afternoone

The first yeare practice in the Bible at the 2d. houre.
The 2d. in *Ezra* and *Danel* at the 3d. houre.
The 3d. at the 4th. houre in *Trestius* New Testament.

The 6th. day reads Rhetorick to all at the 8th. houre

Declamations at the 9th. So ordered that every Scholler may declaime once a moneth. The rest of the day *vacat Rhetoricis studiis.*

The 7th. day reads Divinity Catecheticall at the 8th. houre, Common places at the 9th. houre
Afternoone

The first houre reads history in the Winter,
The nature of plants in the Summer.
The summe of every Lecture shall be examined before the new Lecture be read.

Every Schollar that on proofe is found able to read the Originalls of the *Old* and *New Testament* into the Latine tongue, and to resolve them *Logically;* withall being of godly life and conversation; And at any publick Act hath the Approbation of the Overseers and Master of the Colledge, is fit to be dignified with his first Degree.

Every Schollar that giveth up in writing a *System, or Synopsis,* or summe of *Logick,* Naturall and Morall *Phylosophy, Arithmetick, Geometry* and *Astronomy:* and is ready to defend his *Theses* or positions: withall skilled in the Originalls as abovesaid: and of godly life & conversation: and so approved by the Overseers and Master of the Colledge, at any publique *Act,* is fit to be dignified with his 2d. Degree.

4. The manner of the late Commencement, expressed in a Letter sent over from the Governour, and diverse of the Ministers, their own words these

The Students of the first Classis that have beene there foure yeeres trained up in University-Learning (*for their ripening in the knowledge of the Tongues and Arts) and are apprved for their manners as they have kept their publick Acts in former yeares, our selves being present, at them; so have they lately kept two solemne Acts for their Commencement, when the Governour, Magistrates, and the Ministers from all parts, and did heare their Exercises; which were Latine and Greeke Orations, and Declamations and Hebrew Analysis Grammaticall, Logicall & Rhetoricall of the Psalms: And their Answers and Disputations in Logicall, Ethicall, Physicall and Metaphysicall Questions; and so were found worthy of the first degree, (commonly called Batchelour) pro more Academiarum in Anglia: Being first presented by the President to the Magistrates and Ministers, and by him, upon their Approbation, solemnly admitted unto the same degree, and a Booke of Arts delivered into each of their hands, and power given them to read Lectures in the Hall upon any of the Arts, when they shall be thereunto called, and a liberty of studying in the Library.*

All things in the Colledge are at present, like to proceed even as wee can wish, may it but please the Lord to goe on with his blessing in Christ, and stir up the hearts of his faithfull, and able Servants in our owne Native Country, and here, (as he hath graciously begun) to advance this Honourable and most hopefull worke. The beginnings whereof and progresse hitherto (generally) doe fill our hearts with comfort, and raise them up to much more expectations, of the Lords goodnesse for hereafter, for the good of posterity, and the Churches of Christ Jesus.

  BOSTON in New-England,
   September the 26.
    1642.

        Your very loving
         friends, & c.

Thus farre hath the good hand of God favoured our beginnings; see whether he hath not engaged us to wait still upon his goodnesse for the future, by such further remarkable passages of his providence to our Plantation in such things as these:

1. In sweeping away great multitudes of the Natives by the

Small Pox, a little before we went thither, that he might make room for us there.

2. In giving such merveilous safe Passage from first to last, to so many thousands that went thither, the like hath hardly been ever observed in any Sea-voyages.

3. In blessing us generally with health and strength, as much as ever (we might truly say) more than ever in our Native Land; many that were tender and sickly here, are stronger and heartier there. That whereas diverse other Plantations have been the graves of their Inhabitants and their numbers much decreased: God hath so prospered the climate to us, that our bodies are hailer, and Children there born stronger, whereby our number is exceedingly increased.

4. In giving us such peace and freedome from enemies, when almost all the world is on a fire that (excepting that short trouble with the Pequits) we never heard of any sound of Warres to this day. And in that Warre which we made against them Gods hand from heaven was so manifested, that a very few of our men in a short time pursued through the Wildernesse, slew and took prisoners about 1400 of them, even all they could find, to the great terrour and amazement of all the Indians to this day: so that the name of the Pequits (as of *Amaleck*) is blotted out from under heaven, there being not one that is, or (at least) dare call himselfe a Pequit.

5. In subduing those erroneous opinions carryed over from hence by some of the Passengers, which for a time infested our Churches peace but (through the goodnesse of God) by conference preaching, a generall assembly of learned men. Magistrates timely care and lastly, by Gods own hand from heaven, in most remarkable stroaks upon some of the chief fomenters of them; the matter came to such an happie conclusion, that most of the seduced came humbly and confessed their Errours in our publique Assemblies and abide to this day constant in the Truth; the rest (that remained obstinate) finding no fit market there to vent their wares, departed from us to an Iland farre off; some of whom also since that time, have repented and returned to us, and are received againe into our bosomes. And from that time not any unsound, unsavourie and giddie fancie have dared to lift up his head, or abide the light amongst us.

6. In settling and bringing civil matters to such a maturity in a short time amongst us having planted 50 Townes and Villages built 30. or 40. Churches, and more Ministers houses; a Castle, a Colledge, Prisons, Forts, Cartweies, Causies many, and all there upon our owne charges no publique hand reaching out any helpe: having comfortable Houses, Gardens, Orchards, Grounds fenced, Corne fields &c. and such a forme and face of a Commonwealth appearing in all the Plantation, that Strangers from other parts, seeing how much is done in so few yeares, have wondered at Gods blessing on our indeavours.

7. In giving such plenty of all manner of Food in a Wildernesse insomuch, that all kinds of Flesh amongst the rest, store of Venison in its season. Fish both from Sea and Fresh water. Fowle of all kinds, wild & tame; store of Whit-Meale, together with all sorts of English Graine, as well as Indian, are plentiful amongst us; as also Rootes, Herbs and Fruit, which being better digested by the Sun, are farre more faire pleasant and wholesome than here.

8. In prospering Hempe and Flaxe so well, that its frequently sowen, spun, and woven into linnen Cloath; (and in a short time may serve for Cordage) and so with Cotton-Wooll, (which we may have at very reasonable rates from the Islands) and our linnen Yarne, we can make Dimittees and Fustions for our Summer cloathing. And having a matter of 1000. Sheep, which prosper well, to begin withall, in a competent time we hope to have wollen Cloath there made. And great and small Cattel, being now very frequently killd for food; their skins will afford us Leather for Boots and Shoes, and other uses: so that God is leading us by the hand into a way of cloathing.

9. In affording us many materialls, (which in part already are, and will in time further be improved) for Staple commodities, to supply all other defects: As

1. Furres, Bever, Otter, &c.

2. Clapboord, Hoops, Pipestaves, Masts.

3. English Wheat and other graine for *Spaine* and West Indies; and all other provisions for Victualling of Shippes.

4. Fish, as Cod, Haddock, Herrings, Mackerill, Basse, Sturgeon, Seales, Whales, Sea-horse.

5. Oyle of sundry sorts, of Whale, Sea-horse, &c.

6. Pitch and Tarre, Rosen and Turpentine, having Pines, Spruce, and Pitch-trees in our Countrey to make these on.

7. Hempe and Flaxe.

8. Mineralls discovered and proved, as of Iron in sundry places, Black-lead (many other in hopes) for the improving of which, we are now about to carry over Servants and instruments with us.

9. (Besides many Boates, Shallops, Hows, Lighters, Pinnaces) we are in a way of building Shippes, of an 100, 200, 300. 400. tunne, five of them are already at Sea; many more in hand at this present, we being much incouraged herein by reason of the plenty and excellencie of our Timber for that purpose, and seeing all the materialls will be had there in short time.

10. In giving of such Magistrates, as are all of them godly men, and members of our Churches, who countenance those that be good, and punish evill doers, that a vile person dares not lift up his head; nor need a godly man to hang it down, that (to Gods praise be it spoken) one may live there from yeare to yeare, and not see a drunkard, heare an oath, or meet a beggar. Now where sinne is punished, and judgment executed, God is wont to blesse that place, and protect it, *Psa.* 106. 30, *Jer.* 5. 1, *Jos.* 7. 25 with 8. 1. *e contra Esa.* 20 21.

11. In storing that place with very many of his own people, and diverse of them eminent for godlinesse. Now where his people are, there is his presence, and Promise *to be in the middest of them, a mighty God to save, and to joy over them with singing,* Zeph. 3. 17.

12. Above all our other blessings, in planting *his own Name,* and *precious Ordinances,* among us; (we speak it humbly, and in his feare) our indeavour is to have all his own Institutions, and no more then his own and all those in their native simplicity without any humane dressings; having a liberty to injoy all that God Commands and yet urged to nothing more than he Commands. Now *Where soever he records his Name, thither he will come and blesse,* Ex. 20 24.

Which promise he hath already performed to very many

soules in their effectuall conversion to Christ, and the edification of others in their holy Faith, who daily blesse God that ever he carried them into those parts.

All which blessings named we looke upon, as an earnest-penny of more to come. If we seeke his face, and serve his Providence, wee have no cause to doubt, that he for his part will faile to make seasonable supplies unto us.

1. By some meanes to carry on to their perfection our staple trades begun.

2. By Additions of Ammunition and Powder.

3. By maintenance of Schooles of Learning especially the Colledge, as also additions of building to it and furnishing the Library.

4. By stirring up some well-minded to cloath and transport over poore children Boyes and Girles, which may be a great mercy to their bodies and soules, and a help to us, they being super abundant here, and we wanting hands to carry on our trades, manufacture and husbandry there.

5. By stirring up some to shew mercy to the *Indians,* in affording maintenance to some of our godly active young Schollars, there to make it their worke to studie their Language converse with them and carry light amongst them, that so the Gospell might be spread into those darke parts of the world.

Ob. But all your own cost and ours also will be lost, because there can be no subsistence there for any long time. For,

1. Your ground is barren,

Answ. 1. If you should see our goodly Cornefields, neere harvest, you would answer this yourselfe. Secondly, how could it be thin, that we should have *English* Wheat at 4. s. *per* bushell, and *Indian* at 2.8. and this not only for ready money, but in way of exchange. Thirdly, that in a wildernesse in so few yeares, we should have corne enough for ourselves and our friends that come over, and much to spare.

2. *Obj.* Your ground will not continue above 3. or 4 yeares to beare corne.

Answ. Our ground hath been sowne and planted with corne these 7. 10. 12. yeares already by our selves, and (which is more than can be said here of *English* Land (never yet sum-

mer tild: but have borne corne, every yeare since we first
went, and the same ground planted as long by the *Indians*
before, and yet have good crops upon it still, and is like to
continue as ever: But this is, (as many other slanders against
that good Land) against all sense, reason and experience.

3. *Obj.* But you have no money there.

Answ. It's true we have not much, though some there is,
but wee having those staple commodities named, they will
(still as they·are improved) fetch money from other parts.
Ships, Fish, Iron, Pipestaves, Corn, Bever, Oyle, &c. will help
us with money and other things also.

2. Little money is raised in coyne in *England,* how then comes
it to abound, but by this meane?

3. We can trade amongst our selves by way of exchange, one
commodity for another, and so doe usually.

4. *Obj.* You are like to want clothes hereafter.

Answ. 1. Linnen, Fustians Dimettees we are making already.
Secondly, Sheepe are comming on for woollen cloath. Thirdly,
in meane time we may be supplied by way of trade to other
parts. 4th Cordevant, Deere, Seale; and Moose Skins (which
are beasts as big as Oxen, and their skins are buffe) are there
to be had plentifully, which will help this way, especially for
servants cloathing.

5. *Obj.* Your Winters are cold.

Answ. True, at sometimes when the wind blowes strong a
Nor-West: but it holds not long together, and then it useth to
be very moderate for a good space. First the coldnesse being
not naturall (that place being 42. degrees) but accidentall.
Secondly. The cold there is no impediment to health, but very
wholesome for our bodies, insomuch that all sorts generally,
weake and strong had scarce ever such measure of health in
all there lives as there. Thirdly, Is not a moist and foggie cold,
as in *Holland,* and some parts of *England* but bright, cleare,
and faire wether, that men are seldome troubled in Winter
with coughes and Rheumes. Fourthly, it hinders not our imployment, for people are able to worke or travell usually all
the Winter long, so there is no losse of time, simply in respect
of the cold. Fiftly good fires (wood being so plentifull) will
make amends.

6. *Ob.* Many are growne weaker in their estates since they went over.

Answ. Are not diverse in *London* broken in their Estates? and many in *England* are growne poore, and thousands goe a begging (yet wee never saw a beggar there) and will any taxe the City or Kingdome, and say they are unsubsistable places?

Secondly their Estates now lie in houses, Lands, Horses, Cattel, Corne, &c. though they have not so much money as they had here, and so cannot make appearance of their wealth to those in *England,* yet they have it still, so that their Estates are not lost but changed.

3. Some mens Estates may be weaker through great and vast common charges, which the first planters especially have bin at in makeing the place subsistable and comfortable, which now others reape the fruit of, unknowne summes lye buried underground in such a worke as that is.

4. Some may be poore, (so we are sure) many are rich, that carried nothing at all, that now have House, Land, Corne, Cattel, &c and such as carry something are much encreased.

7. *Ob.* Many speake evill of the place.

Ans. Did not some doe so of the Land of *Canaan* it selfe, yet *Canaan* was never the worse and themselves smarted for so doing. Secondly, some have been punished there for their Delinquencies, or restrained from their exorbitancies; or discountenanced for their ill opinions and not suffered to vent their stuffe: and hence being displeased take revenge by slanderous report. Thirdly, Let such if any such there be as have ought to alleadge, deale fairely and above board, and come and justifie any thing against the Country to our faces while we are here to answer, but such never yet appeared in any of our presence to avouch any thing in this kinde, nor (we beleive) dare do it without blushing.

8. *Ob.* Why doe many come away from thence?

Answ. Doe not many remove from one Country to another, and yet none likes the Country the lesse because some depart from it? Secondly, few that we know of intend to abide here, but doe come on some speciall busines, and purpose to returne. Thirdly of them that are come hither to stay, (on our knowledge) some of the wisest repent them already, and wish themselves there againe. Fourthly, as some went thither upon sudden undigested grounds, and saw not God leading them in their way, but were carryed by an unstayed spirit so have they returned upon as sleight headlesse, unworthy reasons as they went. Fiftly, others must have elbow-roome, and cannot abide to be so pinioned with the strict Government in the *Commonwealth,* or Discipline in the Church, now why should such live there; as *Ireland* will not brooke venemous beasts, so will not that Land vile persons, and loose livers. Sixtly, though some few have removed from them, yet (we may truly say) thousands as wise as themselves would not change their place for any other in the world.

6

Anti-Dutch Documents (1663-1664)

The causes of the three Anglo-Dutch Wars (1652-54, 1664-67, 1672-74) were many and deep-seated with the friction points scattered around the world—the North Atlantic, the Baltic, the Narrow Seas, New Netherlands, Africa, and the East Indies. In the North Atlantic the two nations fought bitterly for control of the fisheries. Their diplomacy clashed in the Baltic region, the major source of naval stores. In America, the English regarded the colony of New Netherlands as an illegal intrusion into their domain. England claimed sovereignty in the Narrow Seas and demanded a symbolic salute; the Dutch denied this right. Along the west coast of Africa the two sea powers struggled for control of the slave trade. Both nations had moved into the East Indian vacuum created by the decline of Portugal, and the rich prize of the oriental trade caused a running commercial conflict that produced bloody incidents.

The reduction of Dutch maritime power became a fixed line of mid-seventeenth century English policy. For example, the Navigation Acts of 1651 and 1660 were pointedly anti-Dutch. The first Dutch War came in Cromwell's time and resulted in an English victory. Though the Dutch acknowledged English sovereignty in the Narrow Seas and recognized the navigation system, the major issues of conflict remained unresolved. The Stuart restoration of 1660 brought with it resurgent mercantilism and nationalism. Within a short time, Samuel Pepys could write in his diary that he had come to understand that the seas of the world were not large enough for the English and the Dutch.

One of the chief executors of the anti-Dutch policy was George Downing, one of the first graduates of Harvard College, who had returned to England. He served Cromwell in the army, Parliament, and the diplomatic service. At the restoration he explained his attachment to Cromwell as a mistake due, he thought, to his New England upbringing. Charles II permitted him to remain as ambassador at The Hague. Downing's correspondence with Charles' first minister, Clarendon, bristles with anti-Dutch feeling. The contemporary opinion was that he avoided a rapprochement and actually provoked the war.

Late in 1664, Downing presented England's grievances to the United Provinces. Subsequently the Dutch government publicly criticized his memorial. Downing countered with the pamphlet, *A Discourse* . . . , which was a specific indictment of Dutch actions. His letters to Clarendon reveal his basic attitude. They show him to have been little concerned with specific grievances. He assumed that war was inevitable and in the national interest. He did what he could to bring on a war and he succeeded.

Alfred T. Mahan's *The Influence of Sea Power Upon History, 1660-1783* (Boston: Little, Brown, 1941) is the classic analysis of the relationship of sea power to commerce and empire; chapter two deals with the Anglo-Dutch conflict. A volume of uniform excellence is *The Old Empire from the beginning to 1783* (New York: Macmillan, 1929), which is Volume I of *The Cambridge History of the British Empire*. Though there is a unity to the volume, each essay can be read separately with profit. For the Anglo-Dutch conflict the relevant chapters are 7, J. A. Williamson, "The Beginnings of an Imperial Policy, 1649-1660"; 10, W. F. Reddaway, "Rivalry for Colonial Power, 1660-1713"; and 15, Eveline C. Martin, "The English Slave Trade and the African Settlements."

In reading the following selections note (1) Downing's judgment of how to treat the Dutch; (2) what advice he gave respecting a possible Anglo-Dutch treaty; (3) what complaints Downing expressed against the Dutch; (4) what grounds he advanced to support the British claim to New Netherlands; and (5) what he implied were the means of achieving satisfaction against the Dutch.

A. Letters of Sir George Downing to the Lord Chancellor Clarendon[1]

Downing to Clarendon, September 18, 1663

THIS TRICK OF THE HOLLANDERS TO DECLARE WARRE with the natives in the East Indies and upon the Coast of Africa, with whom his Majesty's subjects have any trade, and then thereupon to forbid them all trade with them, and to continue the warre till they have brought those natives to an agreement with them, to sell them all their comodities, and

---

1. T. H. Lister, *Life and Administration of Edward, First Earl of Clarendon* (3 vols.; London: Longman, Orme, Brown, Green and Longmans, 1837-38), III, 249-51, 286-88, 298-301.

then to keep the English from tradeing, upon the accompt that the natives have agreed with them, to sell all to them;—this trick, I say, hath not only bin the ruine of numbers of his Majesty's subjects, but beaten them out of many mighty trades, and will certainly in conclusion utterly overthrow the English East Indian, and African Companies, if nothing be applied for remedie but wordes. There is nothing makes them here so proud as to have the English come hither eternally with complaints, while their people are unmolested, advance their trade, and obteine their ends. This state haveing once or twice complained to the King of Spaine of the private men of warre, with Spanish Comissions, that they visited their ships, and troubled their trade, without farther delay sent Vice-Admiral Cortmar upon the coasts of Portugall with a squadron of ships, with order to take all of them he could meet with, who, in pursuance thereof, hath already taken nine of them; and now that the Spaniards crye as well as they, they will have reason; and truly I am of opinion it were better that I should make no complainte at all here, but let his Majesty's subjects patiently suffer whatever it will please the Dutch to doe to them, then to complaine, and nothing to follow thereupon, whereby to lett them see that his Majestie will not be put of with wordes and delays. I am sure this mealie way is not the meanes to hinder a warre between England and this country, but the most certaine and undoubted way to bring it on, making them so farr to presume as (as you finde) to add one injury to another; and believe it, the more they may, the more they will. Whereas, on the other side, pay them in their own kind, and set their subjects a crying as well as his Majesties, and you will have a very faire correspondence, and they will take heede what they does; and his Majesty shall be as much honored and loved here as he hath been dispised: for they love nor honor none but them that they think both can and dare bite them. . . .

Downing to Clarendon, February 12, 1663

. . . I had forgot the last part of Dewitts discourse, which was, that they should be very glad, upon this occasion, to enter into conference with me, and to frame a Treaty for the regulating trade within and without Europe. I replyed, that I came hither at that time, only about the business of the shipps Charles and James; moreover, that any Treaty now to be made, could not opperate backwards, and so will do me no good as to this matter; that I did demand satisfaction and raparation, according to the Treaty already made with his Majestie, and the laws and customes of nations now in practice; neither had I any order or instruction concerning any such Treaty, either at that or any other time. That for our parts, wee should be very well satisfied, so wee may but quietly injoy what is already law and right; but that if they did thinke there were nedd of any such further Treaty, and should make me any overtures thereupon, I should not faile to send the same to the King my master, and to do them all the good offices I could.

This Treaty Marine is that they have bin allwayes hancring at, ever since I knew this country, and upon all occasions donning me about it; and when they could do no good with me, gave orders to Newport to trye what he could do at London. But whenever his Majesty shall make any such Treaty with this country he must take the motto off the poop of the Souveraigne; and not onely so, but being assured never to be visited or troubled by his Majesties shipps of warre, (which is the thing aimed at by such a Treaty,) they will certainly thereby become what they do desire to be, viz. the common carriers of the world; and instead of ending disputes, such a Treaty will make a million more. Being equall at sea, as then they would be, all (Dominium maris) being terminated in a Treaty, they would never cease till they were absolute masters, continually stretching and wresting the words and clauses thereof, construing them to their owne advantage, yea, in that case, breaking them downe right, yet still thundring and exclaiming against his Majesty upon all occasions, let him keepe to it never so exactly, as I could shew they do with France and Spaine, with whom they have such treaties.

Downing to Clarendon, March 18, 1663

. . . Here hath been, and is, a whispring, as if there should be some underhand private transaction on foote, as from the East India Company here, and the hopes of prevailing in it, to have the English East Indie Company quitt all their pretence to Pulo

Run, for a sum of mony, and a yearly recognition of spice for his Majesty family, and something of that nature: but God forbid any such thing should take effect. I know they would give any sugerd wordes, and more, to have that place, and they have reason therein. They begin now to take the allarme att the great talkes in England of warres with this country, especially because of the Parliaments now comeing to sitt, and that complaints will be there made against them; and truly it is but needfull that they be quickned a little, for they regard not wordes alone. But I doe assure you, if they see his Majesty goe about in earnest anything that lookes like a resolution of falling upon them, he may have reason done him here for his subjects; for however they talk bigge, as if they feared nobody, yett at bottome they are sencible what a business it would be for them to grapple with his Majesties; and it is high time that they doe end those differences which are depending here, nor was ever a fitter opportunity to obtaine the same. . . .

B. Sir George Downing, A Discourse....[1]

. . . And as to the *Matter* of the said Paper: Is it enough to say in general terms, *That the said* Memorial *was ill grounded,* or *abusively informed,* without particularizing at all *how,* or *wherein;* or so much as excepting against any one word thereof, much less disproving the same.

And again; If the things wherewith they are charged therein be *true* (as they both are, and must now be taken by all men to be, since nothing is made out by their Lordships to the contrary) To what purpose is the whole sequel of the said Paper? If it be true (as it is) That the *Royal Master* of the said *Envoy* was no sooner returned to His Kingdoms, but that he was immediately, and from day to day troubled and importuned with a Crowd of Complaints of His Subjects against those of this Country; all which notwithstanding, His Majesty did not grant any one *Letter* of *Marque,* nor betake himself to any way of

---

1. Sir George Downing, *A Discourse written by Sir George Downing The King of Great Britain's Envoyee Extraordinary to the States of the United-Provinces.* (London: printed by F. M., 1664). I am indebted to the British Museum for permission to make a photographic copy of this pamphlet.

force for the obtaining of their reparation and satisfaction; But instead thereof, for an Everlasting memorial of his great kindness and good will towards this Country, and for the facilitating of the bringing to a Conclusion the late *Treaty* with them, (finding the *Complaints* and *Pretensions* of his Subjects to be so numerous and great,) was pleased after all to suffer very many of them, and those to a vast value, to be utterly mortified and extinguished; and the rest (except the business of the Ships *Bonadventure,* and *Bon-Esperanza*) after so much mony and time had been already expended in the pursuit thereof, and many of them ready for a determination, to be put in a LIST, and proceeded upon anew according to the fifteenth *Article* thereof; no ways doubting, but that all possible speed would have thereupon been used in bringing the matter to an issue, and that for the future better order would have been observed towards His Subjects: But having waited now above 27 *months* since the *Conclusion* of the said *Treaty;* and in that time their Lordships being continually call'd upon by His Said Majesties *Envoy Extraordinary,* yea by His Majesty Himself in several *Audiences* to their *Embassador;* Yet so it is, that those matters are still so far from being ended, that in truth they seem to be now rather further from it then at the days of the *signing* of the said *Treaty;* and on the other side, new injuries daily heaped, and the same designs of the *East* and *West-Indie-Companies* carried on for the utter overthrow of all the *Trade* of His Majesties Subjects in those parts of the world, as appeared by the business of the Ships *Hopewell, Leopard,* and other Ships in the *East-Indies,* and by the business of the *Charles, James, Mary, Sampson, Hopeful Adventurer, Speedwell,* &c. upon the Coast of *Africa*: All which are matters hapned since the *Conclusion* of the said *Treaty.* And after all this, and notwithstanding His *Parliaments* application to Him upon the account of His aggrieved Subjects, in so solemn and extraordinary a manner; His Majesty was yet so far from being inclined to any other then ways of accommodation, as that he did by a publick Writing, or *Declaration* declare, That he would yet try what could be done by amicable endeavours at the *Hague,* before he would make use of any other means; (the which was also very well known to their Lordships) and did thereupon accordingly give orders to his *Envoy Extraordinary* to press them afresh: And further to make out his peacable and moderate intentions, and to take off all *umbrage* from their Lordships, to let them know, (as accordingly he did in publick Conferences with their Deputies) That His Majesty would not in any kind trouble their Fleets which they then expected from the *Streights,* and *East-Indies,* nor their *Fisheries* upon his Coasts; Yea, further to put them out of all doubt, ordered a far less equipage of Shipping for the *Summerguard* then had been known these many years; but all this was so far from working the desired and intended effect, as that on the contrary their Lordships betook themselves to Arms in an extraordinary manner, ordering the fitting out with all speed a great *Fleet,* and *hundreds* of *Carpenters* forthwith dispatched to work upon it night and day, (holy days as well as working days); whereby His Majesty seeing himself wholly defeated of His good intentions, and instead of *satisfaction* for His Subjects, braved and threatned with those *equipages,* which could have no other regard but upon Himself, was at last inforced for His own defense, (though very much contrary to His inclinations and intentions) to arm also.

And whereas it may be pretended, as if their *Lordships* having fitted *Their Fleet,* did desire that His Majesty would be pleased, (for avoyding of all inconveniences) to keep *His Fleet* within His *Harbours,* and that then they would keep in *Theirs* also; It is to be Considered, that *This Proposition was not made until that they had actually put to Sea, a Fleet near as numerous as the whole that His Majesty was equipping, and which was actually gone towards His Coasts;* so that this could not but be construed to be rather a *mocquerie,* then otherwise; for that thereby they had a Fleet at Sea to do what they pleased, and in the mean while His Majesty had tyed His own hands and obliged Himself to keep within doors; but he was yet pleased to assure them, that His (if it did go out) should not do them the least Injury; still in the meanwhile pressing here at the *Hague* by his *Minister* and Himself urging their *Ambassador* at *London,* to hasten the dispatch of the matters in difference; And as a further testimony of His desires of living in good Correspondence with *This Country,* He did declare His willingness to enter into a *Treaty* for the better regulating of the Trade and Navigation of both, and the prevention of such disorders for the future; and for the quicker dispatch and ripening of so good a work, a project thereof was in His Name tendred to them long ago, and yet to this day not one word of answer thereupon.

And if it be also *true,* (as it is) that their *Lordships* began the *seizing* of Ships in these Parts; stopping the Ship from *Gottenburg* bound for London, and though pressed again and again to set her at liberty, yet still retain'd her, and to this day not so much as a word of answer why or upon what account.

These things being so, can there be any doubt who is the *Attacquer* or *Aggressor,* unless it must be held for a *Maxim,* That let their *Lordships* and *Their Subjects* deal with his aforesaid Majesty and His Subjects from time to time and from year to year as they please, yet they are not *Attacquers* or *Aggressors*; but if His *Majesty* or *His Subjects,* after never so many years sufferings, and all amicable indeavours first tryed to have obtained their satisfaction, without to this very day having been able to obtein it in anyone of those numerous *cases* of *piracy* and *violence* committed by the people of *This Country* against them, whereof complaint hath been made from time to time unto their *Lordships* by His Majesties *Minister*: If after all, any thing be done by them towards the righting of themselves, his *Majesty* must be called and reputed the *Attacquer* and the *Aggressor.* Let their Lordships make out, That the complaints in the said *Memorials* are ungrounded, and His Majesty will yield unto them: but if otherwise, Who will think it strange if at last something be done towards the righting of them.

And as to the *Particulars* mentioned in the Said Paper to have been suffered by them from the *English,* though those matters have not been treated of between their *Lordships* and the said *Envoy Extraordinary,* but between the King his *Master* and their *Ambassador* at *London,* so that it is not properly his business to reply thereunto, but to refer them to that answer which his Majesty hath promised to give concerning the same; yet seeing their *Lordships* have been pleased not only to mention and insist thereupon in the afore-said *paper,* but indeed to say nothing else by way of *answer* to the *complaints* in his *Memorial,* he cannot but say thus much thereunto.

"That the *Places* and *Ships* said to be taken from them, were all belonging to the *West-Indie-Company* of *this Country*; and nothing complain'd of in the paper to have been taken from them belonging to any else of *These Countries*; And when it shall be considered, that in the LIST of *Damages* alone, there appears to have been near *twenty English ships* successively, within a very few years before the conclusion of the late *Treaty,* taken in a hostile manner upon the *Coast* of *Africa,* only by the Shipping of the said *West-Indie-Company,* with their whole Lading, to a very great value; and not onely so, but the men that belonged to them, very many of them most barbarously and inhumanly treated; put into stinking nasty *dungeons* and *holes* at *Casteldelmina,* there to lie in the midst of their own excrements, nothing but bread and water given them, and thereof not enough to sustein Nature, their Bodies tortured with exquisite and horrid tortures; and when any of them dyed, the living and the dead left together, and such as escaped, turned out to perish by hunger, or wild beasts in those miserable Countries, or to be carry'd away Captives by the Natives; by which means, several *hundreds* of his Majesties good Subjects have perished and been destroyed: And to this hour, notwithstanding all solicitations and endeavours, not one penny of satisfaction given to the persons concerned in any of the said Ships; And ever since the *Conclusion* of the said *Treaty,* Ships of *Warr* have been kept by the said *Company* upon the said Coasts; which though they have not proceeded so far as to take more of the Shipping of his Majestie's Subjects, yet they have done that which is equivalent, and as ruinous to that Trade; stopping and hindring every one that they met withall from all Commerce, and to that effect pursuing them in an hostile manner from place to place: And where-ever any *English* anchored by them, hindring and shooting at, and taking by force, with their Ladings, all *Boats* of the *Natives* that indeavored to come aboard them, and their Boats that would go on shoare; yea, depriving them of so much as any provision or refreshment of fresh water (as appears by the *Complaints* made by the said *Envoy Extraordinary* from time to time to their Lordships concerning the same): And publishing a *Declaration* in the name as well of the *States General,* as of the said *Company,* wherein they deduce their right to that *whole Coast,* to the exclusion of all other Nations; And

notwithstanding all *Complaints* to their *Lordships,* neither the
said *Declaration* disavowed, nor any thing of *Satisfaction* given,
but still new *Complaints* coming, and among others, that of their
having stirr'd up the King of *Fantine* by rewards and sums of
mony given him to that end; and supplying him with all sorts
of *Armes* and *Amunition* for the surprize of his Majestie's Castle
at *Cormantine* in those parts; concerning which also *Proofs* have
been since given to their *Lordships* by the said *Envoy Extraordinary,* so that there was an absolute necessity impos'd upon
his Majesty and his Subjects, either of loosing all that had been
actually taken from them, and withall abandoning for ever that
Trade it self, or otherwise of betaking themselves to some other
wayes for their relief. And it will rather be thought strange that
their patience did hold out so long, then that now at last something should be done, towards the righting of themselves."

Besides, as to the business of *Capo Corco,* did not the said
Envoy Extraordinary long agoe complain in the name, and by
Order of the *King* his *Master,* in *Publick Conferences* both with
the *Deputies* of their *Lordships* the *Estates General,* and also
with those of *Holland* in *particular,* of the injurious possessing
and keeping of that place by those of the said *West-Indie-
Company,* deducing and remonstrating at large his Masters Right
thereunto, the *ground* having been bought by *His Subjects,* of
the *King* of *That Country* for a valuable consideration, and a
Lodge or *Factory* built thereupon; and those of the *West-Indie-
Company* of *this Country* being got into the possession of the
place, meerly by *fraud* and *treachery;* but no reflection made
thereupon by their *Lordships,* much less any hopes given of ever
obtaining any restitution thereof from them. And indeed, if His
Majesty had not been able to rescue out of their hands the least
Boat, or pennyworth of Goods since His return to His Kingdoms,
(concerning which) complaint had been made by His *Envoy
Extraordinary,* of its being forceably taken by them from His
Subjects,) what hopes of their quitting to him any such place,
especially rembring that business of the *Island* of *Poleroon* in
the *East-Indies,* which hath been a restoring by them ever since
the year 1622 at which time it was by *solemn* and *particular
Treaty* promised to be done; and again, by *another Treaty,* in
the year 1654 and by Orders of the *Estates General* and *East-*

Indie-Company of this Country, in the year 1661 (and again, by Treaty in the year 1662) and yet to this day we know nothing of its being delivered; and can it be thought strange, if invited thereunto by the *King* of the said *Country*, that His Majesty should after so fair warning condescend to suffer His Subjects to endeavour to reposses themselves thereof?

And as to the business of *New-Netherlands* (so called) this is very far from being a surprize, or anything of that nature, it being notoriously known, that *That spot of Land* lyes within the limits, and is part of the possession of His Subjects of *New-England*, (as appears most evidently by their *Charter*) and that those few Dutch that have lived there, have lived there meerly upon connivence and sufferance, and not as having any right thereunto; and that this hath from time to time, and from year to year been declared unto them, but yet so as that the *English* were contented to suffer them to remain there, provided they would demean themselves peaceably and quietly; but that the said *Dutch,* not contenting themselves therewith, did still endeavour to incroach further and further upon the *English,* imposing their *Laws* and *Customs*, and endeavouring to raise *Contributions* and *Excises* upon them, and in places where no *Dutch* were or had ever been; Whereupon they have formerly been necessitated several times to send Souldiers for the repelling of them. . . .

And as to the business of *Cabo Verde,* and the taking of their Ships, and what else is alleadged to have been done in those parts (except that of *Cabo-Corco*:) 'Twas but in the month of *June last,* that the first Complaint was made thereof to his *Majesty,* and did he not immediately return for Answer, That he had given no Order or Direction to *Captain Holmes,* the Person complained of, for the doing thereof; That he did expect him Home very speedily, and that upon his Return, he would cause those matters to be Examined, and Right to be done them, and the Offendours punished? And did not the said *Envoy Extraordinary* upon the *Twenty Seventh day* of *July last* deliver a *Memoriall* to them to the like Effect? And could more be said or done for their Satisfaction? Yea could their *Lordships* Themselves within their own Countries demand more of any of their

Schepens, or most *Inferiour Court of Justice?* And doth not the
Fourteenth Article of the *Late Treaty* say in express Termes, that
In case any thing should happen upon the Coast of Africa, *either
by Sea or Land, that* Twelve Months time *shall be given after
Complaint, for the doing of Justice*; Yet did they not within
about *Six* or *Seven* weeks after; Resolve to send a Considerable
Fleet of Theirs into those Parts, to the Number of *Ten Men of
War* (besides the Ships of the said *West-Indie Company*,) under
the Command of one *Van Campen*, and strengthened with a
Considerable Body of their *Milice*, under the Command of one
Hertsberg? And did they not within about *Six* or *Seven Weeks*
after that, put a *Resolution* into the hands of the said *Envoy
Extraordinary* by their *Agent de Heyde*, and about the same
time give to the *King*, his *Master* by their *Ambassadour* at Lon-
don, Denoting and Containing the Instruction given to the said
Van Campen?

And whereas they are pleased to Complement His most
Christian Majesty in the said Paper, as if upon his score in hopes
of the good Effects of his good Offices for the Accommodating
of Matters, and for the making their Cause the more clear, they
had hitherto forborn the Proceeding against his *Majesties Subjects* as they might have done: Is it not therein expressly Declared
and set Down, that *That Force was not sent thither barely to
Defend what they had, and to take Care that nothing more
should be Attempted upon them; but in down right Termes*, to
Attacque *and* Fall upon *His Majesties Subjects, and to Carve out
their own Satisfaction and Reparation; And to pass by his door's
for the doing thereof?* And that, *Seconded* and *Backed* with
another Great Fleet under their *Chief Sea Officers*; An Affront
and Indignity too great for the Name of *King* to Suffer, and
Digest without Just Resentment.

And moreover, whereas their *Lordships* had lately invited his
Majesty of *Great Brittain*, and other *Christian Princes* to send
Fleets into the *Mid-land-sea* to Act Joyntly against those *Bar-
barians*; And that he did accordingly Declare unto them (in
Writing, and by his *Envoy Extraordinary*,) his Intentions of
Sending, and that his *Fleet* should Act *Junctis Consilliis* with
theirs; Yet so it is, that while it was Acting there, Pursuant there-

unto, and in Expectation of being *Seconded* and *Appuyed* by theirs, according to their Promise, *De Ruthyer* was on a suddain commanded thence.

And whereas their *Lordships* would make the World believe that they had Proceeded with such Singular and Extraordinary *Franchise*, and *Clearness* towards his said *Majesty*, in Communicating their Intentions and Designs (as abovesaid;) Yet, *Is it not evident that the said Orders must have been given to* De Ruyther *much about the same time?*

And though Sir *John Lawson*, and his *Majesties Fleet* hapned to be in the *same Port* with *De Ruyther*, when he quitted those Parts; yet neither did he in least impart unto him his Intentions of quitting the same, or whither he was going; and though the King of *Great Brittain* hath since, several times pressed their *Ambassadour* at *London* to be Informed whither he was gone, and upon what account, yet to this day his *Majesty* hath not been able to obtain any Satisfaction or Assurance concerning that matter; Wereupon, and all other Circumstances being laid together, He hath Just Reason to suppose and believe, that he is sent, and imployed against Him; And that while his *Majesty* was continuing (according to common Consert and Agreement between them,) his *Fleet* against the *Common Enemies* of the very *Name* of CHRISTIAN, and at a season, when it more then ordinarily becomed every one to shew something of their Zeal against them; Theirs is call'd off and turn'd against him: Nor is it to be imagined that *De Ruythers Instructions*, which are *Concealed*, should be more Favourable then those which were *Avowed* to be given to *Van Campen*.

And is it then to be wondered, that his *Majesty* shews himself a little Concerned? Or is it now to be doubted, who is the *Attacquer*, or *Aggressor*? And if *De Ruyther* is in one part of the World, making War against him, what is to be said against it, if his *Majesty* not having at this time in those Parts a suitable Force to Resist him, doth make use of what he hath nearer home to endeavour to secure himself, or to get something of theirs into his hands? Doth either *Common Right*, or His *Majesties Treaty* with *This Country* oblige to seek Satisfaction only in that part of the World where the Injury is done; and so doth that at all alter the Case, because that their Forces acting against Him out of Europe, *His* do something against *Them, in Europe?*

His Majesty hath been very far from beginning with them in any Part of the World, but if at this time they are Actually with a Considerable *Fleet* of the *Estates* falling upon *Him,* and his *Subjects*; and he hath thereupon given Order to the stopping of some of their Ships in These Parts; Will not all the World Justifie His *Majesty* herein? And when withall, *Themselves* also *began the stopping of Ships in These Parts,* and that he hath all those reasons of *Complaint* against them above mentioned.

7

The Charter of Liberties and Privileges Granted by His Royal Highness to the Inhabitants of New York (1683)[1]

In April 1664, Charles II (1660-85) granted a conglomerate complex of American territory to his brother, the Duke of York. In most particulars the charter of New York resembled the earlier proprietary grants, but it omitted any provision for a representative assembly. In the summer of 1664, Richard Nicolls (1624-72) seized the colony from the Dutch West India Company and became the first governor. Nicolls governed the colony with an appointed council but without a legislature. The Dutch residents of New York registered no complaint. Protest came in part from the English merchants of the city, but primarily from the citizens of the Long Island towns, who were former New Englanders. The governor responded to the popular protest by promulgating a basic civil and criminal code, which came to be known as the Duke's Laws. The code was also a partial concession to the Long Islanders because it included substantial extracts from New England codes, but it in no way satisfied them. They continued to call for a representative assembly and particularly protested the levying of taxes without legislative consent.

Nicolls and his successors reported the popular demands to the Duke of York, whose attitude remained proprietary and paternalistic. He could see no reason for an assembly because he provided the New Yorkers with just government. An assembly, he wrote, "would be of dangerous consequence." Though he undoubtedly continued to hold this opinion, ultimately he yielded. He may well have done so because of the very poor return from executively levied provincial taxes. In 1683, a new governor, Thomas Dongan, came out with instructions to permit the election of an assembly, and later that year the first legislature met.

1. *Laws of the Colony of New York from the Year 1664 to the Revolution* (5 vols.; Albany, J. B. Lyons, 1894), I, 111-21.

In addition to passing routine legislation, the first session produced the famous Charter of Liberties. Better than any other seventeenth-century colonial document, the Charter makes clear what the colonists meant when they claimed the rights of Englishmen. The Charter restated the rights of seventeenth-century Englishmen and in so doing it drew heavily on the very language of the great English constitutional documents.

In seeking knowledge about political action and institutions in the colonies one can do no better than to begin with the appropriate volume of Herbert L. Osgood, *The American Colonies in the Seventeenth Century* (3 vols., New York: Columbia University Press, 1930) and *The American Colonies in the Eighteenth Century* (4 vols., New York: Columbia University Press, 1924). There is no comprehensive work on the development of procedural and substantive rights. Monographs on specific themes are: Mary P. Clarke, *Parliamentary Privilege in the American Colonies* (New Haven: Yale University Press, 1943); Chilton Williamson, *American Suffrage from Property to Democracy* (Princeton: Princeton University Press, 1960); and Leonard W. Levy, *Legacy of Suppression; Freedom of Speech and Press in Early American History* (Cambridge: Belknap Press, 1960). In reading the Charter note (1) what institutional framework of government was provided; (2) how radical or novel the granted rights were; (3) what safeguards against tyranny were included; (4) the extent to which religious toleration was protected; and (5) to what degree the provisions of the Charter derived from English precedents.

FOR THE BETTER ESTABLISHING THE GOVERNMENT of this province of New Yorke and that Justice and Right may be Equally done to all persons within the same BEE It Enacted by the Governour Councell and Representatives now in Generall Assembly mett and assembled and by the authority of the same. THAT The Supreme Legislative Authority under his Majesty and Royall Highnesse James Duke of Yorke Albany &c Lord proprietor of the said province shall forever be and reside in a Governour, Councell, and the peopele mett in General Assembly.

THAT The Exercise of the Cheife Magistracy and Administracon of the Government over the said province shall bee in the said Governour assisted by a Councell with whose advice and Consent or with at least four of them he is to rule and Governe the same according to the Lawes thereof. THAT in

Case the Governour shall dye or be absent out of the province and that there be noe person within the said province Comissionated by his Royal Highnesse his heires or Successours to be Governour or Comander in Cheife there That then the Councell for the time being or Soe many of them as are in the Said province doe take upon them the Administracon of the Governour and the Execucon of the Lawes thereof and powers and authorityes belonging to the Governour and Councell the first in nominacon in which Councell is to preside untill the said Governour shall returne and arrive in the said province againe, or the pleasure of his Royall Highnesse his heires or Successours Shall be further knowne.

THAT According to the usage Custome and practice of the Realme of England a sessions of a Generall Asembly be held in this province once in three yeares at least.

THAT Every ffreeholder within this province and ffreeman in any Corporacon Shall have his free Choise and Vote in the Electing of the Representatives without any manner of constraint or Imposicon. and that in all Eleccons the Majority of Voices shall carry itt and by freeholders is understood every one who is Soe understood according to the Lawes of England.

THAT the persons to be Elected to sitt as representatives in the Generall Assembly from time to time for the severall Cittyes townes Countyes Shires or Divisions of this province and all places within the same shall be according to the proporcon and number hereafter Expressed that is to say for the Citty and County of New Yorke four, for the County of Suffolke two, for Queens County two, for Kings County two, for the County of Richmond two for the County of West Chester two, for the County of Ulster two for the County of Albany two and for Schenectade within the said County one for Dukes County two, for the County of Cornwall two and as many more as his Royall Highnesse shall think fitt to Establish.

THAT All persons Chosen and Assembled in manner aforesaid or the Major part of them shall be deemed and accounted the Representatives of this province which said Representatives together with the Governour and his Councell Shall forever be the Supreame and only Legislative power under his Royall Highnesse of the said province.

THAT The said Representatives may appoint their owne Times of meeting dureing their sessions and may adjourne their house from time to time to such time as to them shall seeme meet and convenient.

THAT The said Representatives are the sole Judges of the Qualificacons of their owne members, and likewise of all undue Eleccons and may from time to time purge their house as they shall see occasion dureing the said sessions.

THAT noe member of the general Assembly or their servants dureing the time of their Sessions and whilest they shall be goeing to and returning from the said Assembly shall be arrested sued imprisoned or any wayes molested or troubled nor be compelled to make answere to any suite, Bill, plaint, Declaracon or otherwise, (Cases of High Treason and felony only Excepted) provided the number of the said servants shall not Exceed three.

THAT All bills agreed upon by the said Representatives or the Major part of them shall be presented unto the Governour and his Councell for their Approbacon and Consent All and Every which Said Bills soe approved of Consented to by the Governour and his Councell shall be Esteemed and accounted the Lawes of the province. Which said Lawes shall continue and remaine of force untill they shall be repealed by the authority aforesaid that is to say the Governour Councell and Representatives in General Assembly by and with the Approbacon of his Royal Highnesse or Expire by their owne Limittacons.

THAT In all Cases of death or removall of any of the said Representatives The Governour shall issue out Sumons by Writt to the Respective Townes Cittyes Shires Countryes or Divisions for which he or they soe removed or deceased were Chosen willing and requireing the ffreeholders of the Same to Elect others in their place and stead.

THAT Noe freeman shall be taken and imprisoned or be disseized of his ffreehold or Libertye or ffree Customes or be outlawed or Exiled or any other wayes destroyed nor shall be passed upon adjudged or condemned But by the Lawfull Judgment of his peers and by the Law of this province. Justice nor Right shall be neither sold denyed or deferred to any man within this province.

THAT Noe aid, Tax, Tallage, Assessment, Custome, Loane,

Benevolence or Imposicon whatsoever shall be layed assessed imposed or levyed on any of his Majestyes Subjects within this province or their Estates upon any manner of Colour or pretence but by the act and Consent of the Governour Councell and Representatives of the people in Generall Assembly mett and Assembled.

THAT Noe man of what Estate or Condicon soever shall be putt out of his Lands or Tenements, nor taken, nor imprisoned, nor disherited, nor banished nor any wayes distroyed without being brought to Answere by due Course of Law.

THAT A ffreeman Shall not be amerced for a small fault, but after the manner of his fault and for a great fault after the Greatnesse thereof Saveing to him his freehold, And a husbandman saveing to him his Wainage and a merchant likewise saveing to him his merchandize And none of the said Amerciaments shall be assessed but by the oath of twelve honest and Lawfull men of the Vicinage provided the faults and misdemeanours be not in Contempt of Courts of Judicature.

ALL Tryalls shall be by the verdict of twelve men, and as neer as may be peers or Equalls And of the neighbourhood and in the County Shire or Division where the fact Shall arise or grow Whether the Same be by indictment Infermacon Declaracon or otherwise against the person Offender or Defendant.

THAT In all Cases Capitall or Criminall there shall be a grand Inquest who shall first present the offence and then twelve men of the neighbourhood to try the Offender who after his plea to the Indictment shall be allowed his reasonable Challenges. THAT In all Cases whatsoever Bayle by sufficient Suretyes Shall be allowed and taken unlesse for treason or felony plainly and specially Expressed and menconed in the Warrant of Committment provided Alwayes that nothing herein contained shall Extend to discharge out of prison upon bayle any person taken in Execucon for debts or otherwise legally sentenced by the Judgment of any of the Courts of Record within the province.

THAT Noe Comissions for proceeding by Marshall Law against any of his Majestyes Subjects within this province shall issue forth to any person or persons whatsoever Least by Colour of them any of his Majestyes Subjects bee destroyed or putt to death Except all such officers persons and Soldiers in pay throughout the Government.

THAT from hence forward Noe Lands Within this province shall be Esteemed or accounted a Chattle or personall Estate but an Estate of Inheritance according to the Custome and practice of his Majesties Realme of England.

THAT Noe Court or Courts within this province have or at any time hereafter Shall have any Jurisdiccon power or authority to grant out any Execucon or other writt whereby any mans Land may be sold or any other way disposed off without the owners Consent provided Alwayes That the issues or meane proffitts of any mans Lands shall or may be Extended by Execucon or otherwise to satisfye just debts Any thing to the Contrary hereof in any wise Notwithstanding.

THAT Noe Estate of a feme Covert shall be sold or conveyed But by Deed acknowledged by her in Some Court of Record the Woman being secretly Examined if She doth it freely without threats or Compulsion of her husband.

THAT All Wills in writeing attested by two Credible Witnesses shall be of the same force to convey Lands as other Conveyances being registered in the Secretaryes Office within forty dayes after the testators death.

THAT A Widdow after the death of her husband shall have her Dower And shall and may tarry in the Cheife house of her husband forty dayes after the death of her husband within which forty dayes her Dower shall be assigned her And for her Dower shall be assigned unto her the third part of all the Lands of her husband dureing Coverture, Except shee were Endowed of Lesse before Marriage.

THAT All Lands and Heritages within this province and Dependencyes shall be free from all fines and Lycences upon Alienacons, and from all Herriotts Ward Shipps Liveryes primer Seizins yeare day and Wast Escheats and forteitures upon the death of parents and Ancestors naturall unaturall casuall or Judiciall, and that forever; Cases of High treason only Excepted.

THAT Noe person or persons which professe ffaith in God by Jesus Christ Shall at any time be any wayes molested punished disquieted or called in Question for any Difference in opinion or

Matter of Religious Concernment, who doe not actually disturb the Civill peace of the province, But that all and Every such person or persons may from time to time and at all times freely have and fully enjoy his or their Judgments or Consciencyes in matters of Religion throughout all the province, they behaveing themselves peaceably and quietly and not useing this Liberty to Lycentiousnesse nor to the civill Injury or outward disturbance of others. . . .

8

Imperial Reorganization

The Stuart Restoration of 1660 coincided with a rising interest in trade expansion and imperial reorganization. Beginning in 1660, Parliament passed the basic laws of navigation and trade. These statutes highlighted the problem of law enforcement, which contained three main elements: (1) the need for English law enforcement officials in America; (2) the need for a central agency in England to plan and supervise colonial policy; and (3) the need to consolidate and make more uniform the individual colonial units.

In 1673 Parliament passed another navigation act, one which required the collection of duties in America. The Commissioners of Customs began sending tax collectors to colonial ports. The most famous, or notorious, of these agents was Edward Randolph (c. 1632-1703), who for a period of twenty years, held a variety of positions in the colonial service. His voluminous reports form a continuous and comprehensive indictment of the colonies. Directly or indirectly, Randolph's recommendations affected the many reforms of the 1690s.

The English agency ultimately responsible for colonial policy was the Privy Council, but because of its multiple responsibilities, the Council could never concentrate its attention on colonial affairs. The early Stuarts had established several special commissions to deal with colonial matters, and the practice was resumed by Charles II. In 1675 a standing committee of the Privy Council, the Lords of Trade, was appointed. The Lords employed a staff of professional civil servants, who gave a degree of continuity to colonial policy. By the 1690s the Lords of Trade had lost their effectiveness, and in 1696, William III (1689-1702) created the Board of Trade, an administrative agency responsible to the Privy Council. Throughout its long career the Board translated the demands of English economic interests into orthodox mercantilist policy.

If colonial diversity was a source of American freedom, it was also a standing frustration to English administrators. The first major effort to override colonial autonomy came in the reign of James II (1685-88). The King combined New York, New Jersey, and the New England colonies into a single unit, installed Sir Edmund Andros (1637-1714) as governor and ruled the Dominion without a legislature. Andros' rule was Spartan and effective. He established executive government, drove out illegal traders, introduced the Anglican Church where it had not been known, revised land tenure in favor of the Crown, and throttled local government. But the Dominion was aborted by the Glorious Revolution. "The Declaration of the Gentlemen, Merchants, and Inhabitants of Boston . . ." was written in the hyperbole of a polemic and it must be read as such. It does, however, outline Andros' actions. Men like Randolph remained convinced that the final answer to the imperial question was the royalization of all colonies. In the 1690s they renewed the attack on the private colonies, and bills "reuniting" the colonies to the Crown were introduced in Parliament on several occasions in the early eighteenth century.

A. Berriedale Keith, *A Constitutional History of the First British Empire* (Oxford: Clarendon, 1930) is a fine study of the administrative structure of the empire. Oliver M. Dickerson, tells the story of the influential Board of Trade in *American Colonial Government, 1696-1765* (Cleveland: Arthur H. Clark, 1912). The problems of enforcing imperial policy are related through the medium of biography in Michael G. Hall, *Edward Randolph and the American Colonies, 1676-1703* (University of North Carolina Press: Chapel Hill, 1960). In reading Edward Randolph's report note (1) the main points in Randolph's bill of particulars against Massachusetts; and (2) the tone and spirit of his report. In reading *The Overthrow of the Dominion of New England* note (1) the principal points in this bill of particulars against the British government and its American agents; and (2) the tone and spirit of the declaration. In reading the *Report of the Board of Trade on Private Colonies* note (1) the major complaints entered against the private colonies; (2) what general recommendation the Board made; (3) the specific complaints lodged against individual colonies; and (4) the tone and spirit of the report. In reading the Reunification Bill note (1) what seemed to be the primary concern of the government in proposing this bill; (2) the means proposed of effecting reunification; and (3) what safeguards to colonial interests were included.

A. A Report of Edward Randolph (1678)[1]

M AY IT PLEASE YO[R] LORDSHIPS

In obedience to yo[r] Lordships Commands signified unto me on the 25th of March last, that I should offer in

---

1. Robert N. Toppan, *Edward Randolph; Including his letters and official papers* (7 vols.; Boston: The Prince Society, 1898-1909), II, 311-19.

writing what I have further to certifie unto yor Lordships touching the evill practices and misdemeanors of the Magistrates
that now hold the Governm^t of the Massachusets Bay contrary
to their Charter and the frequent Advices and Commands
received from his Maj^tie I presume in the first place to take
notice

That the Articles against the Bostoners which I abstracted
from my Narrative stand in no part invalidated by the endeavors
of the Agents now attending, Who have att several times confessed the particulars thereof promising amendment and begging
pardon for what is past.

I doe further declare my self ready to make out unto yor
Lordships all other particulars contained in the several Sheets of
the said Narrative, which indeed the Agents doe confess likewise
by their not having offered any thing to the contrary. But that I
may enter upon New particulars I think it my duty to acquaint
yor Lordships

That these Boston Magistrates have not only injured their
Neighbours on the North and East viz. Mr Mason and Mr Gorges
by a forceable extent of Grounds drawne from the Notion of
their Imaginary Line, but have opprest even the Southerne
Colonyes of New Plimouth and Connecticut violently enlarging
their Bounds upon them as his Maj^ts Comm^rs formerly in 1665
and lately the Lords Cheif Justices have reported, terrifying
those people into a compliance and quiet suffering by their
overawing power.

That many of their Laws that are now in force are not only
disagreable, but repugnant to the Fundamental Laws of England, and contrary to the plaine intent of the Grand Charter,
aswell as his Maj^ts Express Commands, the most Notorious are
as Followes.

It is sufficiently apparent that the First designe of this Colony
was to enjoy liberty of Conscience and that his Maj^tie hath
likewise particularly enjoined That all persons of good and
honest lives be admitted to the Sacrament of the Lords supper
according to the Book of Common prayer, and their Children to
Baptisme, Yet such is their pernicious practice herein, that instead hereof, Farr from the maine designe of bringing Infidels to
Christianity, By the factious distinctions and privations in their

Laws, many English Children, and full grown persons remaine
without the Sacrament of Baptisme, in case their Parents, Grand-
father or Grandmother have not been Church members, And
many more are forbidden the Sacrament of the Lords supper,
such Ministers as would administer the same being prohibited
by that Law Whereby no Minister is to be chosen but such as
is in full communion, And the County Courts are obliged to
purge their Towns and peculiers from all Ministry which shall
be found (as they terme it) Heteradox. P\ua 41. By which they
discourage a voluntary Reformation from their Arbitrary Independency.

Nor will they suffer any man by their Laws to preach publickly to any Company or people, where any Two Organick
Churches, Councill of State, or General Court shall declare their
dissatisfaction thereat either in Doctrine or Practice. Further
they provide That whosoever with draws himself from the
publick ministry setled amongst them shall for every such offence
forfeit Five Shillings, by all which practices they obstruct the
true Protestants in the exercise of their Religion, and terrifie the
seduced people from a Compliance with the Church of England.

His maj^tie doth further enjoine That all Freeholders of Competent Estates not vicious in their conversations, and Orthodox in
their Religion though of different perswasions concerning Church
Government to have their votes in the Elections of all officers
Military and Civill. Yet their Law provides That no man shall
be admitted a Freeman unless he be in full Communion in some
Church amongst them, thereby excluding the most and best
affected to his Maj^tie and the Church of England. And by an
other Law order That all persons which refuse to attend the
publick worshipp of God their established, be made uncapable
of voting in all Civill Assemblies.

That although his Maj^tie commanded that in their Elections of
G[overn^rs &] Magistrates there be only consideration had to the
vertue and integrity of the persons to be chosen and not of any
Faction with reference to their opinion and outward profession.
Their Law directs that all Freemen preferre in their Elections
the former Magistrates under penalty of Tenn pounds. by which
means the first Founders of the Common Wealth are still continued in the Magistracy, and none (Except by Death) removed

how obnoxious soever, Mr Leveret who was in actuall Armes against his Maj^tie and turned out his Maj^ts Justices of the peace in the province of Main, being present Governor, Mr Guggins (who after his Maj^ts Commands of seizing the Murtherers of his late Maj^tie came to that Government) harboured and protected Goffe and Whaley is the last year againe Elected a Magistrate, Mr Hawthorne who being then a Magistrate was commanded by his Maj^ts Letters of 1666 to attend upon his Allegiance at White-hall but refused to appeare, is still in the Magistracy.

That by vertue of a Souveraigne Right (as they give it out) communicated to them in their Charter, they assume a power of allowing or rejecting any Law Royall Commands or Act of Parlement not agreeing with their Frame of Polity & Government.

They sweare their Jurors to determine causes Civill and Criminal according to the Laws of that Country, without respect to the Laws of England, which are neither in the whole or in any part of them valid or pleadable in their Courts till such Laws or such part thereof be received and voted such by a General Assembly.

All these Enormities and crimes I should have willingly passed over were there any hopes of amendment left, Since besides their contempt of all his Maj^ts Letters of 1662. 1664 and 1666, They have had little consideration in order to a redress of these Misdemeanors charged upon them by my Narrative and Articles, their General Court being desirous to be secured only for what is past by his Maj^ts pardon and to be Enriched with the accession of New Government, with leave to pursue their former practice, For the maintenance wherof, Notwithstanding the Signification of his Maj^ts pleasure That they should take the Oaths of Allegiance, They have lately at a General Court held at Boston, cunningly contrived a Test (upon the pretence of a Fire at Boston) to be imposed upon all persons as well Inhabitants as Strangers to take the Oath of Fidelity to their Country throughout their Jurisdiction the Refusers wherof are not to have the benefit of the Law or protection from the Government.

And they have at the same time for avoiding the consequences of their neglect of the Acts of Trade and Navigation made a Specious Law, with a more Specious preamble setting forth

That his Maj^ts pleasure therein had not been before signified unto them Either by Express from his Maj^tie or Ministers, Whereby they doe not only confess their unlimited trading ever since his Maj^ts Restauration But throw all the fault upon his Maj^tie and Ministers, afraid to owne unto the people under their Government That they had for soe long time neglected their Duty and obedience to his Maj^tie least those people which are for the most part loyal, and ready to execute his Maj^ts Commands (if they were permitted thereto by their Superiours) should discover the profitable Intregues of their Government and take occasion (as formerly they have done) to remonstrate against the heavy pressures therof.

And it is further to be observed That they have taken soe little care to conforme themselves to the Decency of Truth, that although the present Magistrates and their Secretary Rawson had in 1663 confessed the Receipt of his Maj^ts Orders to putt in Execution the said Acts of Parliament, as appears by an Act since printed by them, Yet now after soe many years and soe many Transgressions they are not willing to call to Remembrance the former signification of his Maj^ts pleasure, concluding perhaps That the irregularities of their Governm^t and Manners are soe little taken notice of by his Maj^ts Ministers, that any formal assurance or Declaration coming from them shall blot out of all memory what they have formerly acknowledged, and therefore have most dishonorably and untruly taxed his Maj^tie and his Ministers not to have within the Space of above Sixteen years informed the Court of Boston of their dutys whilest they themselves glad of that pretence have shutt their Eyes to such Acts as no part of the trading World but they have pretended ignorance of, and come now most disingeniously to declare That they would have given a more timely obedience if they had been more timely commanded.

Nor may I omitt to take notice That the Bostoners by reenacting this Act of parliament doe Encourage the English under their Government to beleeve That no Acts of Parliament much less Orders from his Maj^tie are in force with them untill such time as their Governors in a General Court doe Enact and order them soe to be.

Lastly it is to be feared that the Boston Magistrates intend by this contrivance to acquit not only themselves and people of all imputation of disobedience, but shutt the Door against such as may lawfully by the said Acts of Parliament impeach them for their former Transgressions, since by this New Law all persons may plead the issue [of] this private Act, and Encourage them to hope that in time to come, another Act of Oblivion shall pass at the General Court of Boston, and his Maj^tie remain soe farre satisfied, as to grant them his Royal pardon in confirmation of their own Acts.

Upon the whole matter it is most certain by what is before alleadged that by the convayance of their Agents They have long since been informed of the charge brought in against them for Misdemeanors contained in my Narrative and Articles. But it doth not appeare that after consideration had of them at Boston, they have thought fitt to give any redress, but have only taken time to order his Maj^ts pardon to be Sollicited with an increase of power upon their Neighbours, Nor am I informed by my Correspondants in New England, that they have gone about to give or take the Oaths of Allegiance or Supremacy, or that they have for any time suspended or repealed any of their unjust Laws, or even held their hand in Coining of money, or testified any inclination to the premises. But in opposition therto, as a greater manifestation of their Authority have given the Test aforesaid, to which they have annexed soe Severe and determinate penalties, Whilest none are imposed on Such as disobey [the] Acts of Trade and Navigation.

Articles abstracted from the precedent paper against the Governm^t of the Massachusets Bay in New England.

1. That the Governm^t of the Massachusets is guilty of all the Crimes & Misdemeanors which I formerly exhibited in my Articles against them, even by the confession of their owne Petition, wherein they desire a pardon for the same.

2. That they have Encroached upon the Bounds of the Southerne Colonies in New England.

3. That the Fundamentall Laws of the Governm^t are repugnant to the Laws of England.

4. That they doe not allow liberty of conscience nor the Exercise of the Religion professed by the Church of England, constraining all persons to be present at their Meetings.

5. That they admitt none to have share in the Govern^t Except such as are in full Communion with them.

6. That they have acted contrary to their Charter and his Maj^{ts} Commands in 1662 and others.

7. That they assume powers not granted in their Charter, intrenching upon his Maj^{ts} Prerogative.

8. That instead of the oaths of Allegiance and Supremacy they have lately enforced an oath of Fidelity to be taken to the Country.

9. They permitt no Law of England, nor Act of Parliament to be in force there, Except first allowed and Enacted by them.

10. That they have falcely charged his Maj^{tie} and his Ministers of State.

11. That they have not proceeded to any amendment of their Crimes and Misdemeanors confessed by them, although timely admonished therto.

ED: RANDOLPH:

B. The Overthrow of the Dominion of New England

The Declaration of the Gentlemen, Marchants, and Inhabitants of Boston, and the Country Adjacent. April 18, 1689.[1]

I. We have seen more than a decad of Years rolled away, since the English World had the Discovery of an horrid Popish Plot; wherein the bloody *Devotoes* of Rome had in their Design and Prospect no less than the Extinction of the *Protestant Religion*: which mighty Work they called *the utter subduing of a Pestilent Heresy; wherein* (they said) there never were such hopes of Success since the Death of Queen *Mary,* as now in our days. And we were of all men the most insensible, if we should apprehend a Countrey so remarkable for the true Profession and pure Exercise of the Protestant Religion as *New-England* is, wholly unconcerned in the Infamous Plot. To crush and break a Countrey so entirely and signally made up of *Reformed Churches,* and at length to involve it in the miseries of an utter Extirpation, must needs carry even a Supererogation of merit with it among

1. William H. Whitmore, ed., *The Andros Tracts* (3 vols.; Boston: The Prince Society, 1868), I, 11-19.

such as were intoxicated with a Bigotry inspired into them by the great *Scarlet Whore.*

II. To get us within the reach of the desolation desired for us, it was no improper thing that we should first have our *Charter* Vacated, and the hedge which kept us from the wild Beasts of the field, effectually broken down. The accomplishment of this was hastened by the unwearied sollicitations, and slanderous accusations of a man, for his *Malice* and *Falshood,* well known unto us all. Our *Charter* was with a most injurious pretence (and scarce that) of Law, condemned before it was possible for us to appear at *Westminster* in the legal defence of it; and without a fair leave to answer for our selves, concerning the Crimes falsly laid to our charge, we were put under a *President* and *Council,* without any liberty for an Assembly, which the other *American Plantations* have, by a Commission from His *Majesty.*

III. The Commission was as *Illegal* for the form of it, as the way of obtaining it was *Malicious* and *unreasonable*: yet we made no Resistance thereunto as we could easily have done; but chose to give all *Mankind* a Demonstration of our being a people sufficiently dutiful and loyal to our King: and this with yet more Satisfaction, because we took pains to make our selves believe as much as ever we could of the Whedle [enticement] then offer'd unto us; That his *Majesty's* Desire was no other than the happy encrease and advance of these *Provinces* by their more immediate Dependance on the *Crown* of *England.* And we were convinced of it by the Courses immediately taken to damp and spoyl our *Trade;* whereof decayes and complaints presently filled all the Country; while in the mean time neither the Honour nor the Treasure of the King was at all advanced by this new Model of our Affairs, but a considerable Charge added unto the Crown.

IV. In little more than half a Year we saw this Commission superseded by another yet more Absolute and Arbitrary, with which Sir *Edmond Andross* arrived as our Governour; who besides his Power, with the Advice and Consent of his Council, to make Laws and raise Taxes as he pleased; had also Authority by himself to Muster and Imploy all Persons residing in the Territory as occasion shall serve; and to transfer such Forces to any English Plantation in *America,* as occasion shall require. And several Companies of Souldiers were now brought from *Europe,* to support what was to be imposed upon us, not without repeated Menaces that some hundreds more were intended for us.

V. The Government was no sooner in these Hands, but care was taken to load Preferments principally upon such Men as were strangers to and haters of the People; and every ones Observation hath noted, what Qualifications recommended a Man to publick Offices and Employments, only here and there a *good Man* was used, where others could not easily be had; the Governour himself, with Assertions now and then falling from him, made us jealous that it would be thought for his Majesties Interest, if this People were removed and another succeeded in their room: And his far-fetch'd Instruments that were growing rich among us, would gravely inform us, that it was not for his Majesties Interest that we should thrive. But of all our Oppressors we were chiefly *squeez'd* by a Crew of abject Persons fetched from *New York,* to be the Tools of the Adversary, standing at our right hand; by these were extraordinary and intollerable Fees extorted from every one upon all occasions, without any Rules but those of their own insatiable Avarice and Beggary; and even the probate of a Will must now cost as many *Pounds* perhaps as it did *Shillings* heretofore; nor could a small Volume contain the other Illegalities done by these *Horse-leeches* in the two or three Years that they have been sucking of us; and what Laws they made it was as impossible for us to know, as dangerous for us to break; but we shall leave the Men of *Ipswich* and of *Plimouth* (among others) to tell the story of the kindness which has been shown them upon this account. Doubtless a Land so ruled as once *New-England* was, has not without many fears and sighs beheld the wicked walking on every side, and the vilest Men exalted.

VI. It was now plainly affirmed, both by some in open Council, and by the same in private converse, that the people in *New-England* were all *Slaves,* and the only difference between them and *Slaves* is their not being bought and sold; and it was a maxim delivered in open Court unto us by one of the Council,

*that we must not think the Priviledges of English men would
follow us to the end of the World*: Accordingly we have been
treated with multiplied contradictions to *Magna Charta,* the
rights of which we laid claim unto. Persons who did but peaceably object against the raising of Taxes without an Assembly,
have been for it fined, some twenty, some thirty, and others fifty
Pounds. Packt and pickt Juries have been very common things
among us, when, under a pretended form of Law, the trouble of
some honest and worthy Men has been aimed at: but when
some of this Gang have been brought upon the Stage, for the
most detestable Enormities that ever the Sun beheld, all Men
have with Admiration seen what methods have been taken that
they might not be treated according to their Crimes. Without a
Verdict, yea, without a Jury sometimes have People been fined
most unrighteously; and some not of the meanest Quality have
been kept in long and close Imprisonment without any the least
Information appearing against them, or an Habeas Corpus allowed unto them. In short, when our Oppressors have been a
little out of Mony, 'twas but pretending some Offence to be
enquired into, and the most innocent of Men were continually
put into no small Expence to answer the Demands of the
Officers, who must have money of them, or a Prison for them,
tho none could accuse them of any Misdemeanour.

VII. To plunge the poor People every where into deeper
Incapacities, there was one very comprehensive Abuse given to
us; Multitudes of pious and sober Men through the Land,
scrupled the Mode of Swearing on the Book, desiring that they
might Swear with an uplifted Hand, agreeable to the ancient
Custom of the Colony; and though we think we can prove that
the Common Law amongst us (as well as in some other places
under the *English Crown*) not only indulges, but even commands and enjoins the Rite of lifting the Hand in *Swearing;* yet
they that had this Doubt, were still put by from serving upon
any Juries; and many of them were most unaccountably Fined
and Imprisoned. Thus one Grievance is a *Trojan Horse,* in the
Belly of which it is not easy to recount how many insufferable
Vexations have been contained.

VIII. Because these Things could not make us miserable fast

enough, there was a notable Discovery made of we know not what *flaw* in all our *Titles to our Lands*; and, tho *besides* our purchase of them from the Natives; and *besides* our actual peaceable unquestioned possession of them for near threescore Years, and besides the Promise of K. *Charles II.* in his Proclamation sent over to us in the Year 1683, That *no Man here shall receive any Prejudice in his Freehold or Estate*: We had the Grant of our Lands, under the Seal of the Council of Plimouth: which Grant was Renewed and Confirmed unto us by King *Charles I.* under the Great Seal of England; and the General Court which consisted of the Patentees and their Associates, had made particular Grants hereof to the several *Towns* (though 'twas now deny'd by the Governour, that there was any such Thing as a *Town*) among us; to all which Grants the General Court annexed for the further securing of them, *A General Act*, published under the Seal of the Colony, in the Year 1684. Yet we were every day told, *That no Man was owner of a Foot of Land in all the Colony.* Accordingly, *Writs of Intrusion* began every where to be served on People, that after all their Sweat and their Cost upon their formerly purchased Lands, thought themselves *Free-holders* of what they had. And the Governor caused the Lands pertaining to these and those *particular Men*, to be measured out for his Creatures to take possession of; and the *Right Owners*, for pulling up the Stakes, have passed through Molestations enough to tire all the patience in the World. They are more than a few, that were by Terrors driven to take *Patents* for their Lands at excessive rates, to save them from the next that might petition for them: and we fear that the forcing of the People at the *Eastward* hereunto, gave too much Rise to the late unhappy Invasion made by the *Indians* on them. *Blanck Patents* were got ready for the rest of us, to be sold at a Price, that all the Mony and Movables in the Territory could scarce have paid. And several *Towns* in the Country had their *Commons* begg'd by Persons (even by some of the Council themselves) who have been privately encouraged thereunto, by those that fought for Occasions to impoverish a Land already *Peeled, Meeted out and Trodden down.*

IX. All the Council were not ingaged in these ill Actions, but those of them which were true Lovers *of their Country,* were seldom admitted to, and seldomer consulted at the Debates which produced these unrighteous Things: Care was taken to keep them under Disadvantages; and the Governor, with five or six more, did what they would. We bore all these, and many more such Things, without making any attempt for any Relief; only Mr. *Mather,* purely out of respect unto the Good of his Afflicted Country, undertook a Voyage into *England;* which when these Men suspected him to be preparing for, they used all manner of Craft and Rage, not only to interrupt his *Voyage,* but to ruin his *Person* too. God having through many Difficulties given him to arrive at *White-hall,* the King, more than once or twice, promised him a certain *Magna Charta* for a speedy Redress of many things which we were groaning under: and in the mean time said, *That our Governor should be written unto, to forbear the Measures that he was upon.* However, after this, we were injured in those very Things which were complained of; and besides what Wrong hath been done in our Civil Concerns, we suppose the *Ministers* and the *Churches* every where have seen our Sacred Concerns apace going after them: How they have been Discountenanced, has had a room in the reflections of every man, that is not a stranger *in our Israel.*

X. And yet that our Calamity might not be terminated here, we are again Briar'd in the Perplexities of another *Indian War;* how, or why, is a mystery too deep for us to unfold. And tho' 'tis judged that our *Indian* Enemies are not above 100, in number, yet an Army of *One thousand* English hath been raised for the Conquering of them; which Army of our poor Friends and Brethren now under *Popish Commanders* (for in the Army as well as in the Council, Papists are in Commission) has been under such a conduct, that not one *Indian* hath been kill'd, but more English are supposed to have died through sickness and hardship, than we have adversaries there alive; and the whole War hath been so managed, that we cannot but suspect in it, a branch of the Plot *to bring us low;* which we leave to be further enquir'd into in due time.

XI. We did nothing against these Proceedings, but only cry to our God; they *have caused the cry of the Poor to come unto him, and he hears the cry of the Afflicted.* We have been quiet hitherto, and so still we should have been, had not the Great God at this time laid us under a *double engagement* to do something for our security: besides, what we have in the strangely unanimous inclination which our Countrymen by extreamest necessities are driven unto. For first, we are informed that the rest of the English *America* is alarmed with just and great fears, that they may be attaqu'd by the *French,* who have lately ('tis said) already treated many of the English with worse then Turkish Cruelties; and while we are in equal danger of being surprised by them, it is high time we should be better guarded, than we are like to be while the Government remains in the hands by which it hath been held of late. Moreover, we have understood, (though the *Governour* has taken all imaginable care to keep us all ignorant thereof) that the Almighty God hath been pleased to prosper the noble undertaking of the Prince of *Orange,* to preserve the three Kingdoms from the horrible brinks of Popery and Slavery, and to bring to a Condign punishment those *worst of men,* by whom *English Liberties* have been destroy'd; in compliance with which Glorious Action we ought surely to follow the Patterns which the Nobility, Gentry and Commonalty in several parts of those Kingdoms have set before us, though *they* therein chiefly proposed to prevent what *we* already endure.

XII. We do therefore seize upon the Persons of those few *Ill Men* which have been (next to our Sins) the grand Authors of our Miseries; resolving to secure them, for what Justice, Orders from his Highness, with the *English Parliament* shall direct, lest, ere we are aware, we find (what we may *fear,* being on all sides in danger) our selves to be by them given away to a Forreign *Power,* before such Orders can reach unto us; for which Orders we now humbly wait. In the mean time firmly believing, that we have endeavoured nothing but what meer Duty to God and our *Country* calls for at our Hands: We commit our *Enterprise* unto the Blessing of Him, *who hears the cry of the Oppressed,* and advise all our Neighbours, for whom we have thus ventured our selves, to joyn with us in Prayers and all just Actions, for the Defence of the Land.

C. Report of the Board of Trade
on Private Colonies (1701)[1]

We have, on many occasions, represented to his Majesty, as we did likewise, in our last report, to the late House of Commons, the state of such plantations in America, as are under the government of proprietors and charters; and how inconsistent these governments are with the trade and welfare of this kingdom:

That these colonies, in general, have no-ways answered the chief design, for which such large tracts of land, and such privileges and immunities, were granted by the crown:

That they have not conformed themselves to the several acts of Parliament for regulating trade and navigation, to which they ought to pay the same obedience, and submit to the same restriction, as the other plantations, which are subject to his Majesty's immediate government; though, on the contrary, in most of these proprietary and charter-governments, the governors have not applied themselves to his Majesty for his approbation, nor have taken the oaths required by the acts of trade; both of which qualifications are made necessary by the late act for preventing frauds, and regulating abuses, in the plantation-trade:

That they have assumed to themselves a power to make laws, contrary and repugnant to the laws of England, and directly prejudicial to our trade, some of them haveing refused to send hither such laws as they have there enacted; and others having sent them, but very imperfectly:

That divers of them have denied appeals to his Majesty in Council; by which, not only the inhabitants of those colonies, but others his Majesty's subjects, are deprived of that benefit enjoyed in the plantations under his Majesty's immediate government; and the parties aggrieved are left without remedy from the arbitrary and illegal proceedings of their courts:

---

1. Leo F. Stock, ed., *Proceedings and Debates of the British Parliaments respecting North America* (5 vols.; Washington: Carnegie Institution, 1924), III, 385-86, 398-401. Reprinted by permission.

That these colonies continue to be the refuge and retreat of pirates and illegal traders, and the receptacle of goods imported thither from foreign parts, contrary to law; in return of which commodities, those of the growth of these colonies are likewise, contrary to law, exported to foreign parts: all which is likewise much encouraged by their not admitting appeals, as aforesaid:

That, by raising or lowering their coin from time to time, to their particular advantage, and to the prejudice of other colonies; by exempting their inhabitants from duties and customs, to which the other colonies are subject; and by harbouring of servants and fugitives; these governments tend greatly to the undermining the trade of the other plantations, and entice and draw away the people thereof; by which diminution of hands, the rest of the colonies, more beneficial to England, do very much suffer.

Nor have we omitted to take notice, that these independent colonies do turn the course of trade to the promoting and propagating woollen and other manufactures proper to England, instead of applying their thoughts and endeavours to the production of such commodities, as are fit to be encouraged in those parts, according to the true design and intention of those settlements:

That these governments do not put themselves into a state of defence against an enemy; nor do they sufficiently provide themselves with arms and ammunition; many of them having not a regular militia, and some of them being no otherwise, at present, than in a state of anarchy and confusion.

To cure these, and other great mischiefs in these colonies, and to introduce such an administration of government, and regulation of trade, as may make them duly subservient and useful to England; we have humbly offered our opinion, that the charters of the several proprietors and others, intitling them to a right of government, should be reassumed to the crown, and these colonies put into the same state and dependency as those of his Majesty's other plantations, without further prejudice to every man's particular property and freehold; which, we conceive, cannot otherwise be well effected, than by the legislative power of this kingdom. . . .

Proprieties

In relation to properties, and charter-governments.

Massachuset-Bay. The inhabitants of the Massachusets-Bay are guilty of carrying on illegal trade: their courts of justice have been very partial in protecting it: they have refused to admit appeals to his Majesty from judgments in those cases; and the very members of his Majesty's council there have declared their averseness to the laws of England.

Though that colony be under the inspection of a governor appointed by his Majesty's commission; yet the power of that governor is so tied up by their pretended privileges, and by their not settling any fixed maintenance either upon him, or other funds, for occasional services; his authority, and his very subsistence amongst them, are so precarious; that it is impossible for him, as the case now stands, to make any considerable step towards their reformation.

Rhode-Island. The irregularities and misdemeanors of the government of Rhode-Island have been so great, that we thought it incumbent upon us to represent to his Majesty the necessity of granting a commission for making a particular inquiry thereinto: the Earl of Bellomont accordingly went thither; but found such a reception, by their opposing his Majesty's authority, and the acts of trade and navigation, that no good effect could be obtained from that commission; they pretending, by their charter, to be independent on the government of England: which we accordingly represented to his Majesty in Council.

Connecticut. Connecticut colony, which lies next, besides the irregularities common to them with other proprieties, are more directly guilty of refusing to admit appeals to England. Upon the petitions of John and Nicolas Hallam, and of Edward Palmes and John Hallam, inhabitants of that colony, complaining of obstruction of justice there, we did write, by his Majesty's Order in Council, to the governor and company of that colony; asserting his Majesty's right to receive and determine appeals from all his colonies in America, and requiring them to admit appeals from thence: but we have since understood, by another petition presented to his Majesty by the said John and Nicholas

Hallam, and by other informations received from thence, that our letter, with his Majesty's foresaid order having been duly delivered, and an appeal accordingly demanded, the superior court of that charter-government did peremptorily refuse the same; and that the governor, who is one of the judges of the said court, did publickly declare, that no appeals should be allowed from thence to his Majesty in Council.

East and West New Jersey. The colonies of East and West New Jersey are at present in utter confusion: there being no governor in East Jersey; and the pretended governor in West Jersey being neither approved by the king, nor acknowledged by the generality of the people; some of the proprietors have thereupon proposed to surrender their pretended right of government to his Majesty; but, others insisting upon it, nothing could yet be done sufficient for the settling of any orderly government amongst them, nor for preventing unlawful trade.

Pennsylvania. The complaints against Mr. Markham, lieutenant-governor of Pensylvania, for the harbouring and protecting of pirates; and against the whole government of that colony, for their opposition to the court of admiralty erected there, as in other places, pursuant to the late act of Parliament for preventing frauds, and regulating abuses, in the plantation-trade; have been very great: but directions having been given, by their excellencies the Lords Justices, to Mr. Penn, upon his going thither, for the reforming of those disorders, we received afterwards an account from Colonel Quary, judge of his Majesty's admiralty court there, as well as from Mr. Penn himself, that he had made several advances in what had been required from him: nevertheless we have of late again received complaints from Colonel Quary, that Mr. Penn, by granting commissions to all the sheriffs of counties to be water-bailiffs, had broke into the admiralty jurisdiction, and invaded the powers thereof; and, by denying the Admiralty any right of jurisdiction within the body of the province, had, in effect, taken it wholly away: we have likewise had fresh informations, from Colonel Quary, of private trade between Pensilvania, and Curassaw [Curacao], a Dutch plantation, carried on chiefly by Scotchmen, who clandestinely and illegally export tobacco, and import such great quantities of iron, linen, wine, and other European commodities, that they are sold there as cheap as in England.

As to pirates; several persons, who have themselves been formerly suspected of piracy, are settled near the capes of Delaware River: these persons, when Kid was there, received his boats, and supplied him: they went on board him constantly, and took on shore quantities of East India goods: Mr. Penn has imprisoned these men; and seized some of the goods, which, as he informs us, shall be sent over.

Carolina, and the Bahama Islands. As to Carolina, and the Bahama Islands; the misbehaviour and ill conduct of the governors and inhabitants of those colonies, in harbouring and protecting Every, and other pirates, is notorious.

In relation to trade; we have, amongst other irregularities of this proprietary government, had information of a practice of conveying tobacco privately out of Virginia into North Carolina, and from thence carrying it to New England, and other charter-plantations, without paying the duty of one penny per pound, established by law. . . .

As to the propriety and charter-governments in general; no governor whereof has qualified himself according to the late act of Parliament, except the Governor of the Bahama Islands; for whose good behaviour security has been refused to be given by the proprietors, their independency making it absolutely necessary, that some speedy and effectual care be taken to render them more subservient and useful to this kingdom; we humbly refer ourselves to our report, dated the 27th March last, wherein we humbly represented to the honorable House, that the charters of the several proprietors, and others, intitling them to absolute government, be re-assumed to the crown; and those colonies put into the same state and dependency as these of his Majesty's other plantations, without prejudice to any man's freehold or property; which, we conceive, cannot otherwise be well effected than by the legislative power of this kingdom.

D. The Reunification Bill (1701)[1]

American Plantations (Re-union with Crown) Bill.—Draft of an Act for reuniting to the Crown the government of several colonies and plantations in America. Whereas, by virtue of

1. Historical Manuscripts Commission, *The Manuscripts of the House of Lords* (London: Eyre & Spottiswoode, 1887——), new series, IV, 314-15.

several Charters and Letters Patent under the Great Seal of England passed and granted by several of his Majesty's royal predecessors, as also by his present Majesty and the late Queen Mary, of blessed memory, the several colonies, provinces, and plantations, of the Massachusetts Bay, New Hampshire, Rhode Island and Providence Plantation, Connecticut in New England, East and West New Jersey, Pennsylvania and the adjacent territories, Maryland, Carolina, and the Bahama or Lucay Islands, in America, have been granted unto several persons, together with the absolute government and authority over his Majesty's subjects in those places, whereby the grantees were not only made proprietors of the soil and lands comprehended within the said places, but also lords and governors thereof, with full power of exercising royal government and other jurisdictions over the inhabitants thereof; and whereas the severing of such power and authority from the Crown and placing the same in the hands of subjects has, by experience, been found prejudicial and repugnant to the trade of this Kingdom and to the welfare of his Majesty's other plantations in America, and to his Majesty's revenue arising from the customs, by reason of the many irregularities committed by the governors of those plantations and by those in authority there under them, by encouraging and countenancing pirates and unlawful traders and otherwise.

Be it therefore enacted, etc., that all and singular the clauses, matters and things contained in any Charters or Letters Patent heretofore passed under the Great Seal of England by any of his Majesty's royal predecessors or by his present Majesty and the said late Queen relating to the government of his Majesty's subjects within the said plantations, colonies, or places, or any of them, or within any other plantation, colony, or place in America, whereby any power or authority is granted to any person or persons from the Crown, be and is hereby declared and enacted to be utterly void and of none effect; and it is hereby further declared and enacted that all such power and authority, privileges, and jurisdictions shall be and are hereby reunited, annexed and vested in his Majesty, his heirs and successors in right of the Crown of England, to all intents and purposes as though no such Charters and Letters Patent had been had or made.

Provided always that nothing herein contained shall be construed to extend any ways to alter, take away, diminish, or abridge the right or title which any person, persons, or bodies politic or corporate have, or lawfully may have or claim, to any land, tenements, or hereditaments, or any other matter or thing, (authority and power of government only excepted), by virtue of the said or any other Charters of Letter Patent, or by virtue of any right or title derived from or under such Charters or Letter Patent by any mean assignments or conveyances or otherwise howsoever.

Provided also that nothing in this Act contained shall be construed to empower his Majesty, his heirs or successors, to govern the said plantations, colonies, or places, or any of them, or the inhabitants thereof, otherwise than according to the laws in force in the said plantations and places respectively, not repugnant to the laws of England and such other laws and constitutions as shall from time to time be made by the general assemblies of the said respective plantations, according to the several and respective privileges at any time heretofore granted to the said several plantations and colonies respectively, by any Charter or Charters or Letters Patent under the Great Seal of England, and according to the usages in his Majesty's other plantations in America.

9

The Royal Governor

In theory, the empire assigned its administration to the prerogative of the king and from this base, a complex system of law enforcement evolved. At the colonial level the key figure was the royal governor. At the beginning of the colonial period there were no royal governors in the continental colonies; at the end there were eight. In the seventeenth century the royalization of private colonies became a settled line of English policy.

From the imperial viewpoint, the governors were largely unsuccessful. The basic explanation of their failure was that they were forced to operate at the point where imperial hopes collided with colonial aspirations. In their day-to-day operations they faced squarely the problems of federalism intrinsic to the imperial relationship. More specific factors caused the governors as a group to write erratic records: their qualifications as administrators were very uneven; too often they were men who had not made the grade in England; and at the extreme, a number of them were outright corruptionists. Regardless of their personal qualities, they were plagued by weaknesses of the system. The colonial administration was centralized in theory but was not so in fact. For example, the agents responsible for the collection of trade duties reported to the commissioners of customs in London rather than to the governor, and this created inefficiency and conflict. Most frustrating to the governors was the necessity to obtain the revenues for the operation of government from the colonial assemblies. The dependence implicit in such a fiscal arrangement created the weakest point in the administrative structure.

The Crown gave the governors their power by commissions issued under the great seal. These powers were then specified in the instructions that passed the privy seal and the trade instructions that emanated from the Board of Trade. By the late seventeenth century these commissions and instructions had been standardized to a large degree. The commission and trade instructions to two New York governors, the Earl of Bellomont and Robert Hunter are typical.

The standard accounts of the powers and problems of the royal governors are Evarts B. Greene, *The Provincial Governor in the English Colonies in North America* (New York: Longmans, Green, 1898) and Leonard W. Labaree, *Royal Government in America, A Study of the British Colonial System Before 1783* (New Haven: Yale University Press, 1930). In reading the commission to the Earl of Bellomont note (1) what authority was granted to him under the traditional headings of executive, legislative, and judicial power; (2) what restrictions were placed on the exercise of his authority; and (3) what powers were granted affecting the various aspects of colonial life placed under his control. In reading the trade instructions given to Governor Hunter note (1) evidence indicating sophistication in the regulation of economic affairs of New York; (2) what features of the instructions display mercantilistic doctrines; (3) some major provisions of the Navigation Acts; (4) to what extent the regulations appear to favor colonial economic growth; and (5) what efforts the Crown made to insure the governor's zealous performance of duty.

A. Commission to the Earl of Bellomont to be Governor of New York (1697)[1]

WILLIAM THE THIRD BY THE GRACE OF GOD KING of England Scotland France and Ireland defender of the faith ettc. To our Right trusty and Right welbeloved Cousin Richard Earl of Bellomont, GREETING. We reposing especial trust and confidence in the prudence courage and loyalty of you the said Richard Earl of Bellomont, out of our especial Grace certain knowledge and meer motion, have thought fit to constitute and appoint, and we do by these presents constitute and appoint you the said Earl of Bellomont to be our Captn General and Govr in chief in, and over our province of New York and the territories depending thereon in America.

And we do hereby require and command you to do and execute all things in due manner that shall belong unto your said command, and the trust we have reposed in you according to the several powers and directions granted or appointed you by this present Commission, and the Instructions herewith given

---

1. Edmund B. O'Callaghan & John R. Brodhead, eds., *Documents Relative to the Colonial History of the State of New York* (15 vols.; Albany: Weed, Parsons & Co., 1853-57), IV, 266-73.

you, or by such further powers, Instructions and Authorities as shall at any time hereafter be granted or appointed you under our signet or sign manual, or by our order in our privy council, and according to such reasonable laws and Statutes, as now are in force, or hereafter shall be made and agreed upon by you with the advice and consent of the Council, and Assembly of our said province under your Govern^t in such manner and forme as is hereafter expressed.

And we do hereby give and grant full power unto you the said Richard Earl of Bellomont after you shall first have taken an oath for the due execution of the Office and trust of our Captn General and Govr in Chief in and over our said province of New York and the territories depending thereon which our said Council or any five of them have hereby full power and authority, and are required to administer unto you, to give and administer to each of the members of our said Council, as well the oaths appointed by act of Parlm^t to be taken instead of the oaths of Allegiance, and supremacy, as the Test and the oath for the due execution of their places and trusts and likewise to require them to subscribe the late association mentioned in an act of Parliament made in the 7th and 8th years of our Reign, entituled: *An act for the better security of His Maj^{tys} Royal person and Government.*

And we do hereby give and grant unto you full power and authority, to suspend any of the members of our said Council, from sitting, voting and assisting therein, if you shall find just cause for so doing.

And if it shall at any time happen that by the death, departure out of our said province, or suspension of any of our Councillors, there shall be a vacancy in our said Council (any three whereof we do hereby appoint to be a quorum) Our will and Pleasure is: that you signify the same unto us, by the first opportunity, that we may under our signet and sign manual, constitute and appoint others in their stead. But that our affairs at that distance, may not suffer for want of a due number of Councillors, if ever it shall happen that there be less than seven of them residing in our said province, we do hereby give and grant unto you full power and authority to choose as many persons out of the principal freeholders inhabitants thereof as will make up the full

number of our said Councill, to be seaven and no more, which
persons by virtue of such choice shall be to all intents & purposes Councillors in our said province, until they shall be
confirmed by us, or that by the nomination of others by us under
our sign manual and signet, the said Council shall have seaven
persons in it.

We do hereby give and grant unto you full power and authority, with the advice and consent of our said Council from
time to time as need shall require, to summon and call General
Assemblys of the Inhabitants being freeholders within your
Govern^t according to the usage of our Colony of N. York.

And our will and pleasure is that the persons thereupon duly
elected by the major part of the Freeholders of the respective
Counties and places, and so returned, and having before their
sitting, taken the oaths appointed by act of Parlm^t to be taken
instead of the oaths of Allegiance and supremacy and subscribed
the Test and the Association aforesaid (which oaths you shall
Comissionate fit persons under our seal of New York to administer and without taking the said oaths and subscribing the
said Test and Association none shall be capable of sitting tho'
elected) shall be called and held the general Assembly of that
our province and territories depending thereon.

And that you the said Earl of Bellomont by and with the
consent of our said Council and Assembly, or the Major part
of them respectively, shall have full power and authority to
make constitute and ordain laws, statutes and ordinances for the
public peace, welfare and good Govern^t of our said province and
of the people and inhabitants thereof, and such others as shall
resort thereto, and for the benefit of us our heirs and successors.

Which said laws, Statutes and ordinances are to be (as near
as may be) agreeable to the laws and Statutes of this our Kingdome of England.

Provided that all such laws, statutes and ordinances of what
nature or duration soever, be within three months or sooner
after the making thereof transmitted unto us under our seal of
New York for our approbation or disallowance of the same, as
also duplicats thereof by the next conveyance.

And in case any or all of them, being not before confirm'd by
us shall at any time be disallowed and not approv'd and so sig-

nified by us our heirs and successors under our or their sign manual and signet, or by order of our or their privy Councill unto you the said Earl of Bellomont or to the Commander in Chief of our said province for the time being then such and so many of them as shall be so disallowed and not approved, shall from thenceforth cease determine and become utterly void and of none effect, any thing to the Contrary thereof notwithstanding.

And to the end nothing may be passed or done by our said Council or Assembly to the prejudice of us, our heirs, and successors, we will and ordain that you, the said Earl of Bellomont, shall have and enjoy, a negative voice, in the making and passing of all laws, statutes, and ordinances as aforesaid.

And that you shall and may likewise from time to time as you shall judge it necessary, adjourn, Prorogue and dissolve all general Assemblies as aforesaid.

Our will and pleasure is, that you shall and may keep and use the publick seal appointed or to be appointed by us for our province of New York.

We do further give and grant unto you the said Earl of Bellomont full power and authority from time to time, and at any time hereafter by yourself or by any other to be authorized by you in that behalf, to administer and give the oaths appointed by act of Parliament to be taken instead of the oaths of allegiance and supremacy, to all and to every such person or persons as you shall think fit, who shall at any time or times pass into our said province or shall be resident or abiding there.

And we do by these presents give and grant unto you, full power and authority with the advice and consent of our said Council, to erect, constitute and establish, such and so many courts of judicature and publick justice, within our said province, and the territories under your Govern^t as you and they shall think fit and necessary, for the hearing and determining of all causes as well criminal as civil according to law and equity, and for awarding of executions thereupon, with all reasonable and necessary powers, authorities, fees and priviledges belonging unto them as also to appoint and commissionate fit persons in the several parts of our Govern^t to administer the oaths appointed by act of Parliam^t to be taken instead of the oaths of allegiance & supremacy and the test, unto such as shall be obliged to take the same.

And we do hereby authorize and empower you to constitute and appoint Judges, Justices of the peace and other necessary officers and Ministers in our said province, for the better administration of Justice and putting the laws in execution and to administer or cause to be administered, such oath or oaths as are usually given for the due execution and performance of offices and places and for the clearing of truth in judicial causes.

We do further by these presents will and require, that appeals be permitted to be made in cases of Errour from our Courts in New York, unto you our Govern^r and to our Council & in your absence from our said province to our Lieut^t Govr and our said Council in civil causes. Provided the value appeal'd for do exceed the sum of one hundred pounds sterling, and that security be first given, by the appellant, to answer such charges as shall be awarded in case the first sentence shall be affirm'd.

And whereas we do judge it necessary, that all our subjects may have liberty to appeal to our Royal person in cases that may deserve the same, Our will and pleasure is, that if either party shall not rest satisfied with the judgm^t or sentence of our Govr or Lieut^t Govr and Council as aforesaid, they may then appeal unto us in our privi Council, Provided the matter in difference exceed the true value and sum of three hundred pounds sterling, and that such appeal be made within fourteen days after sentence and security be likewise duly given by the appellant to answer such charges as shall be awarded in case the sentence of the Govr & Council be confirm'd. And provided also that the execution be not suspended by reason of any such appeal unto us.

And we do hereby give and grant unto you full power and authority where you shall judge any offenders in criminal matters or for any fines or forfeitures fit objects of our mercy, to pardon and remit such offender's fines and forfeitures before or after sentence given. Treason and willful murder only excepted, in which cases you shall likewise have power upon extraordinary occasions to grant reprives to the Offenders, until our Royal pleasure may be known therein.

We do by these presents authorize and empower you to collate any person or persons in any Churches, Chappels or other Ecclesiastical benefices within our said province and territories aforesaid, as often as any of them shall happen to be void.

We do hereby give and grant unto you the said Earl of Bellomont, by yourself, your Capt^ns and Commanders by you to be authorized, full power and authority, to Levy, arm, muster, command and employ, all persons whatsoever within our said province of New York, and other the territories under your Gov^nt and as occasion shall serve them to transfer from one place to another, for the resisting and withstanding of all Enemies, Pirats and Rebells both at sea and at Land, and to transport such forces to any of our plantations in America, as occasion shall require for the defence of the same against the invasion or attempts of any of our Enemies.

And them if occasion shall require to prosecute in or out of the Limits of our said province or Plantations or any of them.

And if it shall please God them to vanquish, apprehend and take, and being taken either, according to law of arms, to put to death or keep and preserve alive at your discretion.

And [to] execute martial law in time of invasion, insurrection or war, and during the continuance of the same as also upon soldiers in pay; and to do and execute all and every other thing or things which to a Captn General doth or ought of right to belong, as fully and amply as any our Captn General doth or hath usually done.

And we do hereby give and grant unto you full power and authority, to erect, raise and build in our said province and territories depending thereon, such and so many Forts and platforms, Castles, Cities, Bourroughs, Townes and fortifications as you by the advice aforesaid shall judge necessary. And the same or any of them to fortify and furnish with ordnance, amunition and all sorts of arms fit and necessary for the security and defence of our said province.

And we do hereby give and grant unto you the said Earl of Bellomont, full power and authority to erect one or more Court or Courts Admiral within our said province and territorys for the hearing and determining of all marine and other causes and matters proper therein to be heard, with all reasonable and necessary powers, authorities fees and privileges.

As also to exercise all powers belonging to the place and office of vice Admiral of and in all the seas and coasts within your Govern^t according to such Commission, Authorities and instructions as you shall receive from ourself, under the seal of our Admiralty or from our high Admiral or Commissioners for executing the office of high Admiral of our foreign plantations for the time being. . . .

Our will and pleasure is, that all publick moneyes raised or to be raised within our said province and other the territories depending thereupon be issued out by warrant from you by and with the advice and consent of the Council and disposed of by you for the support of the Govern^t and not otherwise.

And we do hereby likewise give and grant unto you full power and authority, by and with the advice of our said Council, to agree with the Inhabitants of our province and territories aforesaid, for such lands, tenements and hereditaments as now are or hereafter shall be in our power to dispose of.

And them to grant to any person or p^{r}sons for such terms and under such moderate Quit Rents services and acknowledgements to be thereupon reserved unto us as you by and with the advice aforesaid shall think fitt.

Which said grants are to pass and be sealed by our seal of New York, and being enter'd upon record by such officer or Officers as you shall appoint thereunto shall be good and effectual in law agst us, our heirs & successors—

And we do hereby give you full power, to order and appoint Fairs, Marts, and Markets, as also such and so many Ports, Harbours, Bays, Havens and other places for [the] convenience and security of shipping, and for the better loading and unloading of goods and merchandizes, as by you with the advice and consent of the said Councill shall be thought fit and necessary and in them or any of them to erect, nominate and appoint Customehouses, Warehouses and Officers relating thereunto, and them to alter, change place or displace from time to time as with the advice aforesaid shall be thought fit.

And we do by these presents, Will, Require & Command you

to take all possible care for the discountenance of vice and the encouragement of virtue and good living, that by such example the Infidels may be invited and desire to partake of the Christian faith.

And further Our will and pleasure is, that you shall not at any time hereafter, by colour of any power or Authority, hereby granted or mentioned to be granted take upon you to give, grant or dispose of any Office or place within our said province and territories, which is now or shall be granted under the great seal of England, any further than that you may upon the vacancy of any such Office or suspension of any Officer by you put in any person to officiate in the interval, until the said place be disposed of by us, under the great seal of England, or that our directions be otherwise given therein.

And we do hereby require and command all Officers and Ministers, Civil and Military and all other inhabitants of our said province and the territories depending thereon, to be obedient aiding and Assisting unto you the said Earl of Bellomont, in the execution of this our Commission and of the powers and authorities herein contained. And in case of your death or absence out of our said province and territories aforesaid unto such person as shall be appointed by us to be our Lieut^t Govr or Commander in chief of our said province, to whom we do by these presents give and grant all and singular the power & Authorities aforesaid to be executed and enjoyed by him during our pleasure, or until your return to our said province and territories, and if upon such death or absence there be no person upon the place Commissionated or appointed by us to be our Lieut^t Govr or Commander in Chief Our will and pleasure is, that the then present Councill of our said province, do take upon them the Administration of the Govern^t and execute this Commission and the several powers and authorities herein contained, relating to our said province, and that the first Councillor who shall be at the time of your death or absence residing within the same; do preside in our said Councill with such power and preheminencies as any former president hath used and enjoyed within our said province, or any other our plantations in America, until our pleasure be further known, or your return as aforesaid.

And lastly we do hereby declare ordain and appoint, that you the said Earl of Bellomont shall and may hold execute and enjoy the Office and place of our Captn General and Govr in chief in and over our province of New York and the territories depending thereon, together with all and singular the powers and Authorities hereby granted unto you, for and during our will and pleasure, immediately upon your arrival within our said province of New York and the publication of this our Commission from which time our Commission to our Trusty & welbeloved Benjamin Fletcher Esq: to be Captn Genl and Govr in chief of our said province and territories depending thereon is immediately to cease and become void.

And whereas there are divers Colonies adjoining to our province of New York for the defence and security whereof, it is requisite that due care be taken in this time of war. We have therefore thought it further necessary for our service, and for the better protection and security of our subjects inhabiting those parts to constitute and appoint and we do by these presents constitute and appoint you the said Richard Earl of Bellomont to be our Captain General and Commander in Chief, of the Militia and of all the forces by sea and land within our province of East and West New Jersey and of all our Forts and places of strength within the same.

And for the better ordering Governing and ruling our said Militia and all our forces Forts and places of strength within our said province of East and West New Jersey; We do hereby give and grant unto you the said Richard Earl of Bellomont, and in your absence to your Lieut^t Govr or Commander in chief of our province of New York, all and every the like powers as in these presents are before granted and recited for the ruling, governing and ordering our Militia and all our forces forts and places of strength within our province of New York to be exercised by you the said Richard Earl of Bellomont and in your absence from our territory and Dominion of New York by our said Lieutenant Govr or Commander in Chief of our said province of New York within our said provinces of East and West New Jersey for and during our pleasure. IN WITNESS whereof, We have caused these our letters to be made patents.—Witnesses. Thomas Archbishop of Canterbury, and the rest of the Guardians and Justices of the Kingdome—At Westminster the 18th day of June in the ninth Year of our Reign 1697.

B. Trade Instructions to Governor Robert Hunter of New York (1709)[1]

FIRST, you shall inform your self of the Principal Laws relating to the Plantation Trade, vizt The Act for encouraging and Encreasing of Shipping and Navigation, made in the 12th year of the reign of King Charles the Second; The Act for preventing frauds and regulating abuses in the Customs, made in the 14th year of the said Kings Reign; The Act for encouragement of Trade, made in the 15th year of the said King's Reign; the Act for Regulating the Plantation Trade, made in the 22nd and 23d years of the said King's reign; The Act for the Encouragement of the Eastland and Greenland Trades, and better securing the Plantation Trade made in the 25th year of the said King's reign, and the Act for preventing Frauds and regulating abuses in the Plantation Trade, made in the 7th and 8th years of the Reign of His late Majesty, King William the 3d: All which Laws you will herewith receive and you shall take a solemn oath to do your utmost That all the Clauses, Matters and things contained in the before recited Acts of Parliament heretofore passed and now in force, relating to our Colonies and Plantations be strictly and duly observed according to the true intent and meaning thereof.

2dly And as by the last recited Act the officers appointed by the Governors for performance of certain things mentioned in the aforesaid Act for Encouragement of Trade, commonly known by the name of the Naval officers, are to give security to the Commissioners of our Customs in this Kingdom for the time being, or such as shall be appointed by them for our use, for the true and faithfull performance of their duty. You shall take care that the person by you so employed, do not only give such security to the said Commissioners of our Customs, but be approved of by them in manner as thereby is enjoyned.

3dly Whereas by the said Act of Navigation no Goods or

---

1. O'Callaghan & Brodhead, *Documents Relative to the Colonial History of the State of New York,* V, 144-51.

Commodities whatsoever are to be imported into or exported out
of any of our Colonies or Plantations in any other ship or vessells
whatsoever but in such as do truly and without fraud belong
only to the people of England or Ireland or are of the build of,
and belonging to, any of our Lands, Islands or Territories, as the
Proprietors and right owners thereof, and whereof the Master
and three fourths of the Mariners at least are English, under the
Penalty of the forfeiture and loss of all the goods and commodities which shall be imported into, or exported out of any of the
said Places in any other Ship or vessel with her Guns, Furniture
&c And wheras by a clause in the aforesaid Act of Frauds, no
foreign built ship, that is to say not built in any of our dominions
of Asia, Africa or America, or other than such as shall bona fide
have been bought before the first of October 1662, and expressly named in the list thereby appointed to be made of all
Foreign built ships in all the parts of England shall enjoy the
Privilege of a ship belonging to England or Ireland; altho'
own'd or mann'd by English (except such ships only as shall be
taken at sea by Letters of Mart, or Reprisal, and Condemnation
made in our Court of Admiralty (as lawful prize) but all such
ships shall be deemed as Aliens ships and be lyable to all duties
that Alien's ships are lyable to, by vertue of the aforesaid Act for
Encourageing and Encreasing of Shipping and Navigation, And
whereas by a clause in the aforesaid Act for preventing Frauds
and regulating Abuses in the Plantation Trade, 'tis enacted that
after the Twenty Fifth of March 1698 no goods or merchandizes
whatsoever shall be imported into or exported out of any of our
Colonies or Plantations in Asia, Africa or America, or shall be
laden or carried from any one port or place in the said Colonies
or Plantations to any other port or place in the same our Kingdom of England, Dominion of Wales, or Town of Berwick upon
Tweed in any Ship or Bottom, but what is or shall be of the
build of England, or the build of Ireland, or of the said Colonies
or Plantations, and wholly own'd by the people thereof or any of
them, and Navigated with the Master and three fourths of the
Mariners of the said places only. Except such ships only as shall
be taken prize, and Condemnation thereof made in one of our
Courts of Admiralty in England, Ireland or the said Colonies or
Plantations, to be navigated by the Master and three fourths of

the Mariners English, or of the said Plantations as aforesaid, & whereof the Property doth belong to Englishmen; with an Exception for three years to such Foreign built ships as shall be employed by the Commissioners of Our Navy for the time being, or upon Contract with them, in bringing only Masts, Timber & other Naval Stores for Our service, from the Colonies or Plantations aforesaid to this Kingdom, to be navigated as aforesaid and whereof the Property does belong to Englishmen, on the pain of forfeiture of Ship and Goods: And whereas by another clause in the said Act for the more effectual prevention of Frauds, which may be used by colouring Foreign Ships under English names, 'Tis further enacted That from and after the 25th of March 1698 no ship or vessel whatsoever shall be deemed or pass as a Ship of the build of England, Ireland, Wales, Berwick, Guernsey, Jersey, or of any of our Plantations in America so as to be qualifyed to trade to, from or in any of the said Plantations, until the Person or Persons claiming Property in such ship or vessel, shall register the same in manner thereby appointed; You shall take care and give in charge, that these matters and things be duely observed within Our Province of New York, according to the true intent and meaning of the said Acts, and the Offences and Offenders prosecuted according to the Directions thereof, and where it is required that the Master and three fourths of the Mariners be English, you are to understand that the true intent and meaning thereof is that they shall be such during the whole Voyage, unless in case of sickness, Death or being taken prisoners in the voyage, to be proved by the Oath of the Master or other chief Officer of the Ship, and none but our subjects of England, Ireland, or the Plantations are to be accounted English.

4thly Whereas by the said Act of Navigation 'tis further Enacted, that for every ship or vessell which shall set sail out of or from England, Ireland, Wales or Berwick upon Tweed, for any English Plantations in America, Asia or Africa sufficient Bond shall be given with one surety to the chief Officers of the Customs of such Port or place from whence the said ship shall set sail, to the value of one thousand pounds if the Ship be of less burthen than one hundred Tunns, and of the sum of Two thousand pounds if the ship shall be of greater burthen, That in case the said ship or vessell shall load any of the Commodities therein enumerated, (vizt Sugar, Tobacco, Cotton Wool, Indico, Ginger, Fustick or other dying wood of the growth, production or Manufacture of any English Plantation in America, Asia or Africa) at any of the said English Plantations, the same Commodities shall be by the said ship brought to some port of England, Ireland, Wales or to the Port or Town of Berwick upon Tweed and be there unloaden and put on shoar, the danger of the Seas only excepted, And for all ships coming from any port or place to any of the aforesaid Plantations who by this act are permitted to trade there, That the Governors of such English Plantations shall, before the said ship or vessell be permitted to load on board any of the said Commodities take Bond in manner and to the value aforesaid for each respective Ship or Vessel, that such ship or vessel shall carry all the aforesaid Goods that shall be loaden on board the said ship to some other of our English Plantations or to England, Ireland, Wales or Berwick, and that every ship or vessel which shall load or take on board any of the aforesaid Goods until such Bond be given to the said Governor, or Certificate produced from the Officers of any Custom House of England, Ireland, Wales or Berwick that such Bond hath been there duly given, shall be forfeited with her Guns, Tackle, apparel and Furniture, to be Employ'd and Recovered as therein is directed: You are to take notice that tho' by the said Act the word Ireland is to be incerted in the condition of the Bonds, and permission thereby given to bring the Enumerated Plantation Commodities to Ireland, as well as to England, Wales or Berwick, Yet, by the aforesaid Act for Regulating the Plantation Trade, (which having been expired was afterwards revived and is now in force) the word Ireland is to be left out of the Condition of such Bonds, and you are not to permit any ships or vessels to load any of the Enumerated Goods upon any Certificate of Bonds having been given in Ireland; But in that case before they load any of the said Goods, they are to produce certificates of Bonds given in England, Wales or Berwick under the hands and seals of the Customer and Comptroller of our Customs or their Deputies, in such Port from whence the respective Ships shall come, signed also by four or more of the Commisioners of our Customs in England, or to give Bond to your self or the person appointed to receive the same, with good security as aforesaid, and if any ship or vessell shall load or take on board any of the said Commodities until such Bond be given or Certificate produced, the said ship or vessel is forfeited with her gunns &c^a to be recovered and divided in manner as is therein directed.

5^{ly} You shall carefully examine all Certificates which shall be brought to you of Ships giving security in this Kingdom to bring their lading of Plantation Goods hither; as also certificates of having discharged their Lading of Plantation Goods in this Kingdom, pursuant to their securities, and where there shall be reasonable ground of suspicion that the Certificate of having given security in this Kingdom is false, in such case you or the person appointed under you shall require and take sufficient security for the discharge of the Plantation lading in this our Kingdom; and where there shall be cause to suspect that the certificate of having discharged the lading of Plantation Goods in this Kingdom is false and counterfeit, you shall not cancel or vacate the security given in the Plantations untill you shall be informed from the Commissioners of our Customs here, that the matter of the said Certificate is true, and if any person or persons shall counterfeit, Raze or falsify any such certificate for any vessell or Goods or shall knowingly or wittingly make use thereof, you shall prosecute such person for the forfeiture of the sum of five hundred pounds according to a Clause of the Aforesaid Act for preventing Frauds and regulating abuses in the Plantation Trade; and pursuant to the said Act you shall take care that in all such Bonds to be hereafter given or taken in the Plantations vizt in our Province of New York, the Sureties therein named be persons of known Residence and Ability there for the value mentioned in the said Bonds be within Eighteen Months after the date thereof (the danger of the Seas excepted) to produce Certificates of having landed and discharged the goods therein mentioned, in one of our Plantations, or in this our Kingdom, otherwise to attest the Copy of such Bonds under your hand and Seal, and to cause prosecution thereof.

6^{ly} You are to understand that the Payment of the Rates and Duties imposed by the aforesaid Act for the Encouragement of the Eastland and Greenland Trades, and for the better securing the Plantation Trade on the several Plantation Commodities therein enumerated, doth not give liberty to carry the said goods to any other place, than to some of our Plantations, or to England, Wales or Berwick only, and that notwithstanding the payment of the said Duties Bond must be given to carry the said goods to some of our said Plantations, or to England, Wales, or Berwick, and to no other place.

7^{tly} You shall every three months or Oftener, or otherwise, as there shall be opportunity of conveyance to this Kingdom, transmit to the Commissioners of Our Customs here, a List of all ships and vessells trading within our said Province according to the Form and Specimen hereunto annexed: And you shall cause demand to be made of every Master, at his clearing, of an Invoyce of the Contents and Quality of his lading &^{c}, according to the form hereunto also annexed: And to enclose a copy thereof, by some other ship, or want of such Opportunity, by the same ship under cover, sealed and directed to the said Commissioners of our Customs; and send another Copy thereof in like manner to the Collector thereof of that Port within this Kingdom for the time being, to which such ship shall pretend to be bound.

8^{tly} Whereas by the aforesaid Act for the Encouragement of Trade no commodities of the growth, production, or manufacture of Europe except Salt for the Fishery of New England and New foundland, Wines of the growth of the Maderas or Western Islands, or Azores, Servants and Horses from Scotland or Ireland and all Sorts of Victuals of the Growth and production of Scotland, and Ireland shall be imported into any of our said Colonies or Plantations, but what shall be bona fide and without fraud laden and Shipped in England Wales or Berwick in ships duely qualified, you shall use your utmost endeavours for the due observance thereof; and if, contrary hereunto, any ship or Vessell shall import into our said Province of New York, any Commodities of the Growth, Production or Manufacture of Europe, (but what are before excepted) of which due proof shall not be made, that the same were shipped or laden in some port of this Kingdom by producing Cocquetts or Certificates under the hands and seals of the officers of our Customs in such Port or place where the same were laden, such ship or vessel and goods will be forfeited: And you are to give in charge that the same be seized and prosecuted accordingly.

9[tly] And in order to prevent the acceptance of forged Cocquets or Certificates (which hath been practised to our great prejudice) you are to give effectual orders, that for all such European Goods as by the said Act are to be shipp'd and laden in England, Wales or Berwick, Cocquets for the same, from hence, be produced to the Collectors, or other Officers of the Customs in Our said Province of New York for the time being, before the unlading thereof and you shall give order that no European Goods be landed but by warrant from the said Collector, in the presence of an Officer appointed by him, and for the better prevention of Frauds of this kind you shall take care that, according to the said Act of Trade, no ship or vessell be permitted to lade or unlade any goods or Commodities whatsoever untill the Master or Commander thereof shall first have made known to you or such officer or other person as shall be thereunto authorized and appointed, the arrival of the said ship or vessell with her name and the name and Surname of her Master, and hath shewn that she is a ship duely navigated and otherwise qualified according to Law, and hath delivered to you, or such person as aforesaid, a true and perfect Inventory of her Lading, together with the place or places in which the said Goods were laden and taken into the said Ship or Vessel, under forfeiture of such Ships and Goods.

10[thy] You shall not make or allow of any By-laws, Usages or Customs in our said Province of New York which are repugnant to the Laws herein mentioned or any of them so far as they do relate to our said Plantations or any of them, or to any other law hereafter to be made in this Kingdom, so far as such Law shall relate to and mention the said Plantations; by [but] you shall declare all such Laws, By-Laws, Usages, or Customs in our said Province of New York which are any wise repugnant to the forementioned Laws, or any of them, to be illegall, null and void to all intents and purposes whatsoever.

11[tly] You shall be aiding and assisting to the Collector and other Officers appointed, or that shall hereafter be appointed by the Commissioners of Our Customs in this Kingdom, by and under the authority and direction of our High Treasurer of this Kingdom, or Commissioners of our Treasury for the time being, in putting in execution the several Acts of Parliament before mentioned and you shall cause due prosecution of all such persons as shall any ways hinder or resist any of the said Officers of our Customs in the performance of their Duty.

12tly You shall take care that upon any Actions, suits or informations that shall be brought, commenced or entred in our said Province of New York, upon any Law or Statute concerning our duties, or ships, or goods, to be forfeited by reason of any unlawfull Importations or Exportations there be not any Jury but of such as are natives of this Kingdom or Ireland or are Born in any of our said Plantations.

13tly If you shall discover that any persons or their assines claiming any right or property in any Island or Tract of Land upon the continent of America, by charter or by Letters Patents, shall at any time hereafter alien, sell or dispose of such Island, Tract of Land, or Propriety other than to our Natural born subjects of Great Britain, without lycense and consent of us, our Heirs and Successors, signifyed by our or their order in Councill first had and obtained you shall give notice thereof to us or to our High Treasurer of Great Britain or Commissioners of our Treasury for the time being.

14th You shall take care that all places of Trust in the Courts of Law, or in what relates to the Treasury of our foresaid Province of New York, be in the hands of our native born subjects of this Kingdom or Ireland, or the Plantations.

15ly And that there may be no interruption or delay in matters of Prosecution and Execution of Justice in our said Province, by the death or removal of any of our officers employed therein untill we can be advised thereof and appoint others to succeed in their places, You shall make choice of persons of known loyalty, experience, diligence and fidelity to be employed for the purposes aforesaid untill you shall have our approbation of them or the Nomination of others from hence.

16tly You shall from time to time correspond with the Commissioners of our Customs in this Kingdom for the time being, and advise them of all failures, neglects, frauds and misdemeanours of any of the Officers of our Customs in our said Province of New York, and shall also advise them as occasion shall offer, of all occurrencies necessary for their information relating either to the aforesaid Laws of Trade and Navigation or to our Revenue of Customs and other Duties under their management both in Great Britain and the Plantations.

17[tly] Whereas by the aforesaid Act preventing Frauds and regulating abuses in the Plantation Trade, 'Tis provided for the more effectual prevention of Frauds which may be used to elude the Intention of the said Act, by colouring Foreign Ships under English Names, That from and after the Twenty Fifth of March 1698 no ship or vessell shall be deemed or pass as a Ship of the build of England, Ireland, Wales, Berwick, Guernsey, Jersey, or any of our Plantations in America, so as to be qualifyed to trade to, from, or in, any of our said Plantations, until the Person or Persons claiming Property in such ship or Vessel, shall register the same in manner thereby directed; And whereas by an Act pass'd the 9th and 10th years of His late Majesty King William the third, entituled, An Act for the enlarging the time for registring of ships pursuant to the Act for preventing Frauds and Regulating abuses in the Plantation Trade, nine months longer time from the said 25th day of March 1698, are granted and allowed for the Registring of such ships, and it is provided that all such ships or vessells being Registred within the said Nine Months shall have and enjoy all such benefit and advantage of the aforesaid Act, as they might or could have had, in case they had been Registred before the said 25th day of March 1698; You shall take care that no foreign built ship be permitted to pass as a ship belonging to our Kingdom of England, Ireland, Wales or to the Town of Berwick upon Tweed, untill proof be made upon oath, of one or more of the owners of such ship or vessell, before the Collector and Comptroller of our Customs in such Port to which she belongs or upon like proof before yourself, with the principal officer of our Revenue residing in our foresaid Province of New York, if such ship shall belong to the said Province which Oath you and the Officers of our Customs respectively are authorized to administer in manner thereby directed, and being attested by you and them so administring the same, and Registred in due form, according to the Specimen hereunto annexed, You shall not fail immediately to transmit a

Duplicate thereof to the Commissioners of our Customs in London, in order to be entered in a general Register to be there kept, for that purpose; with penalty upon every ship or vessel trading to, from, or in, any of our said Plantations in America, after the said Twenty Fifth day of March, and nine months longer as aforesaid and not having made proof of her build and property, as by the forementioned Act is directed, that she shall be lyable to such Prosecution and forfeiture as any foreign ship (except Prizes condemned in our High Court of Admiralty) would for Trading with our Plantations by the said Law be lyable unto, with this Proviso, That all such ships as have been or shall be taken at sea by Letters of Mart or Reprisal, and Condemnation thereof, made in our High court of Admiralty of this Kingdom as Lawfull Prize shall be specially Registred, mentioning the Capture and Condemnation instead of the time and place of building with proof also, upon Oath, that the entire Property is British, before any such prize be allowed the Priviledg of a British built Ship according to the meaning of the said Act, and that no Ships names Registred be afterwards changed without registring such Ship de Novo, which by the said Act is required to be done upon any transfer of property to another Port, and delivering up the former Certificate to be cancelled, under the same penalties and in like method; and in case of any alteration of Property in the said Port by the sale of one or more shares in any ship after Registring thereof, such sale shall always be acknowledged by Endorsement on the Certificate of the Register before two witnesses, in order to prove that the entire property in such ship, remains to some of our subjects of this Kingdom if any dispute shall arise concerning the same.

18^{tly} Whereas by an act passed in the 10th year of His late Majesty King William the third To prevent the exportation of Wool out of the Kingdoms of Ireland and England into foreign parts and for the Encouragement of Woollen Manufactures in the Kingdom of England, it is amongst other things thereby enacted, that from and after the first day of December 1699 no Wool, Woolfells, Shortlings, Morlings, Wool Flocks, Worsted, Bay or Woollen Yarn, Cloath, Serge, Bays, Kerseys, Says, Frizes, Druggets, Cloath Serges, Shalloons or any other Drapery, Stuffs or Woollen Manufactures whatsoever, made or mixed with Wool, or Wool Flocks being of the Product or Manufacture of any of the English Plantations in America, shall be laden or laid on board in any ship or Vessell in any place or ports within any of the said English Plantations, upon any Pretence, whatsoever; As also, That no such wool, or other of the said Commodities being of the Product or Manufacture of any of the said English Plantations shall be loaden upon any Hors, Cart or other Carriage, to the Intent and purpose to be Exported, transported, Carried or Conveyed out of the said English Plantations to any other of our Plantations or to any other place whatsoever upon the same and like pains, Penalties and forfeitures to and upon all the Offender and Offenders therein; within all and every of our said English Plantations respectively as are provided and prescribed by the said Act, for the said Offences committed within our Kingdom of Ireland, you are to take effectual care that the true intent and meaning thereof as far forth as it relates to you be duely put in execution.

19^{tly} Whereas an Act of Parliament was pass'd in the 3^d and 4th years of our Reign, entituled an act to permit the Exportation of Irish Cloath to the Plantations and to prohibit the Importation of Scotch Linnen into Ireland, with several Clauses and Provisoes for the due Execution of the said act (a copy whereof will be herewith delivered to you) you are therefore to take care that the said Act with all its clauses and Provisoes be duely observed and complyed with in that our Province under your Govern^t

20^{ly} In an Act of Parliament made in the 10th and 11th years of His late Majesty's Reign, entituled an Act for laying further duties upon Sweets and for lessening the Duties as well upon Vinegar as upon certain low wines and whale Finns, and the Duties upon Brandy Imported &c^a There is a Clause (Copy whereof you shall herewith receive) to prevent Frauds in the Importation of Bulk Tobacco, Enacting that from and after the 29th day of September 1700, no Tobacco shall be brought or imported into this Kingdom of England, Dominion of Wales, or Town of Berwick upon Tweed, in any Ship or Vessel from any of the Plantations on the Continent of America, nor shipped in any of the said Plantations, in order to be so imported, otherwise than in cask, chest or case only, each cask, chest or case whereof shall contain 200 weight of Tobacco at the least and each hundred thereof shall contain 112^l under the Penalties and Forfeitures of all the Tobacco so imported or shipped to be imported, contrary to the said Act, shall be forfeited, and every person or persons offending contrary to the true intent and meaning thereof shall forfeit sixpence for every pound weight thereof ⅔^{ds} thereof to us our Heirs and Sucessors, the other third part thereof to such Persons as shall seize and sue for the same, it being Provided That such small Quantities as shall be necessary for the Ship's Company's smoaking in the Voyage shall not be deemed or construed any breach of the said Act: You shall take care that this Part of the said Act be made Publick, that none may pretend Ignorance, and that the true intent and Meaning thereof be duely put in execution, within Your Government.

21st An Act of Parliament having been pass'd in the 3^d and 4th years of our Reign entituled an Act for granting to Her Majesty a further subsidy on Wines, and Merchandize imported, wherein among others there is a clause in the words following vizt "And Whereas by the Acts made in the 12th and 25th years of the reign of his late Majesty King Charles the 2^d, the former entituled An Act for the encouraging and encreasing of Shipping and Navigation, and the latter Entituled An Act for the Encouragement of the Greenland and Eastland Trade and for the better securing the Plantation Trade, certain Commodities therein enumerated of the growth, production or manufacture of any of the English Plantations in America, Asia or Africa, are obliged to be imported into this Kingdom of England, Dominion of Wales, or Town of Berwick upon Tweed, or to some other of the Said Plantations under the Securities and Penaltys in the said Acts particularly mentioned, to the end this Kingdom might be made a Staple, not only of the Commodities of those Plantations, but also of the Commodities which are not in the said Acts particularly enumerated, such as Rice and Molasses are produced, and made in the said Plantations, and Carried to divers Foreign Markets in Europe without being first brought into this Kingdom, Dominion of Wales and Town of Berwick upon Tweed, contrary to the true intent and meaning of the aforesaid Laws to the great prejudice of the trade of this Kingdom, and the lessening the Correspondence and Relation between this Kingdom & the aforesaid Plantations, for the prevention whereof for the future Be it enacted by the authority aforesaid, That from and after the 29th of September 1705, all Rice and Molasses shall be under the like securities and Penalties restrained to be imported into this Kingdom, dominion of Wales, and Town of Berwick aforesaid, as by the fore recited Acts or either of them is provided for the goods therein particularly enumerated;" You are therefore to take particular care and give the necessary Directions that the true intent and meaning of the said Clause be strictly and duly complyed with.

22nd And whereas you will herewith receive copies of the following Acts of Parliament vizt An Act for Encouraging the Importation of Naval Stores from Her Majesty's Plantations in America, pass'd in the 3d and 4th years of our Reign; An act for an union of the two Kingdoms of Scotland, pass'd in the 5th year of our Reign, in which are certain Articles relating to the Plantation Trade, more particularly the 4th 5th and 6th; An act for ascertaining the Rates of Foreign Coins in Her Majesty's Plantations in America, pass'd in the 6th year of our Reign, and an act for the Encouragement of the Trade to America pass'd in the 1st year of our Reign; You are therefore to use Your best endeavours, that the said Acts with all the Clauses, matters and things therein contained be in like manner strictly and duly observed according to the true Intent and meaning thereof.

23d And whereas notwithstanding the many good Laws made from time to time for preventing of Frauds in the Plantation Trade, which have been enumerated in these and former Instructions, it is manifest, that very great abuses have been and continue still to be practised to the prejudice of the same; which abuses must needs arise, either from the Insolvency of the Persons who are accepted for security or from the remisness or Connivance of such as have been or are Governors in the several Plantations, who ought to take care that those persons who give Bond, should be duely prosecuted in case of non performance; You are to take notice that we take the good of our Plantations, and the Improvement of the Trade thereof by a strict and punctual observance of the several Laws in force concerning the same, to be of so great importance to the Benefit of this Kingdom, and to the advancing the Duty of our Customs here, that if we shall be hereafter informed that at any time there shall be any failure in the due observance of those Laws and of these present Instructions, by any Wilfull Fault or Neglect, on your part, we shall look upon it as a Breach of the Trust reposed in you by us, which we will punish with the Loss of Your place in that government, and such further marks of our displeasure, as Wee shall judge reasonable to be inflicted upon you for your offence, against us in a matter of this Consequence, that We now so particularly charge you with.

10

John Wise

A Vindication of the Government
of New-England Churches (1717)[1]

The life of John Wise (1652-1725) was a model of American social concepts. Though his father had been an indentured servant, Wise began his education in a township school, went on to Harvard, and entered the Congregational ministry. After preaching in several villages, he was called to Chebacco, a subdivision of Ipswich; he remained there as pastor for the rest of his life. His strongly stated views were derived from his experience there with village democracy and an independent church. The picture of Wise that emerges from that village and church is one of a nonpedantic preacher, a scholar with wit, a vigorous athlete, a powerful writer, a man of courage, and, above all, a fighter.

Wise must have been deeply contented with his life at Ipswich; only occasionally did he leave it to move on the larger stage of public life. As his first public protest, Wise led the Ipswich town meeting to refuse to pay the tax levied by the Andros Council, on the ground that it was a violation of fundamental rights. Stern Sir Edmund hauled Wise into court, and it was to him and his fellow defendants that Joseph Dudley addressed his notorious statement that they differed little from slaves. On other occasions Wise advocated vaccination for small pox, and paper money as a solution for economic distress. He also stood out against the witchcraft persecutions.

But Wise is remembered primarily for two pamphlets about church government. In 1705 a document entitled *Questions and Proposals* circulated in the Bay Colony. In a veiled way, it proposed that the nearly autonomous Congregational churches should be placed under the central control of a ministerial synod. The idea was agitated for

1. John Wise, *A Vindication of the Government of New-England Churches* (Boston: J. Bayles, 1772).

a number of years. In 1710, Wise annihilated it in the polemic, *The Churches' Quarrel Espoused.* Upholding the existing system of church government, Wise argued forcefully that the suggested "reforms" moved in the direction of presbyterianism, prelacy, and popery. His most comprehensive work was *A Vindication of the Government of New-England Churches.* The only full biography of Wise is George A. Cook, *John Wise, Early American Democrat* (New York: King's Crown Press, 1952). See also the classic by Vernon L. Parrington, *Main Currents in American Thought* (New York: Harcourt, Brace & World, 1927), vol. I, part 2, ch. 3. Parrington's liberal bias is strong and clear. In reading this selection note (1) what views on natural right Wise held; (2) what he thought regarding the quality of men as political beings; (3) what he thought about the origins of political power; (4) what values he assigned to various forms of government; (5) the extent to which he derived his principles of just Church government from political theory; (6) what arguments he advanced in support of local autonomy and Church democracy; and (7) the nature and quality of his rhetoric.

Chapter II

1. I SHALL DISCLOSE SEVERAL PRINCIPLES OF NATURAL knowledge; plainly discovering the law of nature; or the true sentiments of natural reason, with respect to mans being and government. And in this essay I shall peculiarly confine the discourse to two heads, *viz.*

1. Of the natural (in distinction to the civil) and then,

2. Of the civil being of man. And I shall principally take baron *Puffendorff* for my chief guide and spokes-man.

1. I shall consider man in a state of natural being, as a free-born subject under the crown of heaven, and owing homage to none but God himself. It is certain civil government in general, is a very admirable result of providence, and an incomparable benefit to man-kind, yet must needs be acknowledged to be the effect of human free-compacts and not of divine institution; it is the produce of man reason, of human and rational combinations, and not from any direct orders of infinite wisdom, in any positive law wherein is drawn up this or that scheme of civil government. Government (says the Lord *Warrington*) is necessary—

in that no society of men can subsist without it; and that particular form of government is necessary which best suits the temper and inclination of a people. Nothing can be God's ordinance, but what he has particularly declared to be such; there is no particular form of civil government described in God's word, neither does nature prompt it. The government of the *Jews* was changed five times. Government is not formed by nature, as other births or productions; if it were, it would be the same in all countries; because nature keeps the same method, in the same thing, in all climates. If a common-wealth be changed into a monarchy, is it nature that forms, and brings forth the monarch? Or if a royal family be wholly extinct (as in *Noah's* case, being not heir apparent from descent from *Adam*) is it nature that must go to work (with the kings bees, who themselves alone preserve the royal race in that empire) to breed a monarch before the people can have a king, or a government set over them? And thus we must leave kings to resolve which is their best title to their crowns, whether natural right, or the constitution of government settled by human compacts, under the direction and conduct of reason. But to proceed under the head of a state of natural being, I shall more distinctly explain the state of human nature in its original capacity, as man is placed on earth by his maker, and cloathed with many investitures, and immunities which properly belong to man separately considered. As,

1. The prime immunity in mans state, is that he is most properly the subject of the law of nature. He is the favourite animal on earth; in that this part of God's image, *viz.* reason is congenate with his nature, wherein by a law immutable, instampt upon his frame, God has provided a rule for men in all their actions, obliging each one to the performance of that which is right, not only as to justice, but likewise as to all other moral virtues, the which is nothing but the dictate of right reason founded in the soul of man. That which is to be drawn from mans reason, flowing from the true current of that faculty, when unperverted, may be said to be the law of nature, on which account, the holy scriptures declare it written on mens hearts. For being endowed with a soul, you may know from yourself, how, and what you ought to act, Rom. 2. 14. *These having not a*

law, are a law to themselves. So that the meaning is, when we acknowledge the law of nature to be the dictate of right reason, we must mean that the understanding of man is endowed with such a power, as to be able, from the contemplation of human condition to discover a necessity of living agreably with this law: And likewise to find out some principle, by which the precepts of it, may be clearly and solidly demonstrated. The way to discover the law of nature in our own state, is by a narrow watch, and accurate contemplation of our natural condition, and propensions. Others say this is the way to find out the law of nature. If a man any ways doubts, whether what he is going to do to another man be agreable to the law of nature, then let him suppose himself to be in that other mans room; and by this rule effectually executed. A man must be a very dull scholar to nature not to make proficiency in the knowledge of her laws. But more particularly in pursuing our condition for the discovery of the law of nature, this is very obvious to view, *viz.*

1. A principal of self love, and self preservation, is very predominant in every mans being.

2. A sociable disposition.

3. An affection or love to mankind in general. And to give such sentiments the force of a law, we must suppose a God who takes care of all mankind, and has thus obliged each one, as a subject of higher principles of being, than meer instincts. For that all law properly considered, supposes a capable subject, and a superiour power, and the law of God which is binding, is published by the dictates of right reason as other ways: There-fore says *Plutarch, to follow God and obey reason is the same thing.* But moreover that God has established the law of nature, as the general rule of government, is further illustrable from the many sanctions in providence, and from the peace and guilt of conscience in them that either obey, or violate the law of nature. But moreover, the foundation of the law of nature with relation to government, may be thus discovered. Man is a creature ex-treamly desirous of his own preservation; of himself he is plainly exposed to many wants, unable to secure his own safety, and maintenance without assistance of his fellows; and he is also able of returning kindness by the furtherance of mutual good;

but yet man is often found to be malicious; insolent, and easily
provoked, and as powerful in effecting mischief, as he is ready
in designing it. Now that such a creature may be preserved, it
is necessary that he be sociable; that is, that he be capable and
disposed to unite himself to those of his own species, and to
regulate himself towards them, that they may have no fair
reason to do him harm; but rather incline to promote his interests, and secure his rights and concerns. This then is a
fundamental law of nature, that every man as far as in him lies,
do maintain a sociableness with others, agreable with the main
end and disposition of human nature in general. For this is very
apparent, that reason and society render man the most potent
of all creatures. And finally, from the principles of sociableness
it follows as a fundamental law of nature, that man is not so
wedded to his own interest, but that he can make the common
good the mark of his aim: And hence he becomes capaciated to
enter into a civil state by the law of nature; for without this
property in nature, *viz.* Sociableness, which is for cementing of
parts, every government would soon moulder and dissolve.

2. The second great immunity of man is an original liberty
instampt upon his rational nature. He that intrudes upon this
liberty, violates the law of nature. In this discourse I shall wave
the consideration of mans moral turpitude, but shall view him
physically as a creature which God has made and furnished essentially with many enobling immunities, which render him the
most august animal in the world, and still, whatever has happened since his creation, he remains at the upper-end of nature,
and as such is a creature of a very noble character. For as to his
dominion, the whole frame of the lower part of the universe is
devoted to his use, and at his command; and his liberty under
the conduct of right reason, is equal with his trust. Which liberty
may be briefly considered, internally as to his mind, and externally
as to his person.

1. The native liberty of man's nature implies, a faculty of
doing or omitting things according to the direction of his judgment. But in a more special meaning, this liberty does not consist in a loose and ungovernable freedom, or in an unbounded
license of acting. Such licence is disagreeing with the condition

and dignity of man, and would make man of a lower and meaner constitution than bruit creatures; who in all their liberties are kept under a better and more rational government, by their instincts. Therefore as *Plutarch* says, *Those persons only who live in obedience to reason, are worthy to be accounted free: They alone live as they will, who have learnt what they ought to will.* So that the true natural liberty of man, such as really and truely agrees to him, must be understood, as he is guided and restrained by the types of reason, and laws of nature; all the rest is brutal, if not worse.

2. Mans external personal, natural liberty, antecedent to all human parts, or alliances must also be considered. And so every man must be conceived to be perfectly in his own power and disposal, and not to be controuled by the authority of any other. And thus every man, must be acknowledged equal to every man, since all subjection and all command are equally banished on both sides; and considering all men thus at liberty, every man, has a prerogative to judge for himself, *viz.* What shall be most for his behoof, happiness and well-being.

3. The third capital immunity belonging to mans' nature, is an equality amongst men; which is not to be denied by the law of nature, till man has resigned himself with all his rights for the sake of a civil state; and then his personal liberty and equality is to be cherished, and preserved to the highest degree, as will consist with all just distinctions amongst men of honor, and shall be agreable with the public good. For man has a high valuation of himself, and the passion seems to lay its first foundation (not in pride, but) really in the high and admirable frame and constitution of human nature. The word man, says my author, is thought to carry somewhat of dignity in its sound; and we commonly make use of this as the most proper and prevailing argument against a rude insulter, *viz. I am not a beast or a dog. But am a man as well as yourself.* Since then human nature agrees equally with all persons; and since no one can live a sociable life with another that does not own or respect him as a man; It follows as a command of the law of nature, that every man esteem and treat another as one who is naturally his equal, or who is a man as well as he. There be many popular, or

plausible reasons that greatly illustrate this equality, *viz.* that we all derive our being from one stock, the same common father of human race. . . .

Nothing is more suitable to nature, then that those who excel in understanding and prudence, should rule and controul those who are less happy in those advantages, &c. Yet we must note, that there is room for an answer. That it would be the greatest absurdity to believe, that nature actually invests the wise with a sovereignity over the weak; or with a right of forcing them against their wills; for that no sovereignity can be established, unless some human deed, or covenant precede: Nor does natural fitness for government make a man presently governor over another; for that as *Ulpian* says, *by a natural right all men are born free*; and nature having set all men upon a level and made them equals, no servitude or subjection can be conceived without inequality; and this cannot be made without usurpation or force in others, or voluntary compliance in those who resign their freedom, and give away their degree of natural being. And thus we come,

2. To consider man in a civil state of being; wherein we shall observe the great difference between a natural, and political state; for in the latter state many great disproportions appear, or at least many obvious distinctions are soon made amongst men; which doctrine is to be laid open under a few heads.

1. Every man considered in a natural state, must be allowed to be free, and at his own dispose; yet to suit mans inclinations to society; and in a peculiar manner to gratify the necessity he is in of public rule and order, he is impelled to enter into a civil community; and divests himself of his natural freedom, and puts himself under government; which amongst other things comprehends the power of life and death over him; together with authority to anjoyn him some things to which he has an utter aversion, and to prohibit him other things, for which he may have as strong an inclination; so that he may be often under this authority, obliged to sacrifice his private, for the public good. So that though man is inclined to society, yet he is driven to a combination by great necessity. For that the true and leading cause of forming governments, and yielding up natural liberty,

and throwing mans equality into a common pile to be now cast by the rules of fellowship; was really and truly to guard themselves against the injuries men were lyable to interchangeably; for none so good to man, as man, and yet none a greater enemy. So that,

2. The first human subject and original of civil power is the people. For as they have a power every man over himself in a natural state, so upon a combination they can and do bequeath this power unto others; and settle it according as their united discretion shall determine. For that this is very plain, that when the subject of sovereign power is quite extinct, that power returns to the people again. And· when they are free, they may set up what species of government they please; or if they rather incline to it, they may subside into a state of natural being, if it be plainly for the best. In the *Eastern* country of the *Mogul,* we have some resemblance of the case; for upon the death of an absolute monarch, they live so many days without a civil head; but in that *Interregnum,* those who survive the vacancy, are glad to get into a civil state again; and usually they are in a very bloody condition when they return under the covert of a new monarch; this project is to indear the people to a tyranny, from the experience they have so lately had of an anarchy.

3. The formal reason of government is the will of a community, yielded up and surrendered to some other subject, either of one particular person, or more, conveyed in the following manner.

Let us conceive in our mind a multitude of men, all naturally free and equal; going about voluntarily, to erect themselves into a new common-wealth. Now their condition being such, to bring themselves into a politick body, they must needs enter into divers covenants.

1. They must interchangeably each man covenant to joyn in one lasting society, that they may be capable to concert the measures of their safety, by a publick vote.

2. A vote or decree must then nextly pass to set up some particular species of government over them. And if they are joyned in their first compact upon absolute terms to stand to the decision of the first vote concerning the species of government:

Then all are bound by the majority to acquiesce in that particular form thereby settled, though their own private opinion, incline them to some other model.

3. After a decree has specified the particular form of government, then there will be need of a new covenant, whereby those on whom sovereignty is conferred, engage to take care of the common peace, and welfare. And the subjects on the other hand, to yield them faithful obedience. In which covenant is included that submission and union of wills, by which a state may be conceived to be but one person. So that the most proper definition of a civil state, is this, *viz.* A civil state is a compound moral person. Whose will (united by those covenants before passed) is the will of all; to the end it may use, and apply the strength and riches of private persons towards maintaining the common peace, security, and well-being of all, which may be conceived as tho' the whole state was now become but one man; in which the aforesaid covenants may be supposed under God's providence, to be the divine *Fiat,* pronounced by God, let us make man. And by way of resemblance the aforesaid being may be thus anatomized.

1. The sovereign power is the soul infused, giving life and motion to the whole body.

2. Subordinate officers are the joynts by which the body moves.

3. Wealth and riches are the strength.

4. Equity and laws are the reason.

5. Councellors the memory.

6. *Salus Populi,* or the happiness of the people, is the end of its being; or main business to be attended and done.

7. Concord amongst the members, and all estates, is the health.

8. Sedition is sickness, and civil war death.

4. The parts of sovereignty may be considered: So,

1. As it prescribes the rule of action: It is rightly termed legislative power.

2. As it determines the controversies of subjects by the standard of those rules. So is it justly termed judiciary power.

3. As it arms the subjects against foreigners, or forbids hostility, so its called the power of peace and war.

4. As it takes in ministers for the discharge of business, so it

is called the right of appointing magistrates. So that all great officers and public servants, must needs owe their original to the creating power of sovereignty. So that those whose right it is to create, may dissolve the being of those who are created, unless they cast them into an immortal frame. And yet must needs be dissoluble if they justly forfeit their being to their creators.

5. The chief end of civil communities, is, that men thus conjoyned, may be secured against the injuries, they are liable to from their own kind. For if every man could secure himself singly; it would be great folly for him, to renounce his natural liberty, in which every man is his own king and protector.

6. The sovereign authority besides, that it inheres in every state as in a common and general subject. So farther according as it resides in some one person, or in a council (consisting of some select persons, or of all the members of a community) as in a proper and particular subject, so it produceth different forms of commonwealths, *viz.* Such as are either simple and regular, or mixt.

1. The forms of a regular state are three only, which forms arise from the proper and particular subject, in which the supream power resides. As,

1. A democracy, which is when the sovereign power is lodged in a council consisting of all the members, and where every member has the privilege of a vote. This form of government, appears in the greatest part of the world to have been the most ancient. For that reason seems to shew it to be most probable, that when men (being originally in a condition of natural freedom and equality) had thoughts of joyning in a civil body, would without question be inclined to administer their common affairs, by their common judgment, and so must necessarily to gratify that inclination establish a democracy; neither can it be rationally imagined, that fathers of families being yet free and independent, should in a moment, or little time take off their long delight in governing their own affairs, and devolve all upon some single sovereign commander; for that it seems to have been thought more equitable, that what belonged to all should be managed by all, when all had entered by compact into one community.

A democracy is then erected, when a number of free persons, do assemble together, in order to enter into a covenant for

uniting themselves in a body: And such a preparative assembly
hath some appearance already of a democracy; it is a democracy
in *embrio,* properly in this respect, that every man hath the
priviledge freely to deliver his opinion concerning the common
affairs. Yet he who dissents from the vote of the majority, is not
in the least obliged by what they determine, till by a second
covenant, a popular form be actually established; for not before
then can we call it a democratical government, *viz.* Till the right
of determining all matters relating to the public safety, is actually placed in a general assembly of the whole people; or by
their own compact and mutual agreement, determine themselves
the proper subject for the exercise of sovereign power. And to
compleat this state, and render it capable to exert its power to
answer the end of a civil state: These conditions are necessary.

1. That a certain time and place be assigned for assembling.

2. That when the assembly be orderly met, as to time and
place, that then the vote of the majority must pass for the vote
of the whole body.

3. That magistrates be appointed to exercise the authority of
the whole for the better dispatch of business, of every days oc-
currence; who also may with more mature diligence, search into
more important affairs; and if in case any thing happens of
greater consequence, may report it to the assembly; and be
peculiarly serviceable in putting all public decrees into execution. Because a large body of people is almost useless in respect
of the last service, and of many others as to the more particular
application and exercise of power. Therefore it is most agreable
with the law of nature, that they institute their officers to act
in their name, and stead.

2. The second species of regular governments, is an aristocracy; and this is said then to be constituted when the people,
or assembly united by a first covenant, and having thereby cast
themselves into the first rudiments of a state; do then by common decree, devolve the sovereign power, on a council consisting
of some select members; and these having accepted of the desig-
nation, are then properly invested with sovereign command; and
then an aristocracy is formed.

3. The third species of a regular government, is a monarchy
which is settled when the sovereign power is conferred on some

one worthy person. It differs from the former, because a monarch who is but one person in natural, as well as in moral account, and so is furnished with an immediate power of exercising sovereign command in all instances of government; but the fore-named must needs have particular time and place assigned; but the power and authority is equal in each.

2. Mixt governments, which are various and of divers kinds (not now to be enumerated) yet possibly the fairest in the world is that which has a regular monarchy; settled upon a noble democracy as its basis. And each part of the government is so adjusted by pacts and laws that renders the whole constitution an *elisium*. It is said of the British empire, that it is such a monarchy, as that by the necessary subordinate concurrence of the lords and commons, in the making and repealing all statutes or acts of parliament; it hath the main advantages of an aris-tocracy, and of a democracy, and yet free from the disadvantages and evils of either. It is such a monarchy, as by most admirable temperament affords very much to the industry, liberty, and happiness of the subject, and reserves enough for the majesty and prerogative of any king, who will own his people as sub-pects, not as slaves. It is a kingdom, that of all the kingdoms of the world, is most like to the kingdom of Jesus Christ, whose yoke is easy, and burden light. . . .

1. In general concerning rebellion against government for particular subjects to break in upon regular communities duly established, is from the premises to violate the law of nature; and is a high usurpation upon the first grand immunities of mankind. Such rebels in states, and usurpers in churches affront the world, with a presumption that the best of the brotherhood are a company of fools, and that themselves have fairly monopo-lized all the reason of human nature. Yea, they take upon them the boldness to assume a prerogative of trambling under foot of the natural original equality and liberty of their fellows; for to push the proprietors of settlements out of possession of their old, and impose new schemes upon them, is vertually to declare them in a state of vassalage, or that they were born so; and therefore will the usurper be so gracious as to insure them they shall not be sold at the next market: They must esteem it a favour, for by this time all the original prerogatives of mans

nature are intentionally a victim, smoaking to satiate the usurpers ambition. It is a very tart observation on an *English* monarch, and where it may by proportion be applied to a subject must needs sink very deep, and serve for evidence under this head. It is in the secret history of K. C. 2. and K. J. 2. p. 2 says my author, Where the constitution of a nation is such, that the laws of the land are the measures both of the sovereigns commands, and the obedience of the subjects, whereby it is provided; that as the one are not to invade what by concessions and stipulations is granted to the ruler; so the other is not to deprive them of their lawful and determined rights and liberties; then the prince who strives to subvert the fundamental laws of the society, is the traytor and the rebel, and not the people, who endeavour to preserve and defend their own. It's very applicable to particular men in their rebellions or usurpations in church or state.

2. In special I shall now proceed to enquire, whether any of the aforesaid species of regular, unmixt governments, can with any good shew of reason be predicable of the church of Christ on earth. If the churches of Christ, as churches, are either the object or subject of a sovereign power intrusted in the hands of men, then most certainly one of the fore-cited schemes of a perfect government will be applicable to it.

Before I pursue the enquiry, it may not be improper to pause, and make some caution here, by distinguishing between that which may have some resemblance of civil power, and the thing it self; and so the power of churches is but a faint resemblance of civil power; it comes in reality nothing near to the thing it self; for the one is truly coercive, the other persuasive; the one is sovereign power, the other is delegated and ministerial: But not to delay, I shall proceed with my enquiry, and therein shall endeavour to humour the several great claimers of government in the church of Christ. And,

1. I shall begin with a monarchy. It's certain, his holiness, either by reasonable pleas, or powerful cheats, has assumed an absolute and universal sovereignity; this fills his cathedral chair, and is adorned with a triple crown, and in defence thereof does protest, The Almighty has made him both key-keeper of heaven and hell, with the adjacent territories of purgatory, and vested

in him an absolute sovereignty over the christian world. And his right has so far prevailed, that princes and civil monarchs hold their crowns and donations as his dutiful sons, and loyal subjects; He therefore decks himself with the spoils of the divine attributes, stiling himself, our Lord God, *optimum, maximum et supremum numen in Terris*: a God on earth, a visible deity, and that his power is absolute, and his wisdom infallible. And many of the great potentates of the earth have paid their fealty, as though it was really so. One of them clad in canvas, going barefoot in the depth of winter (in obedience to the decree, stinting the penance in proportion to the wickedness of princes) has waited many days for absolution at his pious gates. Another has thrown himself down prostrate a humble penitent before him: He has placed his holy foot on the monarchs profane neck as crushing a vermine, crawling out of the stable of his sovereignty; and others frequently kiss his toes with very profound devotion. These and such like triumphant signals of his sovereign power does he wear. And indeed if he is the universal monarch of the catholic church, princes that are members of it must needs knock under; for that in one world there cannot possibly be two *Most High's*, any more than two *Infinites*. Thus you see the clergy, or gospel ministry of the christian world have so wisely handled business, and managed the gospel that they have fairly (as they avouch) found a sovereign power bequeathed in it to the ministry of Christ, and rummaging more warily and nicely, at last found a spiritual monarch, very compleatly furnished with the keys of all sorts of power hanging at his girdle; and may we not pronounce the wiser they! seeing the world growing weary of religion, was willing to loll itself down to sleep, and leave them in sole trust with the whole interest of God's kingdom. But the sad enquiry is, whether this sort of government has not plainly subverted the design of the gospel, and the end for which Christ's government was ordained, *viz.* the moral, spiritual, and eternal happiness of men?

But I have no occasion to pursue this remark with tedious demonstrations: It's very plain, it's written with blood in capital letters, to be read at midnight by the flames of *Smithfield*, and other such like consecrated fires. That the government of this ecclesiastical monarch has instead of sanctifying, absolutely debauched the world, and subverted all good christianity in it. So that without the least shew of any vain presumption we may infer, that God and wise nature were never propitious to the birth of this monster.

An aristocracy which places the supream power in a select company of choice persons. Here I freely acknowledge were the gospel ministry established the subject of this power, *viz.* To will and do, in all church affairs without controul, &c. This government might do to support the church in its most valuable rights, &c. If we could be assured they would make the scripture, and not their private will the rule of their personal and ministerial actions: and indeed upon these terms any species of government, might serve the great design of redemption; but considering how great an interest is embarked, and how frail a bottom we trust, though we should rely upon the best of men, especially if we remember what is in the hearts of good men, (*viz.* much ignorance, abundance of small ends, many times cloked with a high pretence in religion; pride skulking and often breeding revenge upon a small affront; and blown up by a pretended zeal; yet really and truly by nothing more divine than interest, or ill nature) and also considering how very uncertain we are of the real goodness of those we esteem good men; and also how impossible it is to secure the intail of it to successors: and also if we remind how christianity by the foresaid principle has been peel'd, rob'd and spoiled already; it cannot consist with the light of nature to venture again upon such perils, especially if we can find a safer way home. More distinctly.

It is very plain (allowing me to speak emblematically) the primitive constitution of the churches was a democracy, as appears by the foregoing parallel. But after the christian churches were received into the favour of the imperial court, under the dominion of *Constantine* the great; there being many praeliminaries which had furnished the ministers with a disposition thereunto, they quickly deprived the fraternities of their rights in the government of the churches, when they were once provided of a plentiful maintenance through the liberality of *Constantine,* that when christianity was so luxuriantly treated, as by his great bounty, and noble settlement, it is said there was a voice heard from heaven, saying, Now is poyson poured into the church. But the subversion of the constitution, is a story too long now to tell. . . .

In a word, an aristocracy is a dangerous constitution in the church of Christ, as it possesses the presbytery of all church power: What has been observed sufficiently evinces it. And not only so but from the nature of the constitution, for it has no more barrier to it, against the ambition, insults, and arbitrary measures of men, then an absolute monarchy. But to abbreviate; it seems most agreable with the light of nature, that if there be any of the regular government settled in the church of God it must needs be,

3. A democracy. This is a form of government, which the light of nature does highly value, and often directs to as most agreable to the just and natural prerogatives of human beings. This was of great account, in the early times of the world. And not only so, but upon the experience of several thousand years, after the world had been tumbled, and tost from one species of government to another, at a great expence of blood and treasure, many of the wise nations of the world have sheltered themselves under it again; or at least have blendished, and balanced their governments with it.

It is certainly a great truth, That mans original liberty after it is resigned, (yet under due restrictions) ought to be cherished in all wise governments; or otherwise a man in making himself a subject, he alters himself from a freeman, into a slave, which to do is repugnant to the law of nature. Also the natural equality of men amongst men must be duly favored; in that government was never established by God or nature, to give one man a prerogative to insult over another; therefore in a civil, as well as in a natural state of being, a just equality is to be indulged so far as that every man, is bound to honor every man, which is agreable both with nature and religion, 1. Pet. 2. 17. *Honor all men.*—The end of all good government is to cultivate humanity, and promote the happiness of all, and the good of every man in all his rights, his life, liberty, estate, honor, &c. without injury or abuse done to any. Then certainly it cannot easily be thought, that a company of men, that shall enter into a voluntary compact, to hold all power in their own hands, thereby to use and improve their united force, wisdom, riches and strength for the common and particular good of every member, as is the nature of a democracy; I say it cannot be that this sort of constitution, will so readily furnish those in government with an appetite, or disposition to prey upon each other, or imbezle the common stock; as some particular persons may be apt to do when set off, and intrusted with the same power. And moreover this appears very natural, that when the aforesaid government or power, settled in all, when they have elected certain capable persons to minister in their affairs, and the said ministers remain accountable to the assembly; these officers must needs be under the influence of many wise cautions from their own thoughts (as well as under confinement by their commission) in their whole administration: And from thence it must needs follow that they will be more apt, and inclined to steer right for the main point, *viz.* The peculiar good, and benefit of the whole, and every particular member fairly and sincerely. And why may not these stand for very rational pleas in church order?

For certainly if Christ has settled any form of power in his church he has done it for his churches safety, and for the benefit of every member: Then he must needs be presumed to have made choice of that government as should least expose his people to hazard, either from the fraud, or arbitrary measures of particular men. And it is as plain as day light, there is no species of government like a democracy to attain this end. There is but about two steps from an aristocracy, to a monarchy, and from thence but one to a tyranny; an able standing force, and an ill-nature, *Ipso facto,* turns an absolute monarch into a tyrant; this is obvious among the Roman Caesars, and through the world. And all these direful transmutations are easier in church affairs (from the different qualities of things) then in civil states. For what is it that cunning and learned men can't make the world swallow as an article of their creed, if they are once invested with an uncontroulable power, and are to be the standing orators to mankind in matters of faith and obedience? indeed some very wise and learned men are pleased to inveigh, and reproach the notion of a democracy in the church, which makes the *Cetu fidelium* or community of the faithful the first subject of the power of government. This they say tends to

Brownism, and abhorred anarchy, and then say they upon such praemises, it must needs follow that every member of the body must be an officer; and then every one must preach and dispence the sacraments, &c.

Reply. Certainly such gentlemen, either designs to pose and baffle their reader with falacy; or they themselves never took up, or understood the true ideas of the several species of government; in that a democracy is as regular a form, and as particular as any other.

For,

1. An absolute or limited monarch can't manage the power or government devolved upon him, without the great officers of the crown, or a large sett of ministers; though possibly he may with the quicker dispatch issue out his degrees, yet he must execute all by his ministry. And why may not a democracy be indulged the same liberty? And this will prevent all anarchy or confusion most apparently. But,

2. The bitter bill to swallow in this doctrine of a democracy in the church, is the terrible power of life and death; or the accountableness of particular members to the assembly, and especially those in the ministry; but yet is agreable with the nature of the constitution, and easily managed without anarchy, or popular confusion also, which would be made very evident, if we should but run the parallel in all points between the democracy of the state and church. But nextly from the premises, I shall

3. Infer, That if these churches are not properly formed, yet are fairly established in their present order by the law of nature. And will they be advised, I would exhort them to try who will be so bold as to dare to disseize them. A monarchy has been tryed in the church with a witness, but it has absolutely failed us. An aristocracy in a deep calm threw the democracy overboard, and took not only the helm in hand, but seized ship and cargo as their right and title; but after some time brought all to ship-wreck, and that in a good harbour too.

A democracy was the noble government which beat out in all the bad weather of ten bloody persecutions under the management of antiquity. And this is our constitution, and what can't we be pleased? This constitution is as agreable with the light and laws of nature as any other whatsoever, as has been fairly laid down and fully evinced, and more accommodated to the concerns of religion than any other. Therefore I shall now conclude my demonstration with this brief appeal to the common reason of mankind, *viz.*

How can it consist with the honourable terms man holds upon here on earth; that the best sort of men that we can find in the world; such men as are adorned with a double sett of enobling immunities, the first from nature, the other from grace; that these men when they enter into charter-party to manage a trade for heaven, must *ipso facto* be clapt under a government, that is arbitrary and dispotick; yea that carries the plain symptoms of a tyranny in it, when the light of nature knows of a better species, and frequently has made use of it? It wants no farther demonstration, for it's most apparent, that nature is so much mistress of herself, that man in a natural state of being, is under God the first subject of all power, and therefore can make his own choice, and by deliberate compacts settles his own conditions for the government of himself in a civil state of being: And when a government so settled shall throw itself from its foundations, or the subjects of sovereign power shall subvert or confound the constitution, they then degrade themselves; and so all power returns again to the people, who are the first owners. And what! Is man become so unfortunate, degraded and debased, as to be without all power in settling a government over himself, relating to the matters of his eternal well-being? Or when he comes back to a fathers house, must he fall into the capacity of a meer passive being, and be put under such tutors, as can easily turn tyrants over him, and no relief left for him in his own hands; this is certainly most repugnant to the light of nature, and very disagreable with the liberty and free genius of a gospel state. Nay, in a word, if the government of the churches be settled by God, either in the hands of a church monarch, or aristocracy, and the people are no ways the subject of church-power: Nay, if they are not under Christ, the fountain of power; then the reformation so called, is but a meer cheat, a schism, and notorious rebellion; neither is there room left for the least paliation, or shadow of excuse, for the reformers in renouncing their obedience to their publick governors. And the Martyrologies which pretend to immortalize the fame of eminent heroes, must be changed into chronicles, handling along an account of the just and deserved fate of a crew of rebels against God and government; for what business had such a company of illeterate and crack brain'd fellows to meddle with their rulers, or examine into their administrations? For if they have no right of power in government, they stand absolutely bound to yield a passive obedience and non-resistance; and if they are so hardy and daring as to oppose their lawful rulers, the sharpest penalty in this world, is too easy for them; the inquisition is but dallying and playing with them, hell is their desert. But how it comes about that a state of grace, when in want of a suitable government, is become such a vassal, and wise and cunning nature is by her creator intrusted, and adorned with more enobling prerogatives, I must leave, and resign unto those learned men to solve, who plead for an aristocracy in the churches of Christ.

But to wind up the whole discourse in a few words, I acknowledge many objections may be here made, and several questions of moment might here fall under debate; but having obtained what I have principally sought for, in traversing the paths of nature, in the three following particulars; therefore with them, and with one objection answered; and also with some brief improvement of the grand hypothesis in this demonstration, I shall finish the argument.

1. Three particulars; or so many golden maxims, securing the honor of congregational churches.

Particular 1. That the people or fraternity under the gospel, are the first subject of power; or else religion sinks the dignity of human nature into a baser capacity with relation to ecclesiastical, then it is in, in a natural state of being with relation to civil government.

Particular 2. That a democracy in church or state, is a very honorable and regular government according to the dictates of right reason. And therefore,

Particular 3. That these churches of *New-England*, in their ancient constitution of church order; it being a democracy, are manifestly justified and defended by the law and light of nature.

2. The objection. The plea from the law of nature for a democracy in the church, is as forceable for any other species of

government; because nature is furnished with such a variety of schemes as has been pleaded to: And why may not the wise christian nations take which likes them best?

Answ. We must distinguish between man left solely to the direction of the law of nature, and as the subject of revelation, wherein divine wisdom may interpose; and determine on some particular species, without hurting or crossing the law of nature. Therefore,

1. I readily grant and acknowledge, a christian people may settle what species of government they please, when they are solely left to determine by the law of nature, what government in the church they will have. But then we must remember, that by the argument or concession, the power is originally in the people; and then our own case is secure and safe enough; both on the account of the reversion of power, and especially, for that the people the first subjects of power, have been pleased to settle a democracy for their government, in the churches of this country. And if after the peaceable possession of about an hundred years, any persons can persuade them to alter their government into any other species, this will be less worthy of blame, than craftily, or unfairly to force it out of their hands.

2. It's granted, that according to the light of nature, there be various regular models of government; but if divine wisdom is pleased to interpose and over-rule natures agitations, and cast the seales for this or that particular form, nature will be but fair manuered to submit to its author and rector. So that if we find that God has disclosed his mind by revelation, that his churches be the subjects of a democracy, then all stand obliged to comply under a double bond. And so we come under a proper crisis to enquire in the next place for scripture-evidence in the justification of these churches.

But before I proceed to it, I shall

3. Make some brief improvement of the main *Hypothesis* in the demonstration; that is to say, if the government of the gospel churches, be a democracy, these consequences must necessarily follow,

1. *Cons.* That the right of convoking councils ecelesiastical, is in the churches.

2. *Cons.* That such a council has only consultative not a jurid-

ical power in it. A juridical power committed to such a representative body is both needless, and also dangerous to the distinct and perfect states they derive from. Compleat states settled upon a body of immutiable and imperial laws as its basis, may want council; but to create a new subject of juridical power, is some way to endanger the being of the creators.

3. *Cons.* That all the members of an ecclesiastical council, deriving from a democracy are subjects of equal power. Whatever the power is, the several delegates must from the nature of the government they derive from, be equal sharers in it. Democratical states, in their representative body can make but one house, because they have but one subject of supream power in their nature, and therefore their delegates, let them be who or what they may be, are under equal trust; so that none can justly claim superiority over their fellows, or pretend to a higher power in their suffrage. Indeed in such kingdoms, where the sovereign power is distributed and settled in divers subjects, that the balance of power may be more even, for the safety of the whole, and of all parts under all acts of sovereign power: From such a settlement of power, there arises several distinct states in the same government, which when convened as one subject of sovereign power, they make different houses in their grand sessions; and so one house or state can negative another. But in every distinct house of these states, the members are equal in their vote; the most ayes makes the affirmative vote, and most no's the negative: They don't weigh the intellectual furniture, or other distinguishing qualifications of the several voters in the scales of the golden rule of fellowship; they only add up the ayes, and the no's, and so determine the suffrage of the house.

11

Hugh Jones
The Present State of Virginia[1]

In 1716, Hugh Jones received the degree of Master of Arts from Oxford. The twenty-four year old graduate asked his clerical superiors for an American assignment. At the same time, the officers of William and Mary College at Williamsburg were seeking a professor of mathematics. Jones was appointed to the position and came out to Virginia in 1717.

In addition to his duties at the college, Jones acted as chaplain of the House of Burgesses and often conducted services in a local Anglican Church. Throughout his American career Jones moved in high circles and enjoyed the confidence of public and social leaders. His brief description of Virginia makes it clear that he relished his life there and respected the Virginians.

Jones returned to England in 1721. While there he published *The Present State of Virginia* and *An Accidence to the English tongue,* the latter a practical grammar of the English language specifically designed for students who had no Latin or Greek. While in England, Jones married a widow with two children and in 1724 again came out to Virginia.

During his first stay in America, Jones had become involved in a dispute with James Blair, president of William and Mary and commissary of the church in Virginia. Blair assigned Jones to a parish known for its contentiousness and in a short time Jones abandoned his position and moved to Maryland. Armed with a letter from Governor Benedict Calvert, he soon became rector of an Eastern Shore parish, a position he held until his death in 1760.

Jones's biography is a minor model of the versatility of the eighteenth-century educated man. In Maryland he continued to be associated with highly placed men. For example, he served the

1. Hugh Jones, *The Present State of Virginia,* ed. Richard L. Morton (Chapel Hill: University of North Carolina Press, 1956). Reprinted by permission of the University Press of Virginia.

governor on the commission that attempted to settle the question of the colony's disputed boundaries. As an orthodox Anglican divine he kept a vigilant watch over Catholics and nonconforming Protestants. Though conservative in religion, he had the inquisitive mind of the scientist. In 1753 his pamphlet, *The Pancronometer*— attracted much attention. In it he argued for calendar reform, a standardization of coinage, weights, and measures, and the adoption of the unit *eight* as the standard unit of computation. Jones corresponded with many of the Philadelphia associates of Benjamin Franklin.

A recent comprehensive history is Richard L. Morton, *Colonial Virginia*. (2 vols.; Chapel Hill: University of North Carolina Press, 1960). Although there is no modern account of slavery in the colonial period, one may profitably refer to Philip A. Bruce, *Economic History of Virginia in the Seventeenth Century* (2 vols. New York: Macmillan, 1895). A panorama of eighteenth-century southern life unfolds in the well-written diaries of William Byrd: Louis B. Wright and Marion Tinling (eds.), *The Secret Diary of William Byrd of Westover*, 1709-1712 (Richmond: Dietz, 1941); Maude H. Woodfin and Marion Tinling (eds.), *Another Secret Diary of William Byrd of Westover, 1739-1741, with Letters and Literary Exercises, 1696-1726* (Richmond: Dietz, 1942). In reading the following selection note (1) what features characterized the Virginia labor system; (2) how agriculture was organized and practiced in the colony; (3) what Jones said concerning the derivation of habits, customs, and standards of living of the people; (4) how the new environment altered the character of the Virginians; (5) what kind of education Jones thought appropriate for Virginians; (6) what advantages he saw in living in Virginia; (7) what value he thought Virginia was to the mother country; and (8) what qualities of style marked his writing.

Chapter IV

Of the Negroes, with the Planting and Management of Indian Corn, Tobacco, etc. and of their Timber, Stock, Fruits, Provision, and Habitations, etc.

THE NEGROES LIVE IN SMALL COTTAGES CALLED quarters, in about six in a gang, under the direction of an overseer or bailiff; who takes care that they tend such land as the owner allots and orders, upon which they raise hogs and cattle, and plant Indian corn (or maize) and tobacco for the use of their master; out of which the overseer has a dividend (or share) in proportion to the number of hands including himself; this with several privileges is his salary and is an ample recompence for his pains, and encouragement of his industrious care, as to the labour, health, and provision of the Negroes.

The Negroes are very numerous, some gentlemen having hundreds of them of all sorts, to whom they bring great profit; for the sake of which they are obliged to keep them well, and not overwork, starve, or famish them, besides other inducements to favour them; which is done in a great degree, to such especially that are laborious, careful, and honest; though indeed some masters, careless of their own interest or reputation, are too cruel and negligent.

The Negroes are not only encreased by fresh supplies from Africa and the West India Islands, but also are very prolifick among themselves; and they that are born there talk good English, and affect our language, habits, and customs; and though they be naturally of a barbarous and cruel temper, yet are they kept under by severe discipline upon occasion, and by good laws are prevented from running away, injuring the English, or neglecting their business.

Their work (or chimerical hard slavery) is not very laborious; their greatest hardship consisting in that they and their posterity are not at their own liberty or disposal, but are the property of their owners; and when they are free, they know not how to provide so well for themselves generally; neither did they live so plentifully nor (many of them) so easily in their own country, where they are made slaves to one another, or taken captive by their enemies.

The children belong to the master of the woman that bears them; and such as are born of a Negroe and an European are called Molattoes; but such as are born of an Indian and Negroe are called Mustees.

Their work is to take care of the stock, and plant corn, tobacco, fruits, etc. which is not harder than thrashing, hedging, or ditching; besides, though they are out in the violent heat, wherein they delight, yet in wet or cold weather there is little occasion for their working in the fields, in which few will let them be abroad, lest by this means they might get sick or die, which would prove a great loss to their owners, a good Negroe being sometimes worth three (nay four) score pounds sterling, if he be a tradesman; so that upon this (if upon no other account) they are obliged not to overwork them, but to cloath and feed them sufficiently, and take care of their health.

Several of them are taught to be sawyers, carpenters, smiths, coopers, etc. and though for the most part they be none of the aptest or nicest; yet they are by nature cut out for hard labour and fatigue, and will perform tolerably well; though they fall much short of an Indian, that has learned and seen the same things; and those Negroes make the best servants, that have been slaves in their own country; for they that have been kings and great men there are generally lazy, haughty, and obstinate; whereas the others are sharper, better humoured, and more laborious.

The languages of the new Negroes are various harsh jargons, and their religions and customs such as are best described by Mr. Bosman in his book intitled (I think) A *Description of the Coasts of Africa.*

The Virginia planters readily learn to become good mechanicks in building, wherein most are capable of directing their servants and slaves.

As for timber they abound with excellent good; having about eight sorts of oak, several kinds of walnut-tree and hickory and pignut, pine, cedar, and cypress for shingles; which covering is lighter than tiles, and being nailed down, are not easily blown off in any tempest or gust.

The oak, etc. is of quick growth, consequently will not last so long as ours; though it has a good grain, and is freer from knots, and will last long enough for shipping, and ordinary uses.

When a tract of land is seated, they clear it by felling the trees about a yard from the ground, lest they should shoot again. What wood they have occasion for they carry off, and burn the rest, or let it lie and rot upon the ground.

The land between the logs and stumps they how up, planting tobacco there in the spring, inclosing it with a slight fence of cleft rails. This will last for tobacco some years, if the land be good; as it is where fine timber, or grape vines grow.

Land when tired is forced to bear tobacco by penning their

cattle upon it; but cowpen tobacco tastes strong, and that planted in wet marshy land is called nonburning tobacco, which smoaks in the pipe like leather, unless it be of a good age.

When land is tired of tobacco, it will bear Indian corn, or English wheat, or any other European grain or seed, with wonderful increase.

Tobacco and Indian corn are planted in hills as hops, and secured by wormfences, which are made of rails supporting one another very firmly in a particular manner.

Tobacco requires a great deal of skill and trouble in the right management of it.

They raise the plants in beds, as we do cabbage plants; which they transplant and replant upon occasion after a shower of rain, which they call a season.

When it is grown up they top it, or nip off the head, succour it, or cut off the ground leaves, weed it, hill it; and when ripe, they cut it down about six or eight leaves on a stalk, which they carry into airy tobacco houses; after it is withered a little in the sun, there it is hung to dry on sticks, as paper at the paper-mills; when it is in proper case, (as they call it) and the air neither too moist, nor too dry, they strike it, or take it down, then cover it up in bulk, or a great heap, where it lies till they have leisure or occasion to stem it (that is pull the leaves from the stalk) or strip it (that is take out the great fibres) and tie it up in hands, or streight lay it; and so by degrees prize or press it with proper engines into great hogsheads, containing from about six to eleven hundred pounds; four of which hogsheads make a tun, by dimension, not by weight; then it is ready for sale or shipping.

There are two sorts of tobacco, viz. Oroonoko the stronger, and sweet scented the milder; the first with a sharper leaf like a fox's ear, and the other rounder and with finer fibres: but each of these are varied into several sorts, much as apples and pears are; and I have been informed by the Indian traders, that the inland Indians have sorts of tobacco much differing from any planted or used by the Europeans.

The Indian corn is planted in hills, and weeded much as Tobacco.

This grain is of great increase and most general use; for with this is made good bread, cakes, and hommony for the Negroes, which with good pork and potatoes (red and white, very nice and different from ours) with other roots and pulse, are their general food.

Indian corn is the best food for cattle, hogs, sheep and horses; and the blades and tops are excellent fodder, when well cured, which is commonly used, though many raise good clover and oats; and some have planted sanfoin, etc.

In the marshes, and woods, and old fields is good range for stock in the spring, summer, and fall; and the hogs will run fat with certain roots of flags and reeds, which abounding in the marshes they root up and eat.

Besides, at the plantations are standard peach-trees, and apple-trees, planted out in orchards, on purpose almost for the hogs.

The peaches abound, and are of a delicious taste, and apple-trees are raised from the seeds very soon, which kind of kernel fruit needs no grafting, and is diversifyed into numberless sorts, and makes, with good management, an excellent cyder, not much inferior to that of Herefordshire, when kept to a good age; which is rarely done, the planters being good companions and guests whilst the cyder lasts. Here cherries thrive much better (I think) than in England; though the fruit-trees soon decay, yet they are soon raised to great perfection.

As for wool, I have had near as good as any near Leominster; and it might be much improved if the sheep were housed every night, and foddered and littered as in Urchinfield, where they have by such means the finest wool; but to do this, would be of little use, since it is contrary to the interest of Great Britain to allow them exportation of their woollen manufactures; and what little woollen is there made might be nearly had as cheap, and better from England.

As for provision, there is variety of excellent fish in great plenty easily taken; especially oysters, sheepheads, rocks, large trouts, crabs, drums, sturgeons, etc.

They have the same tame fowl as in England, only they propagate better; but these exceed in wild geese and ducks, cohoncks, blew-wings, teal, swans, and mallard.

Their beef and veal is small, sweet, and fat enough; their pork is famous, whole Virginia shoots being frequently barbacued in

England; their bacon is excellent, the hams being scarce to be distinguished from those of Westphalia; but their mutton and lamb some folks don't like, though others extol it. Their butter is good and plentiful enough. Their venison in the lower parts of the country is not so plentiful as it has been, though there be enough and tolerably good; but in the frontier counties they abound with venison, wild turkies, etc. where the common people sometimes dress bears, whose flesh they say, is not to be well distinguished from good pork or bacon.

They pull the down of their living geese and wild and tame ducks, wherewith they make the softest and sweetest beds.

The houses stand sometimes two or three together; and in other places a quarter, half a mile, or a mile, or two, asunder, much as in the country in England.

Chapter V

Of the Habits, Customs, Parts, Imployments, Trade, etc. of the Virginians; and of the Weather, Coin, Sickness, Liquors, Servants, Poor, Pitch, Tar, Oar, etc.

The Habits, Life, customs, computations, etc. of the Virginians are much the same as about London, which they esteem their home; and for the most part have contemptible notions of England, and wrong sentiments of Bristol, and the other outports, which they entertain from seeing and hearing the common dealers, sailors, and servants that come from those towns, and the country places in England and Scotland, whose language and manners are strange to them; for the planters, and even the native Negroes generally talk good English without idiom or tone, and can discourse handsomly upon most common subjects; and conversing with persons belonging to trade and navigation from London, for the most part they are much civilized, and wear the best of cloaths according to their station; nay, sometimes too good for their circumstances, being for the generality comely handsom persons, of good features and fine complexions (if they take care) of good manners and address. The climate makes them bright, and of excellent sense, and sharp in trade, an ideot, or deformed native being almost a miracle.

Thus they have good natural notions, and will soon learn arts and sciences; but are generally diverted by business or inclination from profound study, and prying into the depth of things; being ripe for management of their affairs, before they have laid so good a foundation of learning, and had such instructions, and acquired such accomplishments, as might be instilled into such good natural capacities. Nevertheless through their quick apprehension, they have a sufficiency of knowledge, and fluency of tongue, though their learning for the most part be but superficial.

They are more inclinable to read men by business and conversation, than to dive into books, and are for the most part only desirous of learning what is absolutely necessary, in the shortest and best method.

Having this knowledge of their capacities and inclination from sufficient experience, I have composed on purpose some short treatises adapted with my best judgment to a course of education for the gentlemen of the plantations; consisting in a short English grammar; an Accidence to Christianity; an Accidence to the Mathematicks, especially to Arithmetick in all its parts and applications, algebra, geometry, surveying of land, and navigation.

These are the most useful branches of learning for them, and such as they willingly and readily master, if taught in a plain and short method, truly applicable to their genius; which I have endeavoured to do, for the use of them, and all others of their temper and parts.

They are not very easily persuaded to the improvement of useful inventions (except a few, such as sawing mills) neither are they great encouragers of manufactures, because of the trouble and certain expence in attempts of this kind, with uncertain prospect of gain; whereas by their staple commodity, tobacco, they are in hopes to get a plentiful provision; nay, often very great estates.

Upon this account they think it folly to take off their hands (or Negroes) and employ their care and time about any thing, that may make them lessen their crop of tobacco.

So that though they are apt to learn, yet they are fond of, and will follow their own ways, humours, and notions, being not easily brought to new projects and schemes; so that I question, if they would have been imposed upon by the Mississippi or South-Sea, or any other such monstrous bubbles.

In their computations of time, weights and measures both of length, superficies, and solidity, they strictly adhere to what is legal; not running into precarious customs, as they do in England. Thus their quart is the true Winchester, their hundred is 100, not 112, and they survey land by statute measure.

Indeed, what English coin is there, is advanced in value; so that a shilling passes for 14 d. and a guinea goes by tale for 26 s. but the current money is the Spanish; which in reality is about 15 per cent. [hundred] inferior to our English coin, as settled by law; but frequently the value of this varies in respect of sterling bills according to the circumstances of trade; currency and sterling being sometimes at a par; but for the generality 10 per cent. Discount is allowed for sterling bills.

As for education several are sent to England for it; though the Virginians being naturally of good parts, (as I have already hinted) neither require nor admire as much learning, as we do in Britain; yet more would be sent over, were they not afraid of the smallpox, which most commonly proves fatal to them.

But indeed when they come to England they are generally put to learn to persons that know little of their temper, who keep them drudging on in what is of least use to them, in pedantick methods, too tedious for their volatile genius.

For grammar learning taught after the common round-about way is not much beneficial nor delightful to them; so that they are noted to be more apt to spoil their school-fellows than improve themselves; because they are imprisoned and enslaved to what they hate, and think useless, and have not peculiar management proper for their humour and occasion.

A civil treatment with some liberty, if permitted with discretion is most proper for them, and they have most need of, and readily take polite and mathematical learning; and in English may be conveyed to them (without going directly to Rome and Athens) all the arts, sciences, and learned accomplishments of the antients and moderns, without the fatigue and expence of another language, for which most of them have little use or necessity, since (without another) they may understand their own speech; and all other things requisite to be learned by them sooner and better.

Thus the youth might as well be instructed there as here by proper methods, without the expence and danger of coming hither; especially if they make use of the great advantage of the college at Williamsburgh, where they may (and many do) imbibe the principles of all human and divine literature, both in English and in the learned languages.

By the happy opportunity of this college may they be advanced to religious and learned education, according to the discipline and doctrine of the established church of England; in which respect this college may prove of singular service, and be an advantageous and laudable nursery and strong bulwark against the contagious dissentions in Virginia, which is the most antient and loyal, the most plentiful and flourishing, the most extensive and beneficial colony belonging to the crown of Great Britain, upon which it is most directly dependant; wherein is established the Church of England free from faction and sects, being ruled by the laws, customs, and constitutions of Great Britain, which it strictly observes, only where the circumstances and occasion of the country by an absolute necessity require some small alterations; which nevertheless must not be contrary (though different from and subservient) to the laws of England.

Though the violence of neither Whig nor Tory reigns there, yet have they parties; for the very best administration must expect to meet with some opposition in all places; especially where there is a mixture of people of different countries concerned, whose education and interest may propose to them notions and views different from each other.

Most other plantations, especially they that are granted away to proprietors, are inferior to Virginia: where the seeming interest and humour of the owners often divert them from pursuit of the most proper methods; besides, they cannot have such a right claim to the favour of the crown, nor demand its best protection, since they may often interfere with its interest; whereas Virginia is esteemed one of the most valuable gems in the crown of Great Britain.

Thus Virginia having to itself (with Maryland) the staple

commodity of tobacco, has a great advantage of all other plantations on the continent for the encouragement of the crown; whereas others belonging to gentlemen, or having no peculiar trade, cannot expect such power to advance and promote their interest.

To this add, that Virginia equals, if not exceeds all others in goodness of climate, soil, health, rivers, plenty, and all necessaries, and conveniences of life: besides she has, among others these particular advantages of her younger sister Maryland, viz. freedom from popery, and the direction of proprietors; not but that part of Virginia, which is between the rivers Potowmack and Rappahannock belongs to proprietors, as to the quit-rent; yet the government of these counties (called the Northern Neck) is under the same regulation with the other parts of the country.

If New England be called a receptacle of dissenters, and an Amsterdam of religion, Pensylvania the nursery of Quakers, Maryland the retirement of Roman Catholicks, North Carolina the refuge of run-aways, and South Carolina the delight of buccaneers and pyrates, Virginia may be justly esteemed the happy retreat of true Britons and true churchmen for the most part; neither soaring too high nor drooping too low, consequently should merit the greater esteem and encouragement.

The common planters leading easy lives don't much admire labour, or any manly exercise, except horse-racing, nor diversion, except cock-fighting, in which some greatly delight. This easy way of living, and the heat of the summer makes some very lazy, who are then said to be climate-stuck.

The saddle-horses, though not very large, are hardy, strong, and fleet; and will pace naturally and pleasantly at a prodigious rate.

They are such lovers of riding, that almost every ordinary person keeps a horse; and I have known some spend the morning in ranging several miles in the woods to find and catch their horses only to ride two or three miles to church, to the courthouse, or to a horse-race where they generally appoint to meet upon business; and are more certain of finding those that they want to speak or deal with, than at their home.

No people can entertain their friends with better cheer and

welcome; and strangers and travellers are here treated in the most free, plentiful, and hospitable manner; so that a few inns or ordinaries on the road are sufficient.

As to the weather, the spring and fall are not unlike those seasons in England, only the air is never long foggy, nor very cloudy; but clear, sometimes of a bluish colour, occasioned by the thin smoak, dispersed in the air, from the flames of the woods and leaves, which are fired in hunting, to drive the beasts from their lurking places; or in the spring to burn the old leaves and grass, that there may be the better pasture the next summer.

The months of December, January and February are generally much colder, and June, July and August are much hotter than in England; though sometimes 'tis on a sudden very cool in summer and pretty warm in winter, the weather being governed by the wind; which with sudden storms from the north-west, and sometimes from the west and southwest bring violent gusts or tempests, with thunder, lightning, and rain very terrible, but soon over.

The north west winds are exquisitely sharp and cold, proceeding from clouds arising from the vast lakes and prodigious snowy mountains that lie to that quarter; but the southerly winds and others are very warm.

The days and nights are there always much nearer the equality of twelve hours, than in the latitude of England.

At the sudden changes of weather, from heat to cold, people are apt to take cold, often neglecting to shift their cloaths with the weather; which with abundance of damps and mists from the water, and by eating too plentifully of some delicious fruits, makes the people subject to feavers and agues, which is the country distemper, a severe fit of which (called a seasoning) most expect, some time after their arrival in that climate; but the goodness of God has furnished us with a perfect catholicon for that sickness, viz. the bark; which being taken and repeated in a right manner, seldom fails of a cure, unless the morbifick matter comes to a head again from fresh causes, and so returns with mastery; upon which recourse must be had to the same specifick remedy; besides which there are several ways of cure, but none so universal and sure as that.

Some for want of timely care, through ignorance or obstinacy, will permit the distemper to lurk about them so long, till at last it has reduced them to an irrecoverable, lingering, ill habit of body; especially if they live meanly, drinking too much water, and eating too much salt meat; and this cachexy generally ends their lives with a dropsy, consumption, the jaundice, or some such illness.

Besides this, some are troubled with the dry gripes, proceeding from cold (I suppose) which take away for a long time the use of the limbs of some, especially hard drinkers of rum; some that have lain out in mighty cold weather have been frost-bitten, and lost their fingers or toes.

There is no danger of wild beasts in traveling; for the wolves and bears, which are up the country, never attack any, unless they be first assaulted and hurt; and the wolves of late are much destroyed by virtue of a law, which allows good rewards for their heads with the ears on, to prevent imposition and cheating the publick, for the ears are cropped when a head is produced.

The bears are also much destroyed by the out-planters, etc. for the sake of their flesh and skins.

As for rattle-snakes, etc. they make off from you, unless you by carelessness chance to tread on them; and then their bite is found now not to be mortal, if remedies can be applied in time.

The worst inconveniency in travelling a-cross the country, is the circuit that must be taken to head creeks, etc. for the main roads wind along the rising ground between the rivers, though now they much shorten their passage by mending the swamps and building of bridges in several places; and there are established ferries at convenient places, over the great rivers; but in them is often much danger from sudden storms, bad boats, or unskilful or wilful ferrymen; especially if one passes in a boat with horses, of which I have great reason to be most sensible by the loss of a dear brother at Chickohomony Ferry, in February 1723/4.

As for their drink, good springs of excellent water abound every where almost, which is very cooling and pleasant in summer, and the general drink of abundance; not so much out of necessity, as choice.

Some planters, etc. make good small drink with cakes of parsimmons a kind of plumbs, which grow there in great plenty;

but the common small beer is made of molossus, which makes extraordinary brisk good tasted liquor at a cheap rate, with little trouble in brewing; so that they have it fresh and fresh, as they want it in winter and summer.

And as they brew, so do they bake daily, bread or cakes, eating too much hot and new bread, which cannot be wholsom, though it be pleasanter than what has been baked a day or two.

Some raise barley and make malt there, and others have malt from England, with which those that understand it, brew as good beer as in England, at proper seasons of the year; but the common strong malt-drink mostly used, is Bristol beer; of which is consumed vast quantities there yearly; which being well brewed and improved by crossing the sea, drinks exceedingly fine and smooth; but malt liquor is not so much regarded as wine, rack, brandy, and rum, punch, with drams of rum or brandy for the common sort, when they drink in a hurry.

The common wine comes from Madera or Phial, which moderately drank is fittest to cheer the fainting spirits in the heat of summer and to warm the chilled blood in the bitter colds of winter, and seems most peculiarly adapted for this climate: besides this, are plentifully drank with the better sort, of late years, all kinds of French, and other European wine, especially claret and port.

Here is likewise used a great deal of chocolate, tea and coffee, which, with several sorts of apparel, they have as cheap, or cheaper than in England, because of the debenture of such goods upon their exportation thither: besides, they are allowed to have wines directly from Madera, and other commodities are brought from the West-Indies, and the Continent, which cannot be brought to England without spoiling.

As for grinding corn, etc. they have good mills upon the runs and creeks; besides hand-mills, wind-mills, and the Indian invention of pounding hommony in mortars burnt in the stump of a tree, with a log for a pestle hanging at the end of a pole, fixed like the pole of a lave.

Though they are permitted to trade to no parts but Great Britain, except these places; yet have they in many respects better and cheaper commodities than we in England, especially of late years; for the country may be said to be altered and improved in wealth and polite living within these few years, since the beginning of Colonel Spotswood's government, more than in all the scores of years before that, from its first discovery. The country is yearly supplied with vast quantities of goods from Great Britain, chiefly from London, Bristol, Liverpool, Whitehaven, and from Scotland.

The ships that transport these things often call at Ireland to victual, and bring over frequently white servants, which are of three kinds. 1. Such as come upon certain wages by agreement for a certain time. 2. Such as come bound by indenture, commonly called kids, who are usually to serve four or five years; and 3. those convicts or felons that are transported, whose room they had much rather have than their company; for abundance of them do great mischiefs, commit robbery and murder, and spoil servants, that were before very good: But they frequently there meet with the end they deserved at home, though indeed some of them prove indifferent good. Their being sent thither to work as slaves for punishment, is but a mere notion, for few of them ever lived so well and so easy before, especially if they are good for any thing. These are to serve seven, and sometimes fourteen years, and they and servants by indentures have an allowance of corn and cloaths, when they are out of their time, that they may be therewith supported, till they can be provided with services, or otherwise settled. With these three sorts of servants are they supplied from England, Wales, Scotland, and Ireland, among which they that have a mind to it, may serve their time with ease and satisfaction to themselves and their masters, especially if they fall into good hands.

Except the last sort, for the most part who are loose villains, made tame by Wild, and then enslaved by his Forward namesake: To prevent too great a stock of which servants and Negroes many attempts and laws have been in vain made.

These if they forsake their roguery together with the other kids of the later Jonathan, when they are free, may work daylabour, or else rent a small plantation for a trifle almost; or else turn overseers, if they are expert, industrious, and careful, or follow their trade, if they have been brought up to any; especially smiths, carpenters, taylors, sawyers, coopers, bricklayers, etc. The plenty of the country, and the good wages given to work-folks occasion very few poor, who are supported by the parish, being such as are lame, sick, or decrepit through age, distempers, accidents, or some infirmities; for where there is a numerous family of poor children the vestry takes care to bind them out apprentices, till they are able to maintain themselves by their own labour; by which means they are never tormented with vagrant, and vagabond beggars, there being a reward for taking up runaways, that are at a small distance from their home; if they are not known, or are without a pass from their master, and can give no good account of themselves, especially Negroes.

In all convenient places are kept stores or ware-houses of all sorts of goods, managed by store-keepers or factors, either for themselves or others in the country, or in Great Britain.

This trade is carried on in the fairest and genteelest way of merchandize, by a great number of gentlemen of worth and fortune; who with the commanders of their ships, and several Virginians (who come over through business or curiosity, or often to take possession of estates, which every year fall here to some or other of them) make as considerable and handsom a figure, and drive as great and advantageous a trade for the advancement of the publick good, as most merchants upon the Royal-Exchange.

At the stores in Virginia, the planters, etc. may be supplied with what English commodities they want.

The merchants, factors, or store-keepers in Virginia buy up the tobacco of the planters, either for goods or current Spanish money, or with sterling bills payable in Great Britain.

The tobacco is rolled, drawn by horses, or carted to convenient rolling houses, whence it is conveyed on board the ships in flats or sloops, etc.

Some years ago there was made an act to oblige all tobacco to be sent to convenient ware-houses, to the custody and management of proper officers, who were by oath to refuse all bad tobacco, and gave printed bills as receipts for each parcel or hogshead; which quantity was to be delivered according to order upon return of those bills; and for their trouble and care in viewing, weighing, and stamping, the officers were allowed 5 s. per hogshead.

The intent of this law was to improve the commodity, prevent frauds in publick payments; and for ease of the common planters, and expedition and conveniency of shipping.

But though the first design was for publick tobacco only, yet the private crops of gentlemen being included in the law, was esteemed a great grievance; and occasioned complaints, which destroyed a law, that with small amendments might have proved most advantageous.

The abrogation of this law reduced the sailors to their old slavery of rolling the tobacco in some places; where they draw it for some miles, as gardeners draw a roller, which makes them frequently curse the country, and through prejudice give it a very vile character.

The tobacco purchased by the factors or store-keepers, is sent home to their employers, or consigned to their correspondent merchants in Great Britain.

But most gentlemen, and such as are beforehand in the world, lodge money in their merchant's hands here, to whom they send their crop of tobacco, or the greatest part of it.

This money is employed according to the planter's orders; chiefly in sending over yearly such goods, apparel, liquors, etc. as they write for, for the use of themselves, their families, slaves and plantations; by which means they have every thing at the best hand, and the best of its kind.

Besides English goods, several merchants in Virginia import from the West-Indies great quantities of rum, sugar, mollossus, etc. and salt very cheap from the Salt Islands; which things they purchase with money, or generally with pork, beef, wheat, Indian-corn and the like.

In some of the poorer parts of the country abounding in pine, do they gather up the lightwood, or knots of the old trees, which will not decay, which being piled up (as a pit of wood to be burnt to charcoal) and encompassed with a trench, and covered with earth, is set on fire; whereby the tar is melted out, and running into a hole is taken up, and filled into barrels; and being boiled to a greater consistency becomes pitch.

Of pitch and tar they send home great quantities, though not near so much as North Carolina, which formerly was the south part of Virginia; but has long since been given away to proprietors, though the bounds between the colony of Virginia, and the government of North Carolina are disputed; so that there is a very long list of land fifteen miles broad between both colonies (called the disputed bounds) in due subjection to neither; which is an asylum for the runagates of both countries.

The greatest part of Virginia is uneven; and near the water they are free from great stones, rocks, and high hills; but far in the country they have vast rocks, stones, and mountains; and though in the salts there is no stone for lime nor building; (but with oyster-shells they make good lime and enough) yet up the freshes, and above the falls of the rivers are discovered free and common stone or several sorts, among which may be expected lime-stone.

Here are also vast quantities of iron oar, and various kinds of minerals, whose nature and vertues are as yet undiscovered.

Moses's words of exhortation to the Israelites for obedience to God's laws, Deut. viii. 6, 7, 8, 9, may be applied to the Virginians; and particularly when he saith that God had brought them into a land whose stones are iron; and for what we know the following words may also be applied to them, when he saith out of the hills of that land might be digged brass, for which there is no small prospect and expectation; and in all probability there may be found the nobler metals of gold and silver, if we did but search for them in the bowels of the earth, if we would but be at the expence and trouble to seek for them.

Why may not our mountains in America, for what we know, be as rich as those of Mexico and Peru in the same country? Since the little hills so plentifully abound with the best of iron; for the digging, melting, working, and exportation whereof providence has furnished us with all wonderful conveniences; if we would add but a little expence, art, and industry.

This iron has been proved to be good, and it is thought, will come at as cheap a rate as any imported from other places; so that 'tis to be hoped Colonel Spotswood's works will in a small time prove very advantageous to Great Britain, which undoubtedly will be carried to great perfection and universal benefit, by his skillful management and indefatigable application to such noble undertakings and glorious projects.

12

Jeremiah Dummer

A Defence of the New-England Charters (1721)[1]

The English view of the colonial charters was that they established limited corporate franchises, which were revocable for cause. The colonies regarded their charters as permanent grants, at once the bases of local liberties and franchises for freedom of action, but the English government moved against individual charters on several occasions during the seventeenth century. The charter of Virginia was quashed by *quo warranto* proceedings in 1624. For almost a half century after 1632, Crown officials intermittently moved against the charter of Massachusetts Bay, and they brought the colony to book in 1683. Connecticut and Rhode Island lost their charters temporarily during the years of the Dominion of New England.

Edward Randolph conceived the idea of proceeding wholesale against the charters by act of Parliament. Bills to accomplish this were introduced in 1701, 1706 and 1715, but in each instance the bills failed. They did so because the colonial cause enlisted effective advocates—the proprietors and colonial agents. The proprietors were members of the English upper classes who could command influence. Essentially, they based their appeal on the sanctity of private property, an argument that had effect with conservative members of Parliament. The colonial agents were paid advocates; we would call them lobbyists. Sir Henry Ashurst was a colonial agent who worked effectively against the bills of 1701 and 1706.

In 1710, Jeremiah Dummer became the agent for Massachusetts Bay and two years later he also began to represent Connecticut. Dummer, Boston born, was a Harvard graduate who later earned the degree of Doctor of Philosophy at a European university. He settled in London and made his career in the law. He was instrumental in convincing Elihu Yale to divert a part of his fortune to the support of a colonial college. He wrote *A Defence of the New-England Charters* in 1715,

1. Jeremiah Dummer, *A Defence of the New-England Charters* (London: Almon, 1765).

and it was published in 1721 when it appeared that the attack on the charters might be revived.

For colonial writers, whether they were preachers, poets, or pamphleteers, one does well to begin with Moses C. Tyler, *A History of American Literature, 1607-1765* (Ithaca: Cornell University Press, 1949). The best account of the significance of the colonial charters remains Louise P. Kellogg, *The American Colonial Charter*, which was published in vol. I of the *Annual Report of the American Historical Association* for 1903. Colonial and imperial politics of the eighteenth century are described succinctly in the volume II of Edward Channing, *A History of the United States* (6 vols.; New York: Macmillan, 1905-25). In reading this selection note (1) Dummer's arguments supporting the proposition that the colonies had a right to their charters; (2) how Dummer demonstrated the colonists' rights to the soil; (3) what evidence he presented to back his belief that the American governments were just; (4) what points he established in reply to the contention that the colonists should lose their charters because of violations of the Acts of Trade; (5) his defense against the charge that colonial governments enacted laws contrary to those of the mother country; (6) how he answered the complaint that the colonies might soon declare their independence; (7) what side of the argument he thought economic interest would take; and (8) why he thought forfeiture of the charters an injustice.

1st Proposition, That the Charter Governments have a good and undoubted Right to their respective Charters.

AS TO THE FIRST POINT THERE CAN BE NO DIFFICULTY. The charters were granted by the crown, and the King is acknowledged to be the head and fountain of all corporations and franchises. For tho' my Lord Coke takes notice, That a body politick may be established by prescription, yet such prescription is only valid upon a presumption that there was an ancient grant of the crown, which by the injury of time was afterwards lost. I need not insist upon what no body controverts; but it is material to observe, that the American charters are of a higher nature, and stand on a better foot, than the corporations of England. For these latter were granted upon improvements already made, and therefore were acts of mere grace and favor in the crown; whereas the former were given as

premiums for services to be performed, and therefore to be
considered as grants upon a valuable consideration; which adds
weight and strength to the title.

To increase the nations commerce and enlarge her dominions,
must be allowed a work of no little merit, if we consider the
hardships to which the adventurers were exposed; or the expence
in making their settlements; or lastly, the great advantages
thence accruing to the crown and nation. It would be an endless
task to recount all of the disappointments, and disasters that
befel the first planters in these enterprizes. I shall therefore only
say in general, that after many dangers in their voyages over
the Atlantic, which was not such an easy navigation a hundred
years ago as it is now, they arrived at an inhospitable shore and
a waste wilderness, where there were few of the necessaries,
and not one of the accommodations of life; where the climate
was so extreme, the summer heats so scorching, and the winters
so long and so cold, that the country seemed hardly habitable;
to sum up their misfortunes, they found themselves inevitably
engaged in a war with the natives. So that by fatigue and famine,
by the extremity of the seasons, and by a war with the savages,
the first planters soon found their graves, leaving the young
settlements to be perfected by their survivors.

To omit all this, I shall only be particular in the expence,
which was above 200,000 £ pounds sterling in settling the single
province of the Massachusets-Bay. The account stands thus: The
freight of the passengers cost 95,000 £. The transportation of
their first stock of cattle came to 12,000 £. The provisions laid in
for subsistance, till by tillage more could be raised, cost 45,000 £.
The materials for building their first little cottages came to
18,000 £. Their arms and ammunition cost 192,000 £ not taking
into account the very great sums which were expended in things
of private use, that people could not be without, who were
going to possess an uninhabited land. I must add, that 192
ships were employed in making this great plantation, and twelve
years were spent before it was brought to any tolerable degree
of perfection.

As great, however, as this expence was, I believe it will appear
that the settlement of New-England was not more chargeable to
the adventurers, than it has been in its consequence profitable

to Great-Britain. There is no sort of British manufacture, but what the subjects there demand in a greater or less proportion, as they have ability to pay for it; every thing for the use, convenience, ornament, and (I say it with regret) the luxury and pride of life. Some of the oldest and most experienced traders to those parts have by computation made these exports arise to the value of 300,000 £ per annum. The imports from thence are equally beneficial to the kingdom. They brought home bullion as long as they had any left; and now they are so exhausted they can no longer send it directly, they continue to remit it by way of Spain, Portugal and the Streights: It is there they sell their fish, and the produce of it comes hither in gold and silver, or bills of exchange, which is the same thing.

Other and better returns than money itself they make in masts, the fairest and largest in the whole world, besides pitch, tar, turpentine, rosin, plank, knees for ships, and other species of timber for various uses. These, especially pitch and tar, were formerly purchased of the Swede with crown pieces at intolerable prices; but since the encouragement given their importation from New-England, they have fallen to half the value. It is further to be considered, that what we take of these commodities from our own plantations, is brought home in our own ships, and paid for with our manufactures.

New-England also imports logwood for the dying our woollen goods in quantities sufficient for our own use, and a surplus with which we furnish Holland, Hamburgh, and other markets in Europe. It is wholly owing to the industry of the people of New-England, that this useful commodity is reduced from 30 and 40 £ per ton, which we used to pay for it to the Spaniard, to 12 £ per ton, which is the present price, and out of this there is 4 £ 5s paid to the crown for custom.

Other articles might be mentioned, as whale-oil and fins, which are yearly imported from New-England in no contemptible quantities. They are useful in several manufactures; and if not had from thence must have been purchased of the Dutch with ready money at excessive prices.

'Tis true, New-England makes no sugar, but it assists the islands that do; without which assistance they could not make it, at least not cheap enough, and in sufficient quantities to answer the markets in Europe. For if the sugar islands were obliged to sow for wheat, and plant as much Indian corn as they wanted, they must needs plant the fewer canes, and by consequence make less sugar. From thence they are also supplied with horses for their mills, timber for their sugar works, staves for their casks, and what is more considerable, with barrel pork, mackrel, and refuse cod-fish for their negroes, without which their labour would yield nothing to their owners. For were they to feed their slaves with beef and other provisions from Britain and Ireland, the expence of a plantation would devour the whole produce of it. There are now such quantities of sugar made in the French and Dutch plantations, and so much imported from Brazil by the Portuguese, that our sugar islands need all advantages to make that commodity cheap and in plenty, that we may be able to out-do, or at least equal our neighbors in the foreign market.

It may be added, that New-England is a good nursery of seamen for the navy. I believe I may affirm, that there was hardly a ship, during the last war, in the royal navy, without some of *their* sailors on board, which so distressed the New-England merchants, that they were obliged to man their ships with Indians and Negroes.

What I have said amounts to this: THAT New-England received her charters on this express condition, of settling colonies for the benefit of the crown: THAT she was at a vast expence, and through incredible difficulties accomplished the work even beyond what was ever hoped or expected.

And then the conclusion, that I would draw from these premises is this, THAT to strip the country of their charters after the service has been so successfully performed, is abhorrent from all reason, equity and justice.

But it is urg'd, *That the crown does not take back the soil, though it does the charters;* which indeed is saying very little or nothing. The crown, strictly speaking, neither did nor could grant the soil, having no right in itself. Queen Elizabeth gave out the first patent to Sir Walter Rawleigh in 1584; and if she had any right, what was it and whence derived? It was not a *right of inheritance,* because those countries did not descend to her from her ancestors. Not of *conquest,* because she neither conquered nor attempted to conquer them. Besides it would be pretty hard to conceive how a conquest, where there was no preceding injury or provocation, could create a right. Nor did it arise by *purchase,* there being no money or other valuable consideration paid. Nor could she claim by the *prior discovery or pre-occupancy,* as the Civilians speak, because that gives a right only to *derelict lands,* which these were not, being full of inhabitants, who undoubtedly had as good a title to their own country, as the Europeans have to theirs. And sure nobody will say in plain terms, that we have any claim upon the foot that we were *Christians,* and they *Heathens;* which yet I know some persons of no obscure fame have tacitly suggested. Rome itself, as imperious as she is, never carried her pretences to this height: for though some of her doctors have taught, absurdly enough, that *dominion* is founded in grace, none of them ever said that *property* was. There remains then no other right than what is derived from the native lords of the soil, and that is what the honest New-England planters rely on, having purchased it with their money. The *Indian title* therefore, as it is descryed and undervalued here, seems the only fair and just one; and neither Queen Elizabeth by *her* patents, or King James by *his* afterwards, could give any more than a bare *right of pre-emption.*

And yet admitting that the crown granted the soil, to how little must the value of such grants amount, all circumstances considered? The patentees were not only obliged to travel a thousand leagues beyond sea, but to purchase their grants over again of the natives, before they could be put into possession. The land itself was of a rough savage nature, incumbered with unprofitable woods, and of no use, till by vast labour and expence subdued and cultivated. For to speak the truth, those parts were but *bare creation* to the first planters, and their labour *like the beginning of the world.*

So that which way soever we take it, I think it's plain, if the crown resumes the charters, it will take away the whole it gave, and deprive the patentees of the only recompence they were to have for all their toils and fatigues, which they thought to have conveyed to their posterity. Could they have imagined this, could they have forseen that their privileges were such transitory things, as to last no longer than their work should be done, and their settlements compleated, they had never engaged in so hazardous and difficult an enterprize. They would never have parted from their native land, being neither criminals nor necessitous; and those countries which have since added so much to the wealth and greatness of the crown, might have been a barren wilderness to this day; or what is worse, and more probable, might have been filled with French colonies, whereby France would have reigned sole mistress of North America.

I believe it will be generally allowed, that my argument is thus far right, if I can make good my second proposition.

2d Proposition. That these Governments have by no Misbehavior forfeited their Charters.*

The 2d Charge in the Bill against the Charter Governments, that they have exercised arbitrary Power, answered.

The other charge in the bill is, *that they have exercised arbitrary power.* If this be' aimed at the proprietary governments, which however I don't accuse, I have nothing to say, but I am sure that the charter governments stand clear of it. The thing speaks loudly for itself. For the governments, where there are charters, and those charters entire, all officers civil and military are elected by the people, and that annually; than which consitution nothing under heaven can be a stronger barrier against arbitrary rule. For should it be allowed, that the people, *corrupted* or *deceived,* might instead of wise magistrates chuse tyrants and oppressors to lord over them one year; yet it can't be imagined that after they have felt the smart of it, they will do so the next. Nor can there be a greater obligation on the rulers themselves to administer justice than that their election depends on it the next year. Hence the frequent choice of magistrates has been a main pillar, upon which all who have aimed at freedom in their schemes of government have depended.

---

*Dummer's answer to the "1st Charge against the Charter Governments, that they have neglected the Defence of the Inhabitants," is omitted here. In rebutting the charge, Dummer cited the efforts of the New Englanders during the War of the League of Augsburg and the War of the Spanish Succession. Ed.

As the reason is incontestible, so the fact is apparent, that these governments, far from retrenching the liberty of the subject, have improved it in some important articles, which the circumstances of things in Great-Britain perhaps don't require, or won't easily admit.

To instance in a few: There has been from the beginning an office erected by law in every county, where all conveyances of land are entered at large, after the grantors have first acknowledged them before a justice of the peace; by which means much fraud is prevented, no person being able to sell his estate twice, or take up more money upon it than it is worth. Provision has likewise been made for the security of the life and property of the subject in the matter of juries, who are not returned by the sheriff of the county, but are chosen by the inhabitants of the town a convenient time before the sitting of the courts. And this election is under the most exact regulation, in order to prevent corruption, so far as human prudence can do it. . . .

Redress in their courts of law is easy, quick and cheap. All processes are in English, and no special pleadings or demurrers are admitted, but the general issue is always given, and special matters brought in evidence; which saves time and expence; and in this case a man is not liable to lose his estate for a defect in form, nor is the merit of the cause made to depend on the niceties of clerkship . . . I can't but think that every body, except gentlemen of the long robe, and the attornies, will think this a wholesome law and well calculated for the benefit of the subject. . . .

Nor are the people of New-England oppressed with the infinite delays and expence which attend the proceedings in Chancery, where both parties are often ruined by the charge and length of the suit. But as in all other countries, England only excepted, justice and equity are held the same, and never divided; so it is there: a power of Chancery being vested in the judges of the courts of common law as to some particular cases, and they make equitable constructions in others. I must add, that the fees of officers of all sorts, are settled by acts of assembly at moderate prices, for the ease of the subject.

It were easy to mention other articles, but that I persuade

myself it is needless. The charter governments are celebrated for their excellent laws; and mild administration; for the security of liberty and property; for the encouragement of virtue and suppression of vice; for the promoting letters, by erecting free-schools and colleges; and, in a word, for every thing that can make a people happy and prosperous. To these arts it is owing, that New-England, though she has attained but little more than the age of a man, with all the disadvantages under which she labors in respect to her trade and climate, and almost a perpetual Indian war, has hitherto flourished far above any other of the plantations.

This being the case of the charter governments, let us turn the tables, and see how it fared with them when in an *evil reign* they lost their charters. Then the governor of New-England, with four or five strangers of his council, men of desperate fortunes, and bad principles, made what laws, and levied what taxes they pleased on the people. They, without an assembly, raised a penny in the pound on all the estates in the country, and another penny on all imported goods, besides twenty pence per head as poll money, and an immoderate excise on wine, rum, and other liquors. Several worthy persons having, in an humble address represented this proceeding as a grievance, were committed to the common gaol for a high misdemeanor; denied the benefit of the habeas corpus act; tried out of their own county; fined exorbitantly, and obliged to pay 160 £ for fees, when the prosecution would hardly have cost them so many shillings in Great-Britain. And to compleat the oppression, when they, upon their trial claimed the privileges of Englishmen, they were scoffingly told, *those things would not follow them to the ends of the earth.* Unnatural insult; must the brave adventurer, who with the hazard of his life and fortune, seeks out new climates to enrich his mother country, be denied those common rights, which his countrymen enjoy at home in ease and indolence? Is he to be made miserable, and a slave to his own acquisitions? Is the labourer alone unworthy of his hire, and shall they *only* reap, who have neither sowed nor planted? Monstrous absurdity! Horrid inverted order!

These proceedings, however arbitrary and oppressive, were but the prelude: the catastrophe was, if possible, yet more dismal. Having invaded their liberties, by an easy transition the next attack was directly on their properties. Their title to their lands was absolutely denied by the governor and his creatures, upon two pretences: one that their conveyances were not according to the law of England; the other, that if they might be thought to have had something like a title formerly, yet it now ceased by the revocation of their charters. So that they who had fairly purchased their lands, and held them in quiet possession for above fifty years, were now obliged to accept new deeds from the governor, and pay for them a third part of their value, in order to ascertain their titles, or otherwise they would be seized by the crown.

It would be an injury to virtue, if I did not in this place pay distinguished honor to the memory of an honest and worthy patriot, Col. Shrimpton, long since deceased, who being rich in lands, was courted to receive his new patents *gratis*, that others might be drawn in by the authority of his example; but when he was apprized of their design, he chose rather to have his lands seized (and they were seized) than by such a base compliance betray his countrymen into the snares prepared for them. I should not have thus far entered into the detail of things so long past, but to show from experience, as well as from the reason and nature of the thing, that charters are not the *causes* of arbitrary government, but indeed *strong works* raised against it, which once thrown down, oppression rushes in like a tide, and bears down every thing before it.

Having thus answered the allegations of the bill, in a manner which I hope may be satisfactory, I am next to consider such arguments as I have met with in conversation from persons in the ministry and others.

The Third Objection, that the Acts of Trade are disregarded, answered.

What I have heard most insisted on is *That the Act of Trade and Navigation, made on purpose to render the plantations beneficial to Great-Britain, are disregarded in the charter governments; and that this evil cannot be effectually cured, but by a resumption of the charters.* . . .

The complaints on this head are for the most part of an old date, and when the bill against the charters was depending in the house of Commons, were produced from the files of the Plantation Board, whither they had been transmitted in former reigns, when customhouse officers in the plantations were such great rarities, that One collector served Four entire provinces. And can it be thought strange that merchants, whose business is gain, should have sometimes for lucre transgressed the acts of trade, when there were no officers to see them duly observed? The case is vastly different now. Officers of the revenue are multiplied, and are extremely rigorous, so that instead of *their* complaints of unfair traders, the merchants on the other hand, greatly complain of the oppression of the officers. I have seen an account of such intolerable hardships imposed on fair well-meaning traders, under colour of law, that one would hardly give credit to the least of the articles, if the whole had not been delivered publickly in an assembly of one of the provinces by a worthy member, and afterwards printed with his name to it. The author I refer to, after a recital of several facts, in which he is very full as to every circumstance, draws up this melancholy conclusion, That the customhouse officers had, by their violent practices, either seized or driven away all the vessels belonging to that part of the country, so that they had no sloops left to carry their produce to markets in the adjacent colonies . . .

If it were true, that some persons did now and then concern themselves in an illegal trade, can it be thought just or reasonable that the whole community should suffer by their private fault? No body will say that the acts of trade are perfectly observed in the provinces immediately under the crown, or in Great-Britain itself. I believe there is no corporation in the kingdom, being a sea port, wherein there are not at some time or other contraband goods imported, or other goods clandestinely run, to the prejudice of the King's duties. In this port of London great abuses are daily committed in spight of the utmost vigilance to prevent them. The fraud of relanding callicoes after a pretended exportation, only to receive the drawback, is a most flagrant instance, if one either considers the perjuries that attend it, or the immense sums that are thereby robbed from the publick, or the vast injuries that are done by it to the honest linen-draper. And yet, who-ever used this, or any other cheat of the like kind, as an argument to disfranchise this ancient corporation? The rule of law is, *Noxa Caput sequiter* [Let the guilty party suffer]; and it is agreeable to natural justice, that every man should suffer for his own transgression. On the other part, if a corporate body were to forfeit their privileges for every private person's offence, they would be of no value. A charter so limited could not stand a week, nor would be worth the expence of the great-seal. . . .

All the officers of the revenue are *in the present state of things* appointed by the crown; all breaches of the acts of trade, saving a single one excepted by act of parliament, are cognizable only in the court of admiralty, where the judge and every inferior officer are created either by commissions under the broad seal, or by warrants from the Lord high admiral. The laws of the country are not pleaded in that court, but acts of parliament, and where they are silent, the civil and maritime laws take place. The forms of proceedings, were *they* of any consequence, are regulated after the manner practised in Doctors Commons. If then his Majesty should resume the charters, nothing more could be done to preserve the acts of trade than is at present, and therefore how plausible soever this pretext may appear at first sight, it is plain, upon a nearer view that there is no weight in it.

I am apprized that the judge of the vice-admiralty in New-England has often complained home of the frequent prohibitions served on him from the courts of judicature there, which he says, *Weaken and in a manner suppress the authority of that court, and all the good ends for which it was constituted.* But neither does this matter in the least relate to the charters, tho' there were reason for the complaint, as on the other hand, I shall immediately show there is none. The right of the courts of Massachusetts, to restrain the excesses of the admiralty jurisdiction, are not derived from their charter, but from subsequent laws of the province, confirmed afterwards by the crown; which power therefore, whether the charters stand or fall, will remain unhurt, and still the same. But the manner of this complaint is wholly groundless, which I must particularly show, because a handle has been taken from it to hurt New-England in its charters. I therefore take leave to say, That the superior court of judicature for the province of Massachuset's Bay has a legal power to issue prohibitions to the court of vice-admiralty: that it is very fitting and necessary such a power should be lodged in that court: and, lastly, that the particular cases where-in the judges of that superior court have hitherto exercised this power, were apparently without and beyond the admiralty jurisdiction.

To begin with the power itself: 'Tis founded on an act of assembly passed in the 11th year of King William, and by him confirmed, entitled, *An act for establishing a superior court of judicature, court of assizes and general gaol delivery.* The act after a recital of several powers vested in the court, has this general clause: *And the said court is hereby vested with the same power as fully and amply to all intents and purposes whatsoever as the courts of* King's bench a power to restrain the court of *admiralty* in England, this court of judicature must have the same in New-England.

The reasons for such a restraining power are as strong in New-England as in Great-Britain. It has been ever boasted as the peculiar privilege of an Englishman, and the grand security of his property, to be tried by his country and the laws of the land; whereas this admiralty method of trial deprives him of both, as it puts his estate in the disposal of a single person, and makes the civil law the rule of judgment; which though it may not perhaps properly be called foreign, being the law of nations, yet 'tis what he has not consented to himself, or his representative for him. A jurisdiction therefore so founded ought not to extend beyond what necessity requires, that is, to nothing but what is transacted on the high seas, which not being *infra corpus comitatus* [within the body of the county], is not triable at common law. If some bounds are not set to the jurisdiction of the admiralty, beyond which it shall not pass, it may in time, like the element to which it ought to be confined, grow outrageous and overflow the banks of all other courts of justice. This danger is still greater in the plantations, where neither the judge nor any of the inferior officers of the admiralty have salaries, or perhaps other dependance, than upon what they get by their fees, and therefore must be strongly tempted to receive all business that comes before them, however improper for their cognizance.

In vain do the advocates for the admiralty urge on this occasion, that an appeal lies home, and therefore, if a cause tried there be found to be *coram non judice* [not within their jurisdiction], justice will be done to the injured party on the appeal. For if this argument has any force, it would take place in England, because an appeal lies here from the sentences of the admiralty to the court of delegates, and yet that is not thought a sufficient reason to prevent the court of King's-Bench from granting prohibitions when they think them necessary. Besides it is to be remarked, that the appeal does not lie to the King and council as it does from other courts, but to the judge of admiralty, and therefore one may imagine that the appellant will have but a *cold cause* of it; for I believe it has been rarely found that any court was forward to limit its own power. . . .

Another thing alleged against the American charters is, *That their governments have made laws repugnant to the laws of Great Britain, contrary to the powers given them, and thereby have incurred a forfeiture of the charters.* . . . I believe it will be easily allowed, that a law may be *various* from the laws of England, and yet not repugnant to them; or otherwise these governments must make no laws at all, which no body will say, who knows that a right of legislature, is the most essential part of the charters, and what indeed the reason and nature of the thing make absolutely necessary. Every country has circumstances peculiar to it self in respect of its soil, situation, inhabitants, and commerce, to all which, convenient laws must, with the nicest care and judgment, be adapted; whereas the laws of England are calculated for their own meridian, and are many of them no ways suitable to the plantations, and others not possible to be executed there. . . .

I answer the question in direct terms, That *then a law in the plantations may be said to be repugnant to a law made in* Great-Britain, *when it flatly contradicts it, so far as the law here mentions and relates to the plantations* . . .[But] the patentees shall not, under colour of their particular charters, presume to make any laws inconsistent with the great charter and other laws of England, by which the lives, liberties and properties of Englishmen are secured. It seems reasonable to think that the crown might intend by this injunction to provide for all its subjects, that they might not be oppressed by arbitrary power; but in whatever distant part of the world they were settled, being still subjects, they should have the usage of Englishmen, be protected by the same mild laws, and enjoy the same happy government, as if they continued within the realm. . . .

There is one thing more I have heard often urged against the charter colonies, and indeed 'tis what one meets with from people of all conditions and qualities, though, with due respect to their better judgments, I can see neither reason nor colour for it. 'Tis said, *that their increasing numbers and wealth, joined to their great distance from* Great Britain, *will give them an opportunity, in the course of some years, to throw off their dependance on the nation, and declare themselves a free state, if not curbed in time, by being made entirely subject to the crown.* Whereas in truth there is no body, though but little acquainted with these, or any of the northern plantations, who does not know and confess, that their poverty and the declining state of their trade is so great at present, that there is far more danger of their sinking, without some extraordinary support from the crown, than of their ever revolting from it. So that I may say without being ludicrous, that it would not be more absurd to place two of his Majesty's beef-eaters to watch an infant in the cradle that it don't rise to cut its father's throat, than to guard these weak infant colonies to prevent their shaking off the British yoke. Besides, they are so distinct in their forms of government, in their religious rites, in their emulation of trade, and consequently in their affections, that they never can be supposed to unite in so dangerous an enterprize. It is for this reason I have often wondered to hear some great men profess their belief of the feasibleness of it, and the probability of its some time or other actually coming to pass, who yet with the same breath advise that all the governments on the continent be formed into one, by being brought under one vice-roy, and into one assembly. For surely if we in earnest believed that there was, or would be hereafter, a disposition in the provinces to rebel and declare themselves independent, it would be good policy to keep them disunited; because if it were possible they should contrive so wild and rash an undertaking, yet they would not be hardy enough to put it in execution, unless they could first strengthen themselves by a confederacy of all the parts. . . .

Another proposition I advanced was, That if these governments should be adjudged to have forfeited their charters back to the crown, yet it is not the true interest of the crown to resume them.

It is generally received opinion, that the people in the plantations have an interest distinct from that of the crown, when it is supposed, at the same time, that the interest of the governors, they being the King's representatives, are one with the crown; and from these premises it is concluded, that there cannot be too much power given to the governors, or too little to the people. Whereas, with humble submission, I conceive this to be a very wrong judgment, and that the reverse of it is true. The only interest of the people is to thrive and flourish in their trade, which is the true interest of the crown and nation, because they reap the profit of it. When, on the other hand, the view that governors generally have is private gain, which being too often acquired by discouraging and oppressing trade, is not only an interest distinct from that of the crown, but extremely prejudicial to it. The trade of a young plantation is like a tender plant, and should be cherished with the fondest care; but if, instead of that, it meets with the rough hand of oppression, it will soon die. The proper nursery for this plant is a free government, where the laws are sacred, property secure, and justice not only impartially but expeditiously distributed. For to what purpose shall the merchant expose his estate to the danger of the sea, the enemy, and many more accidents, if after all he can't save it at home from rapine and violence?

As this is evident, so is it that whatever injures the trade of the plantations, must in proportion affect Great-Britain, the source and center of their commerce; from whence they have their manufactures, whither they make their returns, and where all their superlucration is lodged. The blow then may strike the colonies first, but it comes home at last, and falls heaviest on ourselves.

[It is not strange that] corruptions must happen, when one considers that few gentlemen will cross the seas for a government, whose circumstances are not a little strait at home, and that they know by how slight and uncertain tenure they hold their commissions; from whence they wisely conclude, that no time is to be lost. . . .

To enlarge then the powers of governors, is to give them greater power to oppress; and to vacate the charters, is to enlarge their power, the government in that case devolving upon them; as we see in those plantations which never had any charters, but are immediately dependent on the crown. They have, in a manner, intire legislative and executive powers, or at least so great an influence on the constituent parts of the former, as leaves them little more than nominal sharers, serving rather as screens to the governor than a defence to the people. The militia is absolutely vested in the governors, which influences all elections of representatives: they appoint judges, justices, sheriffs, and other civil officers, with the consent, it's said indeed, of the council; but that such consent voluntary or involuntary will ever be refused, seems too much to be expected, if we consider that although the governors do not indeed appoint the council, yet they recommend proper persons to the King; and it may be supposed, that a gentleman who is intrusted with the chief command of a province, and is actually on the spot, will be thought the best judge who are fit to serve, and therefore his recommendation will almost always prevail. Besides, if there be a turn to serve, or any emergency real or imaginary, and any of the members should be so refractory as not to give in to his measures with an implicit faith, the governor can suspend as many of them as he pleases; and when he has reduced the board under a number limited in his instructions, he can then fill it up to that number *instanter* with whom he pleases; and who will they be, may we presume, but such as are passively obedient to his will? And too many such there are in all colonies so constituted, who are content to be *saddled* themselves, provided they may *ride* others under the *chief rider.* I must farther observe, that where there are no charters, there are courts of equity established, in which the governor is always chancellor, and for the most part chief justice, and ordinary at the same time; which puts the estates, lives and liberties of the inhabitants, saving the liberty of appeal home, intirely in his disposal; and even an appeal, in all cases under a considerable sum, in all cases of the ordinary jurisdiction, and in all cases capital, is either disallowed by his instructions, or wholly in the governor's breast to allow or not.

The sum of my argument is, that the benefit which Great-Britain receives from the plantations, arises from their commerce: that oppression is the most opposite thing in the world to commerce, and the most destructive enemy it can have: that governors have in all times, and in all countries, been too much inclined to oppress: and consequently it cannot be the interest of the nation to increase their power, and lessen the liberties of the people. I am so sanguine in this opinion, that I really think it would be for the service of the crown and nation, to incorporate those governments which have no charters, rather than disfranchize those that have.

The 4th Proposition, That it seems inconsistent with justice to disfranchize the charter colonies by an act of parliament.

The last thing I proposed to consider, was, how far it may be consistent with justice, to deprive the colonies of the charters, without giving them a fair trial or any previous notice.

It is certain, that bills of attainder, such as this would be, have been seldom used in England, and then only upon the most extraordinary occasions: as when flagrant crimes have been committed, of a new and unusual nature, against which the law had made no provision; or when the witnesses have avoided, and perhaps by the contrivance of the party; or lastly, which is the most common case, when the attainted person having himself absconded, and fled from justice, has thereby made such an extrajudicial proceeding justifiable. It is also certain that neither of these things can be pleaded in the present case, which I need not be particular in shewing, because not suggested, nor is there the least colour for such suggestion. And yet I pretend to know the people in the charter governments so well, and to be so thoroughly acquainted with their meek principles of obedience, that I dare affirm, if such an act should pass, however rigorous and severe they might think it within themselves, they would not let fall an indecent word of their superiors, but would receive the news with the lowest submission: so great is their loyalty to the King, and so profound their regard for the resolutions of a British parliament, the wisest and most august assembly in the world. However, seeing there is no such act already passed, and it is to be hoped from the honor and justice of parliaments, never will, it can't be thought a crime modestly to state the hardship of the case. I don't mean with respect to the merits of it, which have been already considered, but as to the *manner of proceeding by bill in parliament*. It is a most sacred and unalterable rule of justice, and has ever been so esteemed by all the civilized nations of the world, that no person be deprived of life, liberty or estate, till he has had time and opportunity to make his defence. And if the matter in judgment, be of great value, dearly paid for, and long enjoyed, it adds much to the weight of the argument, and aggravates the injury, in depriving the possessors unheard. Now this is the case of the charter governments. How great the purchase consideration was has been before said; but how valuable the charters themselves are, can never be said, liberty being inestimable. And for the time they have enjoyed them, were they not on record, it would be what the civilians call *immemorial*, one of them being above four-score years standing.

It seems therefore a severity without a precedent, that a people who have the misfortune of being a thousand leagues from their Sovereign, a misfortune great enough in itself, should UNSUMMONED, UNHEARD, IN ONE DAY be deprived of all their valuable privileges, which they have enjoyed for near an hundred years. It's true, the legislative power is absolute and unaccountable, and King, Lords and Commons may do what they please; but the question here is not about *power*, but *right*: *and shall not the supreme legislature of all the nation do right?* One may say, that what the parliament can't do justly, they can't do at all. *In maximis minima est licentia.* The higher the power is, the greater caution is to be used in the execution of it, because the sufferer is helpless, and without resort.

When in an arbitrary reign, the charter of New-England was vacated, a *quo warranto* first gave the colony notice to prepare for their trial. Although this was a prosecution at law, and the high court of parliament is not strictly confined to the forms of the courts below, yet it is not doubted but the great fountain of law and justice will have some regard, if not to all the rules made for inferior judicatures, yet to such as are essential to justice. And so in other cases it has. For the purpose: if a bill be brought into the house of Commons that touches any man's property in Ireland, it must lie 30 days, that the party may have notice, and not suffer unheard. Why then should not a reasonable time be allowed to the subjects in America, in proportion to their more distant situation; seeing they are no less subjects of the crown, than the inhabitants of Ireland; and liberty is at least as valuable a property; and surely the concern of whole provinces challenges as much regard as the interest of a single person. If it should be said, as I confess a great minister once said to me, That *the regulation of charters must be looked on as part of the public economy, and not the affair of any particular person or province*; I humbly apprehend, with the utmost deference to ᵗhat great person, that his does not reach the present case. It is indeed very reasonable, that all publick affairs be subject to the determination of the publick wisdom, and there is no occasion to notify anybody, because every body is supposed to be present in the representative body of the whole; but here the provinces to be censured and deprived, have no representative in parliament, and consequently must be considered as absent persons, suffering unheard.

I know of but one thing more that can be said to palliate a proceeding against the charters in this way, which is, *That the provinces always have their respective agents at court, who may be heard by petition before the bill passes into an act.* To which I answer, first, that sometimes they have agents here, and at other times they have not. Next, that a bill may pass into an act without the knowledge of the agents, they having no citation. This had once like to have been the case, when a bill of this nature was formerly brought into the house of Commons, and certainly had proved so, if the agent for New-England had at that nice juncture been indisposed in his health, or but a day's journey out of town, or if he had not been more than ordinary active and diligent when he was in town. And lastly, I must observe that agents are only instructed in things that fall within the ordinary course of business, and when any thing of a new and extraordinary nature is brought on the carpet, they have a general instruction to pray for time, in order to notify their principals, and receive their special commands. Besides, it is well known, that the right hon. the Lords Commissioners for Trade and Plantations were, at the time before mentioned, prepared to urge many complaints both new and old; to which facts it had been impossible for any agent to answer *ore tenus,* without being ever apprized of them. To conclude, what *these governments* desire of their superiors at home is, that they may not be judged and condemned unheard. And I cannot but flatter myself they will obtain it, whether I consider the reasonableness of the demand itself, or the celebrated justice and lenity of his Majesty's government, or the importance of the thing in question to the provinces concerned. I mention this last particular, being sure they would reckon the loss of their privileges a greater calamity than if their houses were all in flames at once. Nor can they be justly blamed, the one being a reparable evil, but the other irreparable. Burnt houses may rise again out of their ashes, and even more beautiful than before, but 'tis to be feared that liberty *once lost, is lost for ever.*

13

Cotton Mather

Manuductio ad Ministerium (1726)[1]

Cotton Mather (1663-1728) was acutely aware of his inheritance, the great tradition of moral and intellectual leadership of the Massachusetts ministers. The son bf Increase (1639-1723), he entered Harvard at the age of twelve and earned his baccalaureate degree in his sixteenth year. His intellectual capacity and performance are astounding. He mastered Hebrew, Greek, and Latin, and knew French and Spanish as well. He was a prodigious writer who produced more than four hundred titles, the most famous of which are *The Wonders of the Invisible World*, which deals with the witchcraft hysteria, and *Magnalia Christi Americana*, a history of early New England. Despite, or perhaps because of, his tremendous gifts, he was arrogant, overzealous and conceited.

His career put him at the center of Massachusetts life. He shared the pulpit of the Second Church at Boston with his father. He was a fellow of Harvard College and became embittered when the presidency was denied him. In politics, he stood as a firm advocate of local autonomy and acted as a leader of the resistance to Governor Andros. He involved himself in the witchcraft mess. He advocated the practice of inoculation for smallpox, and his interest in science won him election to the Royal Society.

That Mather was a man within whom there were deep inner contradictions is apparent. A man of intense intelligence, he lived at a time when society was poised on the point of great change. In him the forces of fundamentalism and enlightenment, which would agitate and instruct the eighteenth century, were united. The pamphlet *Manuductio ad Ministerium* announces Mather's ideal of an educated man and demonstrates the wide sweep of his learning.

---

1. Cotton Mather, *Manuductio ad Ministerium or Directions for a Candidate of the Ministry* (New York: Columbia University Press for the Facsimile Text Society, 1938).

The best biography of Mather is Barrett Wendell, *Cotton Mather, The Puritan Priest* (Dodd, Mead & Co.; New York, 1891, reprinted 1926). See also Otho T. Beall and Richard H. Shyrock, *Cotton Mather, First Significant Figure in American Medicine* (Baltimore: Johns Hopkins Press, 1954). The changing pattern of Puritanism is the theme of Perry Miller, *The New England Mind: From Colony to Province* (Cambridge: Harvard University Press, 1953). Concerning Mather and all other colonial writers, the best book is Moses C. Tyler, *A History of American Literature* (New York: G. P. Putnam's Sons, 1878, reprinted Ithaca: Cornell University Press, 1949). In reading this selection note (1) Mather's first and basic admonition and what kind of attitude toward life it was calculated to inspire; (2) what role he assigned to foreign languages; (3) what suggestions he made to improve the quality of one's writing; (4) his judgment of the subjects of logic, metaphysics, and ethics; (5) what advice he gave concerning the cultivation of poetry; (6) what he advised respecting style in writing; (7) how one should approach the study of natural philosophy; (8) his opinion of Aristotle's worth; (9) what basic lesson he thought one should learn from natural philosophy; (10) what advice he gave respecting mathematics, astronomy, astrology, and geography; (11) what purpose he saw in the study of history and what warnings he voiced to the reader of history; and (12) evidences of Mather's erudition.

#**1** INTENDING TO GIVE YOU SOME DIRECTIONS for your Proceeding in the STUDIES, upon which you are Entring, that you may be prepared and furnished for the Work of the Evangelical MINISTRY, to which you are designed; I shall not consult the Method which any of the twice Twelve, *Dissertationes de Studius,* (Collected by *Elzivir* in one little Volumn) have given you. But the Contemplation of DEATH shall be the FIRST Point of the *Wisdom* that my Advice must lead you to. In the FIRST Place, *My Son,* I advise you to consider yourself as a *Dying Person,* and one that must *shortly put off this Earthly Tabernacle.* I move you, I press you, To *Remember how short your Time is,* yea, though it should reach to the *longest* that is ordinarily known among the Children of Men; and how much more *short* it may be made for ought you know, in the *Early Anticipations* of Mortality. Do this, that you may do nothing like *Living in Vain.* Place yourself in the

Circumstances of a *Dying Person;* your *Breath* failing, your *Throat* rattling, your *Eyes* with a dim Cloud, and your *Hands* with a damp Sweat upon them, and your Weeping Friends no longer able to retain you with them: And *then* entertain such Sentiments of *this World,* and of the *Work* to be done in this World, that such a *View* must needs inspire you withal. Such a *Numbring of your Days,* I hope, will compel you to *Apply your Hearts unto Wisdom.* . . .

#7 The *Languages* you will consider, but as *Instruments* to come at the *Sciences,* wherewith you would propose to go *Skilfully* about the Work which your GOD shall call you to. And esteeming them as rather *Helps to Erudition* than any *Parts* of it, you will no more Value yourself as a *Scholar* for *Them,* than the Bare having of *Tools* would make one to boast himself an *Artist.*

If you would make a short Work of all the *Sciences,* and find out a *North-West Passage* to them, I cannot think of any One Author, that would answer every Intention so well as ALSTED. I take him, to have been as learned a Man as ever was in the World; and there being so little Use made of his *Concise Exhibitions,* is to me, One of the Things that I can't but wonder at, and scarce know what to make of.

Instead of Squandering away your Time, on the RHETORIC, whereof no doubt, you tho't your *Dugard* gave you enough at School; and upon all the *Tropes* and *Schemes* whereof a just Censurer well observes, *Possunt una atq; altera Hora ita novari, ut eorum Notitia per omnen Aetatem sufficiat* [that in an hour here and there, can be so refreshed that the knowledge suffices for a lifetime]; And the very Profession whereof usually is little more than to furnish out a *Stage-Player;* My advice to you, is That you observe the Flowres and Airs of such *Writings,* as are most in Reputation for their *Elegancy.* Yet I am willing that you should attentively Read over *Smith,* his *Mystery of Rhetoric Unveiled,* that you may not be Ignorant of what *Figures* they pretend unto.

But I will take this Opportunity to tell you, That there is no where to be found any such *Rhetoric,* as there is in our *Sacred Scriptures.* Even a Pagan *Longinus* himself, will confess,

The *Sublime,* shining in them. There can be nothing so *Beauti-ful,* or so *Affectuous* as the *Figures* every where used in them. They are *Life.* All meer *Humane Flourishes* are but *Chaff* to the *Wheat* that is there. Yea, they are an *Hammer that breaks the Rocks to Pieces.* In them the *GOD of Glory Thunders,* yea does it very *marvellously!* There is in them that *Voice of the Lord* which is *full of Majesty.* For the *Pulpit Oratory,* which is what you have in View, there can be nothing more adviseable, than to be a Master of *Scripture-Phrases,* and employ them with an agreeable Ingenuity, on all fit Occasions. I will add, I know not but a *Lamy,* in his *L'Art de Parler,* may give you some hints that may be not unuseful to you.

Nor can I encourage you to spend very much Time, in that which goes under the Name of LOGIC. If my excellent Friend *Langius,* in his Noble *Medicina Mentis,* [which I commend unto you, to be diligently perused, as an *Introduction* to all your Studies of the *Sciences,*] had not compelled me to a Contempt of the *Vulgar Logic,* learnt in our Colleges, as a sort of meer *Morology,* yet a little serious Recollection would have brought me to it. What is there usually got by the *Vulgar Logic,* but only to be furnished with a Parcel of *Terms,* which instead of leading the Mind into the *Truth,* enables one rather to carry on *Alterca-tions,* and *Logomachies,* by which the Force of *Truth* may be at Pleasure, and by some little *Trick,* evaded. The Power and Process of *Reason* is *Natural* to the Soul of Man; And those *Masters of Reason,* who argue the most *Rationally,* and make the most *Rational Researches* into the true State of Things, and who take the most *Reasonable Measures* for their Conduct, and who in all things arrive to the most notable Discoveries, I pray, what sort of *Logicians* are they? Either they never once read a Page of any Burgesdicius, or else they have unlearnt and forgot all their *Vulgar Logic.* I am sure, they rarely trouble their Heads to recall the *Old Rules* which they have recited unto their Tutors. To exhibit in the pompous Form of an *Art,* what every One does by meer *Nature* and *Custom,* and fabricate it into such a shape as that of the *Vulgar Logic,* and with such trifling Applications and Illustrations, as 'tis usually done, appears as impertinent, as if one should with much Formality teach the *Art* of *Eating* or *Drinking* or *Walking.* And it might with equal Solemnity be

shown, what Points or *Regular Management* are exemplified by
the Boys playing at their Marbles. The most Valuable Thing in
Logic, and the very Termination of it, is, *The Doctrine of
Syllogisms.* And yet it is notorious, that as all *Syllogizing,* is only
to confirm you in a *Truth* which you are already the Owner of,
so, no *Logic* has yet given us all the several Ways of *Syllogizing*
that may be run into; And it is as notorious, that while an
expanded *Syllogizing* is reckoned no other than an Indecency in
ordinary *Writing* as well as *Talking,* our only *Syllogizing* is that
which we call, *An Enthymeme*: Such a thing is evident. *Notwithstanding, lest we should offend them,* go dip into your
Logic. But count it enough, if you have gone through a *Milton,*
or a *Gutherleth,* or a *Watts.* Indeed, some Treatises, that clear
up the *Maxims of Reason,* and may Strengthen you and Sharpen
you in the Use of it, you may do well to look into. The *Ars
Cogitandi,* [The Art of Thinking], may pass for One of those:
And tho' for some Reasons, I would be excused from Recom-
mending an *Essay of Humane Understanding,* which is much in
Vogue, yet I can approve of your perusing *Oldfield,* his *Improvement of Reason.* But for the *Vulgar Logic,* I must freely say,
you lose Time, if you steer any otherwise in it, than, *Touch
and Go.*

What I say of *Logic,* I say of *Metaphysicks*; which a learned
Man too justly calls, *Disciplinarum Omnium Excrementum* [the
excrement of all the disciplines], tho' she would set up for the
Queen of Sciences. If you have got a *Maccovius* or a *Jacchaeus*
into your Head, you have as much as I should care for: To
which indeed some Acquaintance with a *Castanaeus,* or some
such *Fencer* for *Distinctions,* may be added. But then to weave
any more *Cobwebs* in your Brains; to what Purpose is it? This
however, is one of the *Things,* which I will *Affirm constantly;*
That as a *Suarez,* than whom you cannot easily find a greater
dealer in *Metaphysicks,* after all declared, The *Hours* which he
took in Studying and Examing and Rectifying his *own Heart,*
were of infinitely more Use and Worth to him than all his
Metaphysical and Imaginary Disquisitions.

As for ETHICS, tho' such Things as the, *Ethica Christiana* of
a *Daneus,* be among the *Things which cannot be spoken against,*
yet *That* whereon they employ the Plough so long in many

Academies, I will venture to say, 'tis a *Vile Thing*; and no other
than what honest *Vockerodus* has justly called it; *Impietas in
Artis forman redacta.* [impiety reduced to the shape of art].
It is all over a *Sham*; It presents you with a *Mock-Happiness*; It
prescribes to you *Mock Vertues* for the coming at it: And it
pretends to give you a Religion without a CHRIST, and a *Life*
of PIETY without a Living Principle; a Good Life with no other
than *Dead Works* filling of it. It is not amiss for you, to know
what this Paganism is: and therefore you may, if you please,
bestow a short Reading upon a *Galius,* or a *More*: But be more
of a *Christian,* than to look on the *Enchiridion* of the Author
last mentioned, as, *Next the Bible, the best Book in the World.*
Study no other *Ethics,* but what is in the *Bible*; and consult such
Books, as the, *Verus Christianismus* of an *Arndt,* whereby Hundreds of Thousands have been bro't into the Life of GOD.

So much Ethics as treats, *De Decoro,* and may instruct you in
the, *Rules of Behaviour,* I heartily commend unto you. And yet,
even *these* are best learnt by a Wise Observation of what you
see passes in the Conversation of Politer People: And by wisely
considering how they are indeed all Embryo'd in that one Word,
MODESTY; which Renders every one his Due, and assumes
nothing *undue* to ones self: Or, comprized in that one Maxim,
Do and Say nothing that may be justly offensive to the Company.
The Truth is; The most exact and constant *Rules of Behaviour,*
will be found *Rules of Christianity*: For which Cause it pleased
our Glorious Redeemer more than once to give them. Every
Christian as far as he keeps to his own *Rules* will be so far a
Gentleman. And for this Cause, I again advise you to a Careful
Study of them.

#8 POETRY, whereof we have now even an *Antediluvian Piece*
in our Hands, has from the Beginning been in such Request, that
I must needs recommend unto you some Acquaintance with it.
Though some have had a Soul so *Unmusical,* that they have
decried all *Verse,* as being but a meer *Playing* and *Fiddling*
upon *Words*; All *Versifying,* as if it were more *Unnatural* than
if we should chuse *Dancing* instead of *Walking*; and *Ryme,* as
if it were but a sort of *Morisco Dancing* with *Bells*: Yet I cannot
wish you a Soul that shall be wholly *Unpoetical.* An old *Horace*

has left us an *Art of Poetry,* which you may do well to bestow
a Perusal on. And besides your *Lyrick Hours,* I wish you may
so far understand an *Epic Poem,* that the Beauties of an *Homer*
and a *Virgil* may be discerned with you. As to the *Moral* Part
of *Homer,* 'tis true, and let me not be counted a *Zoilus* for saying
so, that by first exhibiting their *Gods* as no better than *Rogues,*
he set open the Floodgates for a prodigious Inundation of
Wickedness to break in upon the Nations, and was one of the
greatest Apostles the *Devil* ever had in the World. Among the
rest that felt the Ill Impressions of this *Universal Corrupter,* (as
Men of the best Sentiments have called him,) One was that
overgrown Robber, of execrable Memory, whom we celebrate
under the *Name of Alexander the Great;* who by his continual
Admiring and Studying of his *Iliad* and by following that false
Model of Heroic Virtue set before him in his *Achilles,* became
one of the worst of Men, and at length inflated with the Ridiculous Pride of being himself a *Deity,* exposed himself to all the
Scorn that could belong unto a *Lunatick.* And hence, notwithstanding the Veneration which this Idol has had, yet *Plato*
banishes him out of a *Common-Wealth,* the Welfare whereof he
was concerned for. Nevertheless, *Custom* or *Conscience* obliges
him to bear Testimonies unto many Points of *Morality.* And it is
especially observable, That he commonly propounds *Prayer* to
Heaven as a most necessary Preface unto all Important Enterprizes; and when the Action comes on too suddenly for a more
extended *Supplication,* he yet will not let it come on without an
Ejaculation; and he never speaks of any *Supplication* but he
brings in a Gracious Answer to it. I have seen a Travesteering
High-Flyer, not much to our Dishonour, Scoff at *Homer* for
this; as making his Actors to be like those whom the English
call *Dissenters.* But then, we are so much led into the Knowledge
of *Antiquities,* by reading of this *Poet,* and into so many Parts
of *Recondite Learning,* that notwithstanding some little *Nods*
in him, not a few Acute Pens besides the old Bishop of *Thessa-
lonica's,* have got a Reputation by regaling us with *Annotations*
upon him. Yea, Tho' One can't but smile at the Fancy of *Croese,*
who tries with much Ostentation of Erudition, to show, That
Homer has all along tendred us in a Disguise and Fable, the
History of the Old Testament, yet many Illustrations of the

sacred Scriptures, I find are to be fetched from him; who indeed had probably read what was Extant of them in his Days; Particularly, Our *Eighteenth Psalm* is what he has evidently imitated. *Virgil,* too, who so much lived upon him, as well as after him, is unaccountably mad upon his *Fate,* which he makes to be he knows not what himself, but Superiour to *Gods* as well as to *Men,* and thro' his whole Composures he so asserts the Doctrine of this Nonsensical Power, as is plainly inconsistent with all Virtue. And what *fatal Mischief* did *Fascinator* do to the *Roman Empire,* when by Deifying one Great Emperor, he taught the Successors to claim the Adoration of *Gods,* while they were perpetrating the Crimes of *Devils?* I will not be a *Carbilius* upon him; nor will I say any thing, how little the *Married State* owes unto One who writes as if he were a *Woman hater:* Nor what his Blunders are about his poor-spirited and inconsistent *Hero,* for which many havè taxed him. Nevertheless, 'tis observed, That the Pagans had no *Rules of Manners,* that were more Laudable and Regular than what are to be found in him. And some have said, It is *hardly possible seriously to Read his Works without being more disposed unto Goodness, as well as being agreeably entertained.* Be sure, had *Virgil* writ before *Plato,* his Works had not been any of the *Books prohibited.* But then, This *Poet* also has abundance of Rare *Antiquities* for us: And such Things, as others besides a *Servius,* have imagined that they have instructed and obliged Mankind, by employing all their Days upon. Wherefore if his *Aeneis,* which tho' it were once near twenty times as big as he has left it, yet he has left it unfinished, may not appear so valuable to you, that you may think *Twenty seven Verses* of the Part that is the most finished in it, worth One and Twenty Hundred Pounds and odd Money, yet his *Georgicks,* which he put his last Hand unto, will furnish you with many things far from Despicable. But after all, when I said, I was willing that the *Beauties* of these *Two Poets,* might become *Visible* to your *Visive Faculty* in *Poetry,* I did not mean, that you should Judge nothing to be Admittable into an *Epic Poem,* which is not Authorised by their Example; but I perfectly concur with One who is inexpressibly more capable to be a Judge of such a Matter than I can be: That it is a *false Critic who with a petulant Air, will insult Reason itself, if it presumes to oppose such Authority.*

I proceed now to say, That if (under the Guidance of a *Vida*) you try your young Wings now and then to see what Flights you can make, at least for an *Epigram*, it may a little sharpen your *Sense*, and polish your *Style*, for more important Performances; For this Purpose you are now even overstock'd with *Patterns*, and _____ Poemata Passim [poems everywhere]. You may, like *Nazianzen*, all your Days, make a little *Recreation* of *Poetry* in the midst of your more painful Studies. Nevertheless, I cannot but advise you, *Withold thy Throat from Thirst.* Be not so set upon *Poetry*, as to be always poring on the *Passionate* and *Measured* Pages. Let not what should be *Sauce* rather than *Food* for you, Engross all your Application. Beware of a *Boundless* and *Sickly* Appetite, for the Reading of the *Poems*, which now the *Rickety* Nation swarms withal: And let not the *Circaean* Cup intoxicate you. But especially preserve the *Chastity* of your Soul from the Dangers you may incur, by a Conversation with *Muses* that are no better than *Harlots*: Among which are others besides *Ovid's* Epistles, which for their Tendency to excite and foment Impure *Flames*, and cast *Coals* into your *Bosom*, deserve rather to be thrown into the *Fire*, than to be laid before the *Eye* which a *Covenant* should be *made* withal. Indeed, not meerly for the *Impurities* which they convey, but also on some other Accounts, the *Powers of Darkness* have a *Library* among us, whereof the *Poets* have been the most *Numerous* as well as the most *Venemous* Authors. Most of the Modern *Plays*, as well as the *Romances* and *Novels* and *Fictions*, which are a sort of *Poems,* do belong to the *Catalogue* of this cursed Library. The *Plays,* I say, in which there are so many Passages, that have a Tendency to overthrow all *Piety*, that one whose Name is *Bedford*, has extracted near Seven Thousand Instances of them, from the Plays chiefly of but Five Years preceeding; and says awfully upon them, *They are National Sins, and therefore call for National Plagues; And if GOD should enter into Judgment all the Blood in the Nation would not be able to atone for them.* How much do I wish that such Pestilences, and indeed all those worse than *Egyptian Toades,* [the Spawns of a *Butler,* & a

Brown, and a Ward, and a Company *whose Name is Legion!*] might never crawl into your Chamber! The *unclean Spirits* that *come like Frogs out of the Mouth of the Dragon, and of the Beast;* which *go forth* unto the young People of *the Earth,* and expose them to be dealt withal as the Enemies of GOD, in *the Battle of the Great Day of the Almighty.* As for those wretched *Scribbles* of *Madmen,* My Son, *Touch them not, Taste them* not, *Handle them not:* Thou wilt *perish* in the *using* of them. They are, *The Dragons whose Contagious Breath Peoples the dark Retreats of Death.* To much better Purpose will an Exellent but an Envied *Blackmore* feast you, than those Vile *Rapsodies* (of that *Vinum Daemonum*) which you will find always leave a Taint upon your Mind, and among other ill Effects will sensibly indispose you to converse with the *Holy Oracles* of GOD your SAVIOUR.

But there is, what I may rather call a *Parenthesis* than a *Digression,* which this may be not altogether an Improper Place for the introducing of.

There has been a deal of a do about a STYLE; So much, that I must offer you my Sentiments upon it. There is a *Way of Writing,* wherein the Author endeavours, that the Reader may have *something to the Purpose* in every Paragraph. There is not only a *Vigour* sensible in every *Sentence,* but the Paragraph is embellished with *Profitable References,* even to something beyond what is *directly spoken.* Formal and Painful *Quotations* are not studied; yet all that could be learnt from them is insinuated. The Writer pretends not unto *Reading,* yet he could not have writ as he does if he had not *Read* very much in his Time; and his Composures are not only a *Cloth of God,* but also stuck with as many *Jewels,* as the Gown of a Russian Embassador. This *Way of Writing* has been decried by many, and is at this Day more than ever so, for the same Reason, that in the old Story, the *Grapes* were decried *That they were not Ripe.* A Lazy, Ignorant, Conceited Sett of Authors, would perswade the whole Tribe, to lay aside that *Way of Writing,* for the same Reason that one would have perswaded his Brethren to part with the Encumbrance of their *Bushy Tails.* But however *Fashion* and *Humour* may prevail, they must not think that the Club at their *Coffee-House* is, *All the World*; but there will always be those, who will in this case be governed by *Indis-putable Reason*: And who will think that the real Excellency of a Book will never ly in *saying of little*; That the less one has for his Money in a Book, 'tis really the more Valuable for it; and that the less one is instructed in a Book, and the more of Superfluous *Margin,* and Superficial *Harangue,* and the less of *Substantial Matter* one has in it, the more tis to be accounted of. And if a more Massy *Way of Writing* be never so much disgusted at This Day, a *Better Gust* will come on, as will some other Thing, *quae iam Cecidere.* In the mean time, Nothing appears to me more Impertinent and Ridiculous than the *Modern Way,* [I cannot say, *Rule*; For they have None!] of *Criticising.* The Blades that set up for *Criticks,* I know not who constituted or commission'd 'em!—they appear to me, for the most part as *Contemptible,* as they are a *Supercilious* Generation. For indeed no Two of them have the same Style; and they are as intollerably Cross-grain'd and severe in their Censures upon one another, as they are upon the rest of Mankind. But while each of them, conceitedly enough, sets up for the *Standard of Perfection,* we are entirely at a Loss which *Fire* to follow. Nor can you easily find any one thing wherein they agree for their *Style,* except perhaps a perpetual Care to give us Jejune and Empty Pages, without such *Touches of Erudition* (to speak in the *Style* of an Ingenious Traveller) as may make the Discourses less *Tedious,* and more *Enriching,* to the Mind of him that peruses them. There is much Talk of a *Florid Style,* obtaining among the Pens, that are most in Vogue; but how often would it puzzle one, even with the best Glasses to find the *Flowres*! And if they were to be Chastized for it, it would be with much what as much of Justice, [sic] as Jerom was, for being a *Ciceronian.* After all, Every Man will have his own *Style,* which will distinguish him as much as his *Gate*: And if you can attain to that which I have newly described, but always writing so as to give an *Easy Conveyance* unto your Idea's, I would not have you by any *Scourging* be driven out of your *Gate,* but if you must confess a *Fault* in it, make a Confession like that of the Lad, unto his Father while he was beating him for his *Versifying.*

However, since every Man will have his own Style, I would pray, that we may learn to treat one another with mutual

Civilities, and *Condescensions,* and handsomely *indulge* one another in this, as *Gentlemen* do in other Matters.

I wonder what ails People, that they can't let *Cicero* write in the *Style of Cicero,* and *Seneca* write in the (much other!) *Style* of *Seneca;* and own that *Both* may please in their *several Ways.* —But I will freely tell you; what has made me consider the *Humourists* that set up for *Criticks upon Style,* as the most *Unregardable Set of Mortals* in the World, is This! Far more Illustrious *Criticks* than any of those to whom I am now bidding Defiance, and no less Men than your *Erasmus's* and your *Grotius's,* have taxed the *Greek Style* of the *New Testament,* with I know not what *Solacisms* and *Barbarisms;* And, how many *learned Folks* have Obsequiously run away with the Notion! Whereas 'tis an Ignorant and an Insolent *Whimsey;* which they have been guilty of. It may be (and particularly by an Ingenious *Blackwal,* it has been) Demonstrated, That the Gentlemen are mistaken in every one of their pretended Instances; All the Unquestionable *Classicks,* may be brought in, to convince them of their Mistakes. These Glorious Oracles are as *pure Greek* as ever was written in the World; and so Correct, so Noble, so Sublime is their *Style,* that never any thing under the Cope of Heaven, but the *Old Testament* has equall'd it.]

#9 What we call NATURAL PHILOSOPHY, is what I must encourage you to spend much more Time in the Study of.

Do it, with continual *Contemplations* and agreeable *Acknowledgements* of the Infinite GOD, whose Perfections are so display'd in His *Works* before you, that from them, you cannot but be perpetually ravished into the Acclamations of, *How Great is His Goodness and His Beauty!*

Do it, with a *Design* to be led into those *Views* wherewith you will in Ways most Worthy of a *Man* effectually *Show yourself a Man,* and may with Unutterable Satisfaction answer the main END of your Being, which is, To Glorify GOD; and therein also Discharge the Office of a *Priest* for the Creation; which, how sweet a, *Token for Good,* must it be unto you!

When I said, *Natural Phylosophy,* you may be sure, I did not mean, the *Peripatetic:* For I heartily subscribe to the Censure of *Christianus Thomasius* upon it; *Omne Tempus pro Perdito judicandum, quod in Physicam Peripateticorum impenditur; ita inepta et stulta ibi sunt Omnia* [that all of the time which is spent on the natural philosophy of the peripatetics is to be judged for lost; so inept and foolish are all things there.] It is indeed amazing to see the Fate of the Writings which go under the Name of *Aristotle.* First falling into the hands of those, who could not *Read* them, and yet for the sake of the Famous Author were willing to *keep* them; they were for a long while hid *under Ground,* where many of them *deserved* a Lodging. And from this Place of Darkness the Torn or Worn Manuscripts were anon fetched out; and imperfectly and unfaithfully enough transcribed, and conveyed from *Athens* to *Rome,* where *Copies* were in like Manner taken of them. The *Saracens* by and by got them, and (the Concise and Broken Style a little suiting them) they spoke *Arabic*; and even in *Africa* there were many *Aristotelean Schools* erected. They were from thence brought over into *Spain,* and Exhibited with such *Translations* and *Commentaries* as it pleased the *Arabians* to bestow upon them. When *Learning* revived under *Charlemaigne,* all *Europe* turned *Aristotelean*; yea, in some *Universities* they swore Allegiance to him; and, O Monstrous! if I am not misinformed, they do in some *Universities* at this Day foolishly and profanely on their Knees continue to do so. With the *Vile Person* that made himself the Head of the Church at *Rome,* this Muddy-headed Pagan *divided the Empire* over the Christian World; but extended his Empire further than *he,* or ever any *Tamerlane.* For the very *Jews* themselves became his Vassals, with a Tradition of his having some *Relation* to, or at least some *Acquaintance* with, their Fathers. And tho' *Europe* has, with fierce and long Struggles about it, begun to shake off the Shackles, he does to This Day, under the Name of *Axlis,* continue to Tyrannize over Humane Understanding in a great Part of the *Oriental World.* No Mortal else ever had such a Prerogative to *Govern Mankind,* as this *Philosopher*; who after the prodigious Cartloads of Stuff, that has been Written to explain him [For within a few Centuries after *Albertus Magnus,* there were Twelve Thousand Authors that wrote upon him; or followed him and defended him; and by a probable Computation, there have since been more than as many more!] he yet remains in many other Things besides his *Entelechia* sufficiently

Unintelligible, and forever in almost all things *Unprofitable.*
Avicen, after he had read his *Metaphysicks* Forty times over,
and had them all by Heart, was forced after all, to lay them
aside, in Despair of ever Understanding them. Have done then,
with your *Magirus,* and your *Eustachius,* and your *Heereboord;*
and the rest of the *Jargon-Writers.* Just so far as to *see a little
what they say,* you may look into them; *Whatsoever is more,
cometh of Evil,* and *Evil* will *Come* of it.

Some Eminent Persons, besides a *Sennertus* and a *Valesius,*
tired with the *Academical Futilities,* have at length betaken
themselves to the best School of *Philosophy* as well as for
Theology. The *Mosaic Philosophy* in the Scheme that *Comenius*
has given of it, is much admired and embraced in some Reforming Universities; and you will do well to bestow a deliberate
Reading upon it. The *Philosophia Vetus ac Vera* [True and
Ancient Philosophy], of the rare Dickinson, has given us a yet
finer Piece of *Mosaic Work,* which must always be honourably
spoken of. But, tho' it be true, that the *Sacred Scriptures* have
a *wondrous Philosophy* in them, and a Memorable *Dutchman* has
lately demonstrated, that, according to what every Day makes
more and more Evident, the *Prophetic Spirit* from whose *Inspira-
tion* they are given to us, *knew* and *own'd,* the now most indis-
puted Things which occur in the Discoveries of our *Modern
Philosophy;* yet it is now plain, the First Chapter of *Genesis,* (as
well as the rest of the *Bible,* which refers to the *System of the
World,* has not been well understood by most of the Gentlemen
that have writ upon it. However, because of the Regard therein
paid unto *Moses,* and the *Traduction of our Philosophy from
the Holy Fountains,* (tho' *Plato* be advanced with him) I do
particularly approve your perusing of the *Philosophia generalis,*
written by our equally Modest and Learned *Gale,* for as to make
yourself a Master of it. I cannot but confess, that the *Hypotheses*
which the more Ingenious and Inquisitive *Sons of the Wild Asses
Colt,* have hitherto mostly valued themselves upon, have been
to justly called, *Philosophical Romances,* and it may be, what is
now most in Vogue, may anon be refuted and refused like its
Predecessors. Nevertheless, I would have you take what may
appear least likely to prove *Romantic.* And therefore, as thorough
an Insight as you can get into the *Principles* of our *Perpetual*

Dictator, the Incomparable Sr. *Isaac Newton,* is what I mightily commend unto you.

Be sure, The *Experimental Philosophy* is that, in which alone your Mind can be at all established. For this Purpose, besides your more occasionally Conversing with such things as, Our *Philosophical Transactions,* and several Communications of our Illustrious *Boyl,* and of *Hook,* and of *Grew,* and *Cheyne,* and *Keil,* and those also that have written the *Natural History* of several Places, [and such Outlandish Writings as those of *Bartholinus,* and *Borellus,* and the *German Ephemerides*] I would Commend unto you, *The Religious Philsopher,* of the Admirable *Nieuentyt*; and what has been communicated by our Industrious *Ray,* and our Ingenuous *Derham,* who still nobly serve *Religion* as well as *Philosophy.* And whatever it might be for *me* to say so unto *any One else,* I hope, it will be no Indecency for me to say so unto *you*; That if you desire to see the largest Collection, I have yet seen of the *Discoveries* which the last Age has made in *Philosophy,* adapted unto the general Capacity of Readers; and short Essays upon every Article, to Show and Raise those Dispositions of PIETY, wherein the *Works* of the Holy and Blessed GOD invite us to *Live* unto Him; together with the *First Claim* that I have ever yet seen so explicitly made on the behalf of a Glorious CHRIST, and the Consideration due to him in our *Philosophy*; you have this prepared for you in a Book Entituled, THE CHRISTIAN PHILOSOPHER.

Above all, I would have you see to it, that you be not, like some haughty, and short-sighted, and half-witted, *Smatterers in Philosophy,* seduced into the *Folly* of doubting the *Existence* or *Providence* of a Glorious GOD, by a Study, which, if well-persued, would *Compel you to come in* to a *Strong Faith,* where with you would *give Glory* to Him, on all Occasions. I hope, every step of your Study, will give you more and more Satisfaction, of what One of our Best Philosophers, the Author of, *The Natural History of the Earth,* adheres unto; *That as the World was at first Created, so it has been ever since preserved, by the Immediate Hand of GOD.* You will see, That the Influences of one thing upon another in the *Course of Nature* are purely from the Omnipotent and Omnipresent GOD, actually forever at

Work, according to His own *Laws,* and putting His *Laws* in Execution, and as the *Universal Cause* producing those Effects, whereof the *Creatures* are but what One may call, *The Occasional Causes.* You will also be often and quickly carried up into those *Immechanical Principles,* from whence, *The next step is into GOD!* The *Gravitation* of Bodies is One of them; For which *No Cause* can be assigned, but the *Will* of the Glorious GOD, who is the *First Cause* of all. *Child, See GOD in every Thing!* Own Him, Fear Him, Love Him; Study *Philosophy* with a perpetual Intention to do so. Remember GOD is to *Spirits,* what *Center* is to *Bodies.* And, A Mind that from the View of the Glorious GOD in his *Works,* is carried into Acknowledgments of a GOD *infinitely Worthy to be Loved and Praised and Served and Relied upon,* becomes a *Temple* filled with *the Glory of the Lord.* Visit for this Purpose the several Classes of the Creatures: Walk thro' the World; [and be so far a Peripatetic!] and in this generous Exercise, *Fear GOD and Give Glory unto Him.*

#10 The MATHEMATICKS will be, next unto *Philosophy,* a noble Study for you; The most Essential Parts whereof, you have in the *Cursus Mathematicus* of an *Ozanam* so delivered unto you, that indeed you will hardly need any more. Tho' you are shaping for a *Divine,* yet I should not be sorry to see you as Exquisite a *Mathematician* as the Excellent *Pitiscus,* who, tho' he were a *Divine,* yet without a Tutor became such an *High Attainer* in this *Real Learning,* that *Melchior Adam* cries out, *Illud Mirandum* [That is to marvelled at]! upon it: And it caused the Noble *Tycho Brahe* to say, *Optarem plures ejusmodi Conciona-tores reperiri: forte plus esset in iis Circumspecti et Solidi Judicii* [I should desire several preachers of that sort to be found, indeed in them would be more of wise and sound judgment]. I should not be sorry to see a *Wallis,* or a *Wilkins,* or a *Barrow,* revived in you, if your *Genius* lead you to it.

Besides the other Uses of ARITHMETIC and GEOMETRY, [wherein an *Hill* and an *Euclid,* or *The Young Mathematicians Guide* of a *Ward,* instead of Both, may singularly be commended for you.] you will find this Benefit by the Study of them; They will Necessitate and Habituate your Mind unto that

Strong Attention, which will marvellously Qualify you for more *Important Services,* and make a *Strong Reasoner* of you, and a very Regular and Coharent *Speaker.* They were distinguished by the Name of *Mathesis,* and made the *First Learning* in some Ancient Schools, for this very Reason. And you may be sure, I should reckon it a further Encouragement unto the Study, if the *General Rule* might hold without any *Exception,* That *Great Mathematicians* use to be Men of *Good Morals;* It seems that their Intense *Applications* and *Speculations* are inconsistent with *Debaucheries.* While you are thus employed, Methinks, it might be a pretty Diversion to go thro' some of Leybourn's *Mathematical Recreations.*

But you must also *soar Upwards,* to the Attainments of ASTRONOMY. For though of *Later Ages,* the voluminous *Tostatus* whom they complemented as having all the Learning in the World, were no better an *Astronomer,* than *Justin Martyr,* and *Ambrose,* and *Theodores,* and *Chrysostom,* and *Austin* himself, who in the more *Early Ages* declaimed violently against the *Spherical Figure* of the Heavens; I should be loth you should thro' Ignorance in *Astronomy,* ever fall into what even a *Jerom* would call *Stultiloquium* in *Ecclesia* [Foolish talk in Church]. Wherefore, I cannot but advise you to be well instructed in the *Astronomical Lectures,* as of an Accurate *Keill,* so of the Acute *Whiston;* while we are Mourning, that he who so excellently serves us in *Astronomy,* should so unhappily hurt us in *Divinity,* and call into Question, (as Dubious *Problem*) the Infinite and Eternal *Godhead* of Him FOR whom, as well as BY whom, the *Sun* and the *Stars* were created.

At the same time, I hope, there is no need of my saying any thing to disswade you from the Study of JUDICIAL ASTROLOGY: The most *Injudicious* Thing in the World: All Futility; All Impiety; All of a Piece with the ridiculous Whim of a *Gassarel,* who maintains, That the *Stars* in the Heavens do stand ranged in the form of *Hebrew Letters,* and that it is possible to *Read there* whatever is to happen of Importance throughout the Universe. And yet perhaps, there may be some Need for me to Caution you against being *Dismay'd at the Signs of the Heavens,* or having any Superstitious Fancies upon *Eclipses* and the like Occurrences, or thinking that if there were a *Conjunction of all*

the Planets in Pisces, it would portend that the World should
be *Drowned.* Yea, I am willing that the *Cometomancy* which
has hitherto so much reigned, even the most *Honest Minds,* be
laid aside with you; and that you be apprehensive of nothing
Portentous in *Blazing Stars,* except it should be apprehended, that
in their *Elliptic Motions* they may make so near an Appulse unto
this Globe as to bring some Confusion upon it. For my Part, I
know not whether all our *Worlds,* and even the *Sun* it self, may
not fare the better for them. Some, that know more than I, do
think so. Indeed, if you perswade a World, here *lying in Wickedness,* there to see a *Prasage,* and to take a *Warning,* from the
tremendous View of a *World in a State of Punishment,* I will
say, *Go on and Prosper.*

But I will now so far fetch you down from the *Stars,* and set
you down on your Native Soyl, as to tell you, That there is
nothing *Mathematical* to which I more advise you, than the easy
Study of GEOGRAPHY. Perhaps the Scituation of *Paradise* and
of *Palestine,* and of the Places mentioned in the Sacred Scriptures,
may be what you would be willing to be first of all acquainted
with. And for this, Let the Admirable *Bochart* be your principal
Instructor. What has been chiefly taken from *him,* and from two
or three more, in three or four *Octavo's* under the Title of
Sacred Geography, [by one *Wells,*] may herein also be of some
Use to you. The *Pisgah Sight* of a *Fuller,* will be read with a
Pleasure equal to the *Profit;* and the *Palestina Illustrata* of a
Reland, perhaps with a *Profit* greater than the *Pleasure.* But you
will not give over, till more of the World, has come into your
Knowledge, than the *Decree* of an *Augustus* could reach unto.
Wherefore, after a *Morden* or a *Gordon,* [together with a
Varenius,] has given you a more Compendious View of the
World, I say no thing of a Work Entituled, *Geography Rectified,*
because 'tis not easy to find a *Work* that more wants to be *Rectified;* but what I say next, is, that the *Atlas Geographus,* will be a
yet more instructive Guide for you, in your taking the Tour of the
several Regions in it. You may then, as your Inclinations may carry
you, with *Delight* and *Safety* make your Visits to particular Countrys and Citys, in the Descriptions given of them. And here, while I
suppose, that what a *Cambden* has given you in his *Britannia,*
will be no unacceptable Entertainment for you, I cannot but

notify it unto you, that, *The English Empire in America*, described by One *Oldmixon*, is the most foolish and faithless Performance in this Kind, that ever Mankind was abused withal. I am desirous, that you proceed and peruse many of the *Travels* that have been published; and (if you dare not venture upon a *Purchas*) by conversing with many more than what are exhibited in that Rich Collection which goes under the Name of, *Itinerantium atque Navigantium Bibliotheca [A Library of Books of Travel and Navigations]*, you may with little Expense or Hazard become a notable *Traveller*. In your thus *Riding a Circuit*, you will especially inform yourself about, *The State of Religion*, in the World: [And methinks, *Pagets Christianography*, and *Brierwood's Enquiries*, may particularly deserve a Reading with you:] And you will have your Heart thereupon raised in Sentiments of *Gratitude* unto a *Sovereign* GOD, who has cast your Lot among a People whom *He has known above* most of *the Families of the Earth: Even so Righteous Father, for so it pleases thee!*— and *Compassion* for a World over so much of which the *Powers of Darkness* continue to Tyrannize: Disposed like an Owner of, *Sellers New System of Geography*, whom I found inserting with his Pen this Note at the End of it; *Peccantis et Perditi tam vasti Mundi, misere Deus* [God have mercy on the sinner and damned of so fearful a world]! Yea, In fine, Let me tell you, This *Easy Study* will not only furnish you to maintain a *Profitable Conversation*, and a *Communication that may minister Grace*, and be ever Acceptable, to the *Hearers*: But if you prove a *Man of Concern for the Kingdom of* GOD in the World, it may bring you to form those *Projections*, by which, as *little as you are in your own Eyes*, whole Nations may anon come to fare the better for you.

For MUSIC, I know not what well to say.—Do as you please. If you *Fancy* it, I don't *Forbid* it. Only do not for the sake of it, Alienate your Time too much, from those that are more Important Matters. It may be so, that you may serve your GOD the better, for the Refreshment of *One that can play well on an Instrument*. However, to accomplish yourself at *Regular Singing*, is a thing that will be of *Daily Use* to you. For I would not have a Day pass you without *Singing*, but so as at the same time to *make a Melody in your Heart unto the Lord;* Besides the Part you may bear, *In Hymnis suavisonantis Ecclesia* [In the sweet singing of the hymns of the church].

I will conclude this Article, with a Remark made by Perault, in his Account of *Illustrious Men*. Some Reproached *Gassendus*, for not knowing enough certain parts of the *Mathematicks*. Whereupon he says; "Whether he was actually *Ignorant* of what was most Abstruse in these Sciences, or whether he *Neglected* it, he could not but be the more Commendable for it. There is something of *Little*, in tying ones self up too much to *little Things*; and even of *Imprudence* too, to consume therein a *Time*, which may be employed more usefully on other Knowledge."

#11 If the Emperor Basil had in his Instructions to *a Son*, recommended unto him HISTORY, as a *Way of Travelling without Fatigue*, yet you may be sure, My SON, I should have recommended unto you an Acquaintance with HISTORY, as one of the most Needful and Useful Accomplishments, for a Man that would serve GOD as you Propose to do. The Praises of that Method which they that *handle the Pen of the Writer*, have taken to *stop the Flood of things*, and give a *Consistency* and a *Duration* unto them, that *Historians* usually begin their Works withal, and the Flourishes about, *Lux Veritatis, Vita Memoriae, Magistra Vitae* [The light of truth, the life of tradition, the mistress of life], and I know not what, areas unnecessary on *this* Occasion, as they are on *that* whereon we commonly have them. And tho' perhaps we cannot meet with such *Historians*, as *Le Moyne* pleases to require, but such as he says, *Will not appear until the Year when the Philosophers Stone shall be discovered;* yet I would not have you discouraged from Reading the *Best we have*. But for this Purpose, I shall be far from advising you to impose on yourself, the tedious Task of Reading over the Hundreds of *Histories*, which *Degory Whear*, or the Frenchman who has more lately written, *L'Histoire des Histoires*, may obtrude upon you, except you were to have the long Life of an *Antediluvian;* and even *then* also, to Read them *all* would be to spend much Time impertinently. Perhaps a Concise *Body of Universal History*, may be very properly laid in the Foundation of your *Historical Studies*. And tho' *Hornius*, his *Arca Noa [The Arc of Noah]*, be Admriable, and *Sleidans* little Book, *De quatuor summis imperiis* [*Concerning The Four Greatest Empires*], be far from Despicable; yet I can't presently think of a Better, than *Mathias Prideaux*, his *Easy and Compendious Introduction for the Reading all sorts of Histories*. Proceed then, to some Volumns of larger Dimensions; Among which I can tell of none that I could more heartily commend unto you, than *Howel*, his *Institution of General History*: And upon this, add, *Puffendorf's Introduction*. But I will here Betimes lay in for this; In Reading of all *History*, ever now and then make a convenient Pause; to think, *What can I see of the Glorious GOD in these Occurrences?* And always remember, *The Providence of the Glorious GOD in governing the World, is now under my Contemplation.*

Doubtless you will have a *Desire*, if you can find a *Leisure*, to Read some *Histories* of *Particular Countrys*. And here, as I know none better than *Mezary*, for *France*; *Mariana*, for *Spain*; *Grotius*, for *Holland*; *Knoles* with *Rycaut*, for the *Ottoman Empire*; *Ludolphus*, for *Abyssinia*; *Crull*, for *Russia*; [there are several small *Story-tellers* for *Persia*, and *Indoustan*,] *Martinius*, and some other *Jesuites* [but you must Remember, they are *Jesuites*!] for China; *Martyr*, or *Acosta*, or *Ogilby*, for *America*; *Buchanan*, for *Scotland*; and *Cox* for *Ireland*; So, I would prefer *Baker*, for *England*; especially, if you could come at an Edition that was printed before what they call, *The Restauration*. *The Memorials of English Affairs, from the supposed Expedition of Brute into the Island, until the coming of K. James, I.* [Don't something in the Title sound a little *oddly?*] written by *Whitlock*, or the little, *Medulla Historiae Angelicane* [The Heart of English History], may also be to you a pretty Abstract of our *English History*.

But the mention of *English Affairs* pushes me, even with some Anticipation, into the Caution which I am to give you, about Reading all our *Common Histories*, but none more than the *English* ones; That is, *To believe with Discretion*. Alas, The *Vanity* which attends Humane Affairs! As there are many Men and Things that are scarce mentioned in *True History*, which deserve a mention more than some that are universally celebrated; What *Hero's* are buried among those who lived before the Days of *Agmemmon?* And *Walter Plettenberg* is less known than a Turkish Pyrate: What has been *ponderous* has (as my

Lord *Bacon* expresses it) been *sunk* to the Bottom in the Stream
of *Time*, while we have *Straw* and *Stubble* swimming a top:
So, 'tis a thing, that may be too *truly*, but can't be too *sadly*,
complained of; That the Instances wherein *False History* has
been imposed upon the World, are what *cannot be numbred*.
Historians have generally taken after their Father *Herodotus*:
And even *One of themselves*, *Vopiscus* by Name, has expresly
said of them, *They are all them Lyars: This Witness is True!* Tho'
they have not all of them always been such Mercenary Villains as
Bishop *Jovius*, or that Scandalous Fellow, who more lately so
hired himself out as an *History Writer* for the highest Bidder,
that his Countrymen, the *Italians*, fixed that Motto on him *Not*
according to the History but the Salary; yet Once who *gently*
enough Criticises on them, too *Justly* questions, *Whether any*
Modern Historian has *thought of any more than pleasing the*
Prince or Party for which he wrote. The *Ancient* are not much
better than the *Modern*; Whereof we have a notorious and
amazing Example in *Josephus*. It would be too long a Digression
to relate his *Vile Prevarications*; which have compelled us to
concur unto the Censure passed by our *Gregory* upon him; That
being Ambitious to have his Work find Acceptance among the
Heathen, he did so compose his *History* as to propose nothing
that might appear Incredible to *them*, and not have some Con-
gruity with what *had been*, and was likely again *to be* among
them. Indeed all honest Men are scandalized, no less than
Castrius, at the Pains he takes to make his Court unto the *Roman*
Princes by his *Heathen Judiasm;* wherein, as One says, he was
more Impious than the *Philistines* who placed the *Ark* by *Dagon*.

What a fine Story are we like to have, of as Infamous a Reign
as ever was in the World, and a *Tyranny* all made up of
Treacheries, and Robberries, and Cruelties that cannot be parallel'd, when it comes from Three Poets, each of them, with a
Pension of Twelve Thousand Livres a Year, to give us a
Panegyric instead of an *History,* and outdo a *Paterculus* blanch-
ing his *Tiberius!* How little many Representations of Matters in
Histories are to be relied upon, methinks, it may be a little illustrated from the *Two chief Commanders* in a Memorable
Battle of *Belgrade*, both of which, wrote the History of the Battle, without the least mention made by one of the other each

assuming to himself the entire Honour of the Day. You will certainly say, *Who can understand his Errors?*—When the Admirable *Erasmus* himself mistakes one Man for two, in writing of what was a great while ago; and three professed and eminent Historians give us a very wrong Account of the Gentleman who a much less while ago, founded the *Charter-House;* and tho' no Writer of History ever were more Meritorious, than the Incomparable *Thuanus,* yet Learned Men have said of his Performance, that it contained, *Multa Falsissima et indigna* [Many things most false and unworthy]. Yea, there are *Historians,* of whom one can scarce tell which to admire most, the *Nature* of their *Lies,* or their *Manner* of telling them; I mean, the *Impudence* with which they tell them. For Instance, it is pretty well, that *Hozier* the French King's Genealogist, has discovered no less than *Four Thousand* wrong Things in *Varillas,* the same King's Historian; And another observes, every single Page in him, has almost as many Errors, as a Printers ordinary Table of *Errata.* But then, what an *Impudent*: Fellow was *Philanan Anglicus,* when he accused *Calvin* of *Delicacy,* and *Epicureanism* in his Way of Living; and quotes *Florimond de Remond* for a Witness of it; who, he says, has *left us a lively Image of him.* Whereas, if you consult this *Florimond de Remond,* the *lively Image* which he gives of Calvin, is, That *from his Youth he macerated his Body with Fasting, and that hardly could be found a Man that equalled him for his Laboriousness.* Be sure, the *late Historians,* that pretend unto an, *History of England,* for us, write such flagrant *Partialities,* and are such evident *Leafing-makers,* and palm upon you so very wrong and base Exhibitions, especially of *late Occurences,* that one may as well believe the *True History* of a *Lucian,* as yield any Credit unto them. If you must read them, yet as to things that passed in the former Century, I would hardly so much as look upon many of them. And among These, tho' several are bad enough, yet there is none that done so Ill as an Eachard, (I mean, in his *English,* and not in his *Roman* History,) who should not be admitted into the Library of a Gentleman that has any Concern for Truth; except he'll assign him a Place on the same Shelf, with the *Grand Cyrus,* or *Cleopatra.* A late *Critical History of England,* has done some Justice upon him. Indeed the *Historians* never keep closer to the *Way of*

Lying, than in the Relation they give of those *Twenty Years,* which passed after the Beginning of our *Civil Wars,* and afforded a very ample and fertile Field, for their Faculty to work upon. Among these, the *Romance* that goes under the Title of, *The History of the Grand Rebellions,* and is fathered on the Earl of *Clarendon,* I would have you more particularly treat with the Disregard that is proper for it. If you would come at all near to the *Truth* of what Concerns those Times, you must look for it, in *Whitlock,* his *Memorial of English Affairs, from the Beginning of K. Charles I. To the Restoring of K. Charles II.* And *Rushworth* his *Collections.* And yet even there, some of the greatest Persons and Actions have not always *Full Justice* done them. I do particularly Advertise you, That the *Mighty Man,* whom not only our King *William* (as *Fleming* reports had a very high Esteem for, but also his most bigotted and bitterest Enemies confess to have been a *Matchless Hero,* and (as even Sr. Roger Manly himself, as well as many more of his Bran, acknowledges) *Not unworthy of the Supreme Heights of Empire which he attain'd to,* has never yet had his *History* fairly and fully given; and when you read it given (as they are now *Approaching towards it*) with the greatest *Impartiality* wherein you have hitherto seen it, you may bear this in your Mind, that the *Principal Stroke* in his Character, and the *Principal Spring* of his Conduct, is forever *defectively* Related.

As for such Abominable Pens, as what the *Athenae Oxonienes* of a *Wood* have been Excretions from, you cannot sufficiently Despise them & Abhor them. And I will further tell you, That if in any *History,* you happen to find any Vindicating or Favourable Passages of old A. Bishop *Laud,* Let these be *Shibboleth* enough with you, to do the Office which the *Rattle* does for the *Serpent,* which our Country is no Stranger to. *Yea,* and when you Read. even such *Consciencious Historians,* as a Baxter, and a *Burnet,* you must make Allowances for some *Hearsays,* which led them into Mistakes; and for certain *Prejudices,* the Tincture whereof a little influenced their *Views* of what they were disaffected to.

14

Selections from the Writings of Benjamin Franklin (1735-1754)[1]

Benjamin Franklin (1706-90) was born in Boston. At an early age he became an apprentice to his half brother, a printer. At the age of seventeen he moved to Philadelphia, and worked there and in London as a printer. By 1730, the twenty-four year old printer owned his shop and had established himself as a successful businessman. A mere list of Franklin's accomplishments is impressive, even astounding. Possessed by a "passion for improvement," he worked in a variety of ways to improve life in Philadelphia. He either established or encouraged the paving and lighting of streets, a municipal police force, a hospital, a circulating library, an academy which became the University of Pennsylvania, and The American Philosophical Society. As a politician and statesman, Franklin served his city, colony, state, and nation. He was clerk of the Pennsylvania Assembly, assemblyman, deputy postmaster for the colonies, author of the Albany Plan of Union, agent for four colonies, member of the Second Continental Congress and delegate to the Constitutional Convention. Franklin was also a scientist with wide ranging interests and an inventor of many practical devices. His literary output was huge. Much that he wrote was occasional or polemic by nature. Everything that he wrote shows wit, grace and force. Included in this collection is one edition of the famous Almanac of Poor Richard.

Carl Van Doren has written one of the better one-volume biographies, *Benjamin Franklin* (New York: The Viking Press, 1938). For a survey of social and cultural history during the eighteenth century see James T. Adams, *Provincial Society 1690-1763* (New York: Macmillan, 1927). Urban life and problems in Franklin's time are

1. Leonard W. Labaree, ed., *The Papers of Benjamin Franklin* (New Haven: Yale University Press, 1959——), II, 12-15, "On the Protection of Towns from Fire"; 150-52, Articles of the Union Fire Co.; V, 284-87, 325-27, "Some Account of the Pennsylvania Hospital"; II, 136-45, *Poor Richard*. Reprinted by permission.

described in Carl Bridenbaugh, *Cities in Revolt: Urban Life in America, 1743-1776* (New York: Knopf, 1955). Perhaps one can do no better than to read Franklin's *Autobiography*, which has been reprinted by many publishers. In reading the documents relating to fire protection, the library, and the hospital note (1) what organizational methods Franklin used to accomplish his ends; (2) what practical suggestions he advanced for the abatement and control of fires; (3) how the library was financed; (4) what objectives the hospital was to serve; and (5) what estimate of its success he made. In reading *Poor Richard* note (1) the quality of humor or wit displayed; (2) evidence of Puritan, middle-class virtues and attitudes; (3) the level of sophistication exhibited; and (4) the tone and style of the language used.

A. On the Protection of Towns from Fire (1735)

M R. FRANKLIN,
          Being old and lame of my Hands, and thereby uncapable of assisting my Fellow Citizens, when their Houses are on Fire; I must beg them to take in good Part the following Hints on the Subject of Fires.

In the first Place, as *an Ounce of Prevention is worth a Pound of Cure,* I would advise 'em to take Care how they suffer living Brands-ends, or Coals in a full Shovel, to be carried out of one Room into another, or up or down Stairs, unless in a Warming-pan shut; for Scraps of Fire may fall into Chinks, and make no Appearance till Midnight; when your Stairs being in Flames, you may be forced, (as I once was) to leap out of your Windows, and hazard your Necks to avoid being over-roasted.

And now we talk of Prevention, where would be the Damage, if, to the Act for preventing Fires, by regulating Bakehouses and Coopers Shops, a Clause were added to regulate all other Houses in the particulars of too shallow Hearths, and the detestable Practice of putting wooden Mouldings on each side the Fire Place, which being commonly of Heart-of-Pine and full of Turpentine, stand ready to flame as soon as a Coal or a small Brand shall roul [roll] against them.

Once more; if Chimneys were more frequently and more carefully clean'd, some Fires might thereby be prevented. I have known foul Chimneys burn most furiously a few Days after they were swept: People in Confidence that they are clean, making large Fires. Every Body among us is allow'd to sweep Chimneys, that please to undertake that Business; and if a Chimney fires thro' fault of the Sweeper, the Owner pays the Fine, and the Sweeper goes free. This Thing is not right. Those who undertake Sweeping of Chimneys, and employ Servants for that Purpose, ought to be licensed by the Mayor; and if any Chimney fires and flames out 15 Days after Sweeping, the Fine should be paid by the Sweeper; for it is his Fault.

We have at present got Engines enough in the Town, but I question, whether in many Parts of the Town, Water enough can be had to keep them going for half an Hour together. It seems to me some Publick Pumps are wanting; but that I submit to better Judgments.

As to our Conduct in the Affair of Extinguishing Fires, tho' we do not want Hands or Good-will, yet we seem to want Order and Method, and therefore I believe I cannot do better than to offer for our Imitation, the Example of a City in a Neighbouring Province. There is, as I am well inform'd, a Club or Society of active Men belonging to each Fire Engine; whose Business is to attend all Fires with it whenever they happen; and to work it once a Quarter, and see it kept in order: Some of these are to handle the Firehooks, and others the Axes, which are always kept with the Engine; and for this Service they are consider'd in an Abatement or Exemption in the Taxes. In Time of Fire, they are commanded by Officers appointed by Law, called *Fire-wards,* who are distinguish'd by a Red Staff of five Feet long, headed with a Brass Flame of 6 Inches; And being Men of Prudence and Authority, they direct the opening and stripping of Roofs by the Ax-Men, the pulling down burning Timbers by the Hookmen, and the playing of the Engines, and command the making of Lanes, &c. and they are impowered to require Assistance for the Removing of Goods out of Houses on fire or in Danger of Fire, and to appoint Guards for securing such Goods; and Disobedience, to these Officers in any, at such Times, is punished by a Fine of 40s. or Ten Days Imprisonment. These Officers, with the Men belonging to the Engine, at their Quarterly Meetings, discourse of Fires, of the Faults committed at some, the good Management in some Cases at others, and thus communicating their Thoughts and Experience they grow wise in the Thing, and know how to command and to execute in the best manner upon every Emergency. Since the Establishment of this Regulation, it seems there has been no extraordinary Fire in that Place; and I wish there never may be any here. But they suffer'd before they made such a Regulation, and so must we; for Englishmen feel but cannot see; as the Italian says of us. And it has pleased God, that in the Fires we have hitherto had, all the bad Circumstances have never happened together, such as dry Season, high Wind, narrow Street, and little or low Water: which perhaps tends to make us secure in our own Minds; but if a Fire with those Circumstances, which God forbid, should happen, we should afterwards be careful enough.

Let me say one thing more, and I will be silent. I could wish, that either Tiles would come in use for a Covering to Buildings; or else that those who build, would make their Roofs more safe to walk upon, by carrying the Wall above the Eves, in the Manner of the new Buildings in London, and as Mr. Turner's House in Front-Street, or Mr. Nichols's in Chesnut-Street, are built; which I conceive would tend considerably to their Preservation.

Let others communicate their Thoughts as freely as I have done mine, and perhaps something useful may be drawn from the Whole. I am yours, &c.

A. A.

B. Articles of the Union Fire Company (1736)

The seventh Day of *December,* in the Year of our Lord One thousand seven hundred and thirty six, We Whose Names are hereunto subscribed, reposing special Confidence in each others Friendship, Do, for the better preserving our Goods and Effects from Fire, mutually agree in Manner following, *That is to say.*

1. THAT we will each of us at his own proper Charge provide Two Leathern Buckets, and Four Baggs of good Oznabrigs or wider Linnen, Whereof each Bagg shall contain four Yards at least, and shall have a running Cord near the Mouth; Which

said Buckets and Baggs shall be marked with the Initial Letters of our respective Names and Company Thus [A.B. & Company] and shall be apply'd to no other Use than for preserving our Goods and Effects in Case of Fire as aforesaid.

2. THAT if any one of us shall fail to provide and keep his Buckets and Baggs as aforesaid he shall forfeit and pay unto the Clerk for the Time being, for the Use of the Company, the Sum of *Five Shillings* for every Bucket and Bagg wanting.

3. THAT if any of the Buckets or Baggs aforesaid shall be lost or damaged at any Fire aforesaid The same shall be supplyed and repaired at the Charge of the whole Company.

4. THAT we will all of us, upon hearing of Fire breaking out at or near any of our Dwelling Houses, immediately repair to the same with all our Buckets and Baggs, and there employ our best Endeavours to preserve the Goods and Effects of such of us as shall be in Danger by Packing the same into our Baggs: And if more than one of us shall be in Danger at the same time, we will divide our selves as near as may be to be equally helpful. And to prevent suspicious Persons from coming into, or carrying any Goods out of, any such House, Two of our Number shall constantly attend at the Doors until all the Goods and Effects that can be saved shall be secured in our Baggs, and carried to some safe Place, to be appointed by such of our Company as shall be present, Where one or more of such shall attend them 'till they can be conveniently delivered to, or secured for, the Owner.

5. THAT we will meet together in the Ev'ning of the last Second Day of the Week commonly called Monday, in every Month, at some convenient Place and Time to be appointed at each Meeting, to consider of what may be further useful in the Premises; And whatsoever shall be expended at every Meeting aforesaid shall be paid by the Members met. And if any Member shall neglect to meet as aforesaid, he shall forfeit and pay the Sum of *One Shilling*.

6. THAT we will each of us in our Turns, according to the Order of our Subscriptions, serve the Company as Clerk for the Space of one Month, Viz. That Member whose Name is hereunto first subscribed shall serve first, and so on to the last, Whose Business shall be to inspect the Condition of each of our Buckets

and Baggs, and to make Report thereof at every Monthly Meeting aforesaid, To collect all the Fines and Forfeitures accruing by Virtue hereof; to warn every Member of the Time and Place of Meeting, at least Six Hours before Hand. And if any new Member be proposed to be admitted, or any Alteration to be made in any of the present Articles, he shall inform every Member thereof at the Time of Warning a[foresaid.] And shall also read over a Copy of these Presents, and a List of all the Subscribers Names, at every Monthly Meeting, before the Company proceeds to any other Bu[siness,] Which said Clerk shall be accountable to the Rest of the Company for, and pay [to] the next succeeding Clerk, all the Monies accruing or belonging unto the Company by virtue of these presents. And if any Member shall refuse to serve as Clerk in his Turn aforesaid, he shall forfeit the Sum of *Five Shillings.*

7. THAT our Company shall not exceed the Number of twenty-five Persons a[t a] time, no new Member be admitted, nor any Alteration made in these present Ar[ticles] until the Monthly Meeting after the same is first proposed, and the whole Company acquainted therewith by the Clerk as aforesaid; Nor without the Consent of Three Fourths of our whole Number, the whole Three Fourths being met. But the other Affairs relating to the Company shall be determined by Three Fourths of Members met. And that the Time of entring upon Business shall be one Hour after the Time appointed for Meeting as aforesaid.

8. THAT each Member shall keep two Lists of all the Subscribers Names, [one] to be fixed in open View near the Buckets and Baggs, and the Other to be pr[oduced] at every Monthly Meeting if required under pain of forfeiting the Sum of [six?] Pence.

9. THAT all Fines and Forfeitures arising by Virtue hereof, shall be paid unto the Clerk for the Time being, for the Use of the Company, and shall be erected into a common Stock. And if any Member shall refuse to pay any Fine or Forfeiture aforesaid when due, his Name shall be razed out, And he shall from thenceforth be excluded the Company.

10. LASTLY THAT upon the Death of any of our Company, the Survivors shall in time of Danger as aforesaid, be aiding to

the Widow of such Decedent during her Widowhood, in the same Manner as if her Husband had been living; she only keeping the Buckets and Baggs as aforesaid. IN WITNESS whereof we have hereunto set our Hands; Dated the Day and Year abovesaid.

C. A short Account of the LIBRARY (1741)

The Library-Company was form'd in 1731, by Constitutions or Articles entred into by 50 Persons, each obliging himself to pay 40s. for purchasing the first Parcel of Books, and 10s. *per annum* to defray Charges and encrease the Library.

Ten Directors or Managers of the Library, and a Treasurer, are chosen yearly by Vote, at a General Meeting of the Company.

The Number of Members are now encreased to upwards of 70. Persons enclining to be admitted, apply to any one of the Directors, who nominates them at the next monthly Meeting of Directors; and being allowed, and paying to the Treasurer the Value of a Share at the Time, and signing the Articles, they become Members.

Any Member may borrow a Book for 2, 3, or 4 Weeks, leaving his Note for double Value, and paying a small Penalty if 'tis not return'd at the Time agreed; which Penalties are applied to defraying Charges, or purchasing more Books.

Every Member has an absolute Property in his Share; may devise it in his Will, or dispose of it when he pleases to any Person the Directors approve. And Shares so sold have always hitherto yielded as much as they had cost. As Shares encrease yearly in Value 10s. so much being yearly added by each Subscriber to the Stock of Books, a Share which at first was worth but 40s. is now valued at £6 10s. But for this small Sum, which, laid out in Books, would go but a little Way, every Member has the Use of a Library now worth upwards of £500, whereby *Knowledge* is in this City render'd more cheap and easy to be come at, to the great Pleasure and Advantage of the studious Part of the Inhabitants.

Those who are not Subscribers may notwithstanding borrow Books, leaving in the Hands of the Librarian, as a Pledge, a

Sum of Money proportion'd to the Value of the Book borrow'd and paying a small Acknowledgment for the Reading, which is apply'd to the Use of the Library.

The Library is open and Attendance given every Saturday Afternoon from 4 a Clock 'til 8.

Besides the Books in this Catalogue given to the Library, the Company have been favour'd with several generous Donations; as, a curious Air-Pump, with its Apparatus, a large double Microscope, and other valuable Instruments, from the Hon. JOHN PENN, Esq; A handsome Lot of Ground whereon to build a House for the Library, from the Hon. THOMAS PENN, Esq; Proprietaries of the Province; and the Sum of £34 *Sterl.* (to be laid out in Books) from Dr. Sydserfe, late of Antigua.

At present the Books are deposited in the West Wing of the State-House, by Favour of the General Assembly.

It is now Ten Years since the Company was first established; and we have the Pleasure of observing, That tho' 'tis compos'd of so many Persons of different Sects, Parties and Ways of Thinking, yet no Differences relating to the Affairs of the Library, have arisen among us; but every Thing has been conducted with great Harmony, and to general Satisfaction. Which happy Circumstance will, we hope, always continue.

Note, *A Copy of the Articles or Constitutions is left in the Library, for the Perusal of all that desire to be more fully informed.*

D. Some Account of the Pennsylvania Hospital (1754)

ABOUT the End of the Year 1750, some Persons, who had frequent Opportunities of observing the Distress of such distemper'd Poor as from Time to Time came to Philadelphia, for the Advice and Assistance of the Physicians and Surgeons of that City; how difficult it was for them to procure suitable Lodgings, and other Conveniences proper for their respective Cases, and how expensive the Providing good and careful Nurses, and other Attendants, for want whereof, many must suffer greatly, and some probably perish, that might otherwise have been restored to Health and Comfort, and become useful to themselves, their Families, and the Publick, for many Years after; and considering moreover, that even the poor Inhabitants of this City, tho' they had Homes, yet were therein but badly accommodated in Sickness, and could not be so well and so easily taken Care of in their separate Habitations, as they might in one convenient House, under one Inspection, and in the Hands of skilful Practitioners; and several of the Inhabitants of the Province, who unhappily became disorder'd in their Senses, wander'd about to the Terror of their Neighbours, there being no Place (except the House of Correction) in which they might be confined, and subjected to proper Management for their Recovery, and that House was by no Means fitted for such Purposes; did charitably consult together, and confer with their Friends and Acquaintances, on the best Means of relieving the Distressed, under those Circumstances; and an Infirmary, or Hospital, in the Manner of several lately established in Great Britain, being proposed, was so generally approved, that there was Reason to expect a considerable Subscription from the Inhabitants of this City, towards the Support of such an Hospital; but the Expense of erecting a Building sufficiently large and commodious for the Purpose, it was thought would be too heavy, unless the Subscription could be made general through the Province, and some Assistance could be obtained from the Assembly; the following Petition was therefore drawn, and presented to the House on the 23d of January, 1750-51.

To the Honourable House of REPRESENTATIVES
of the Province of Pennsylvania,
    The PETITION of sundry Inhabitants of the said Province.
    Humbly sheweth,
THAT with the Numbers of People the Number of Lunaticks, or Persons distemper'd in Mind, and deprived of their rational Faculties, hath greatly encreased in this Province.
    THAT some of them going at large, are a Terror to their Neighbours, who are daily apprehensive of the Violences they may commit; and others are continually wasting their Substance, to the great Injury of themselves and Families, ill disposed

Persons wickedly taking Advantage of their unhappy Condition, and drawing them into unreasonable Bargains, &c.

THAT few or none of them are so sensible of their Condition as to submit voluntarily to the Treatment their respective Cases require, and therefore continue in the same deplorable State during their Lives; whereas it has been found, by the Experience of many Years, that above two Thirds of the mad People received into Bethlehem Hospital, and there treated properly, have been perfectly cured.

YOUR Petitioners beg Leave farther to represent, that tho' the good Laws of this Province have made many compassionate and charitable Provisions for the Relief of the Poor, yet something farther seems wanting in Favour of such whose Poverty is made more miserable by the additional Weight of a grievous Disease, from which they might easily be relieved, if they were not situated at too great a Distance from regular Advice and Assistance, whereby many languish out their Lives, tortur'd perhaps with the Stone, devour'd by the Cancer, depriv'd of Sight by Cataracts, or gradually decaying by loathsome Distempers; who, if the Expence in the present Manner of nursing and attending them separately when they come to Town, were not so discouraging, might again, by the judicious Assistance of Physick and Surgery, be enabled to taste the Blessings of Health, and be made in a few Weeks useful Members of the Community, able to provide for themselves and Families.

THE kind Care our Assemblies have heretofore taken for the Relief of sick and distemper'd Strangers, by providing a Place for their Reception and Accommodation, leaves us no Room to doubt their shewing an equal tender Concern for the Inhabitants. And we hope they will be of Opinion with us, that a small Provincial Hospital, erected and put under proper Regulations, in the Care of Persons to be appointed by this House, or otherwise, as they shall think meet, with Power to receive and apply the charitable Benefactions of good People towards enlarging and supporting the same, and some other Provisions in a Law for the Purposes abovementioned, will be a good Work, acceptable to GOD, and to all the good People they represent.

WE therefore humbly recommend the Premises to their serious Consideration.

ON the second Reading of the Petition, January 29, the House gave Leave to the Petitioners to bring in a Bill, which was read the first Time on the first of February. For some Time it was doubtful whether the Bill would not miscarry, many of the Members not readily conceiving the Necessity or Usefulness of the Design; and apprehending moreover, that the Expence of paying Physicians and Surgeons, would eat up the whole of any Fund that could be reasonably expected to be raised; but three of the Profession, viz. Doctors Lloyd Zachary, Thomas Bond, and Phineas Bond, generously offering to attend the Hospital *gratis* for three Years, and the other Objections being by Degrees got over, the Bill, on the seventh of the same Month, passed the House, *Nemine Contradicente,* and in May following it received the Governor's Assent. . . . from the Tenth of February, 1752, to the Twenty-seventh of April, 1754, which is but about two Years and two Months, sixty Persons, afflicted with various Distempers, have been cured, besides many others that have received considerable Relief, both In and Out-patients; and if so much Good has been done by so small a Number of Contributors, how much more then may reasonably be expected from the liberal Aid and Assistance of the Well-disposed who hitherto have not join'd in the Undertaking? Experience has more and more convinced all concerned, of the great Usefulness of this Charity. The careful Attendance afforded to the Sick Poor; the Neatness, Cleanness, and Regularity of Diet with which they are kept in the Hospital, are found to contribute to their Recovery much sooner than their own Manner of Living at Home, and render the Physick they take more effectual. Here they have the best Advice, and the best Medicines, which are Helps to Recovery, that many in better Circumstances in different Parts of the Province do not enjoy. In short, there is scarce any one Kind of doing Good, which is not hereby in some Manner promoted; for not only the Sick are visited and relieved, but the Stranger is taken in, the Ignorant instructed, and the Bad reclaimed; present Wants are supplied, and the future prevented, and (by easing poor Families of the Burthen of supporting and curing their Sick) it is also the Means of feeding the Hungry, and cloathing the Naked.

IT is therefore hoped, that by additional Benefactions from

pious and benevolent Persons (an Account of which will be published yearly according to Law) this Charity may be farther extended, so as to embrace with open Arms all the Sick Poor that need the Relief it affords, and that the Managers will not, in Time to come, be under a Necessity, from the Narrowness of the Funds, of refusing Admittance to any proper Object. "It is hoped that a deaf Ear will not be turn'd to the Cries of those, in whose Favour both Religion and Humanity strongly plead; who are recommended by the great Pattern of human Conduct; who in Sickness are lost to Society; who contribute greatly to the Instruction of those Youth to whom the Lives of High and Low may hereafter be entrusted, whose Prayers are to be sent up for their Deliverers; but that all will assist to render the Funds of this Hospital answerable to the Necessities of the Poor. Incapacity of contributing can by none be pleaded; the Rich only indeed can bestow large Sums, but most can spare something yearly, which collected from many might make a handsome Revenue, by which great Numbers of distress'd Objects can be taken Care of, and relieved, many of whom may possibly one Day make a Part of the blessed Company above, when a Cup of cold Water given to them will not be unrewarded. Let People but reflect what unnecessary Expences they have been at in any Year for vain Superfluities or Entertainments, for mere Amusements or Diversions, or perhaps in vicious Debauches; and then let them put the Question to themselves, Whether they do not wish that Money had been given in the Way now proposed? If this Reflection has Influence on their future Conduct, the Poor will be provided for. The least Mite may be here given without a Blush; for what People would not chuse to give the Treasurer, or any Manager, the Trouble to receive, may be put into their Charity-boxes, or into the Box which is fixed in the Entry of the Hospital: Where Money cannot so well be spared, Provision or Linen, Blankets, and any Kind of Furniture, Herbs and Roots for the Kitchen, or the Apothecary, or other Necessaries of a Family, may be delivered to the Matron or Governess; old Linen, and even Rags, for Lint, Bandages, and other chyrugical Dressings, are acceptable, being scarce to be purchas'd sometimes for Money; and tho' they are of little or no Value to those who have them, they are absolutely necessary in such an Hospital, and will be thankfully received.

IT ought in Justice to be here observed, that the Practitioners have not only given their Advice and Attendance *gratis,* but have made their Visits with even greater Assiduity and Constancy than is sometimes used to their richer Patients; and that the Managers have attended their Monthly Boards, and the Committees the Visitations of two Days in every Week, with greater Readiness and Punctuality than has been usually known in any other publick Business, where Interest was not immediately concerned; owing, no Doubt, to that Satisfaction which naturally arises in humane Minds from a Consciousness of doing Good, and from the frequent pleasing Sight of Misery relieved, Distress removed, grievous Diseases healed, Health restored, and those who were admitted languishing, groaning, and almost despairing of Recovery, discharged sound and hearty, with chearful and thankful Countenances, gratefully acknowledging the Care that has been taken of them, praising GOD, and blessing their Benefactors, who by their bountiful Contributions founded so excellent an Institution.

E. Poor Richard (1736)

Loving Readers,

Your kind Acceptance of my former Labours, has encouraged me to continue writing, tho' the general Approbation you have been so good as to favour me with, has excited the Envy of some and drawn upon me the Malice of others. These Ill-willers of mine, despited at the great Reputation I gain'd by exactly predicting another Man's Death, have endeavour'd to deprive me of it all at once in the most effectual Manner, by reporting that I my self was never alive. They say in short, *That there is no such a Man as I am*; and have spread this Notion so thoroughly in the Country, that I have been frequently told it to my Face by those that don't know me. This is not civil Treatment, to endeavour to deprive me of my very Being, and reduce me to a Non-entity in the Opinion of the publick. But so long as I know my self to walk about, eat, drink and sleep, I am satisfied that *there is really such a Man as I am,* whatever they may say to the contrary: And the World may be satisfied likewise; for if there were no such Man as I am, how is it possible I should appear publickly to hundreds of People, as I have done for several Years past, in print? I need not, indeed, have taken any Notice of so idle a Report, if it had not been for the sake of my Printer, to whom my Enemies are pleased to ascribe my Productions; and who it seems is as unwilling to father my Offspring, as I am to lose the Credit of it. Therefore to clear him entirely, as well as to vindicate my own Honour, I make this publick and serious Declaration, which I desire may be believed, to wit, *That what I have written heretofore, and do now write, neither was nor is written by any other Man or Men, Person or Persons whatsoever.* Those who are not satisfied with this, must needs be very unreasonable.

My Performance for this Year follows; it submits itself, kind Reader, to thy Censure, but hopes for thy Candor, to forgive its Faults. It devotes itself entirely to thy Service, and will serve thee faithfully: And if it has the good Fortune to please its Master, 'tis Gratification enough for the Labour of Poor   R. SAUNDERS

> Presumptuous Man! the Reason wouldst thou find
> Why form'd so weak, so little, and so blind?
> First, if thou canst, the harder reason guess
> Why form'd no weaker, blinder, and no less?
> Ask of thy Mother Earth, why Oaks are made,
> Taller or stronger than the Weeds they shade?
> Or ask of yonder argent Fields above,
> Why JOVE'S Satellites are less than JOVE?

XI Mon. January hath xxxi days.
> Some have learnt many Tricks of sly Evasion,
> Instead of Truth they use Equivocation,
> And eke it out with mental Reservation,
> Which to good Men is an Abomination.
> Our Smith of late most wonderfully swore,
> That whilst he breathed he would drink no more;
> But since, I know his Meaning, for I think
> He meant he would not breath whilst he did drink.

He is no clown that drives the plow, but he that doth clownish
  things.
If you know how to spend less than you get, you have the
  Philosophers-Stone.
The good Paymaster is Lord of another man's Purse.
Fish and Visitors stink in 3 days.

  XII Mon. February hath xxix days.
    Sam's Wife provok'd him once; he broke her Crown,
  The Surgeon's Bill amounted to Five Pound;
  This Blow (she brags) *has cost my Husband dear,*
  He'll ne'er strike more. Sam chanc'd to over-hear.
  Therefore before his Wife the Bill he pays,
  And to the Surgeon in her Hearing says:
  Doctor, you charge Five Pound, here e'en take Ten;
  My Wife may chance to want your Help again.

He that has neither fools, whores nor beggars among his kindred,
  is the son of a thunder gust.
Diligence is the Mother of Good-luck.
He that lives upon Hope, dies farting.
Do not do that which you would not have known.

  I Mon. March hath xxxi days.
    Whate'er's desired, Knowledge, Fame, or Pelf,
  Not one will change his Neighbour with himself.
  The learn'd are happy Nature to explore,
  The Fool is happy that he knows no more.
  The Rich are happy in the Plenty given;
  The Poor contents him with the Care of Heav'n.
  Thus does some Comfort ev'ry State attend,
  And Pride's bestow'd on all, a common Friend.

Never praise your Cyder, Horse, or Bedfellow.
Wealth is not his that has it, but his that enjoys it.
Tis easy to see, hard to foresee.
In a discreet man's mouth, a publick thing is private.

  II Mon. April hath xxx days.
    By nought is Man from Beast distinguished
  More than by Knowledge in his learned Head.

Then Youth improve thy Time, but cautious see
That what thou learnest some how useful be.
Each Day improving, Solon waxed old;
For Time he knew was better far than Gold:
Fortune might give him Gold which would decay,
But Fortune cannot give him Yesterday.

Let thy maidservant be faithful, strong, and homely.
Keep flax from fire, youth from gaming.
Bargaining has neither friends nor relations.
Admiration is the Daughter of Ignorance.
There's more old Drunkards than old Doctors.

III Mon. May hath xxxi days.
Lalus who loves to hear himself discourse
    Keeps talking still as if he frantick were,
And tho' himself might no where hear a worse,
    Yet he no other but himself will hear.
Stop not his Mouth, if he be troublesome,
But stop his ears, and then the Man is dumb.

She that paints her Face, thinks of her Tail.
Here comes Courage! that seiz'd the lion absent, and run away
    from the present mouse.
He that takes a wife, takes care.
Nor Eye in a letter, nor Hand in a purse, nor Ear in the secret of
    another.
He that buys by the penny, maintains not only himself, but other
    people.

IV Mon. June hath xxx days.
    Things that are bitter, bitterer than Gall
Physicians say are always physical:
Now Women's Tongues if into Powder beaten,
May in a Potion or a Pill be eaten,
And as there's nought more bitter, I do muse,
That Women's Tongues in Physick they ne'er use.
My self and others who lead restless Lives,
Would spare that bitter Member of our Wives.

He that can have Patience, can have what he will.
Now I've a sheep and a cow, every body bids me good morrow.
God helps them that help themselves.
Why does the blind man's wife paint herself?

> V *Mon.* July hath xxxi days.
> Who can charge Ebrio with Thirst of Wealth?
> See he consumes his Money, Time and Health,
> In drunken Frolicks which will all confound,
> Neglects his Farm, forgets to till his Ground,
> His Stock grows less that might be kept with ease;
> In nought but Guts and Debts he finds Encrease.
> In Town reels as if he'd shove down each Wall,
> Yet Walls must stand, poor Soul, or he must fall.

None preaches better than the ant, and she says nothing.
The absent are never without fault, nor the present without
   excuse.
Gifts burst rocks.

> If wind blows on you thro' a hole,
> Make your will and take care of your soul.

The rotten apple spoils his companion.

> VI *Mon.* *August* hath xxxi days.
> The Tongue was once a Servant to the Heart,
> And what it gave she freely did impart;
> But now Hypocrisy is grown so strong
> The Heart's become a Servant to the Tongue.
> Virtue we praise, but practise not her good,
> (Athenian-like), we act not what we know,
> As many Men do talk of Robin Hood
> Who never did shoot Arrow in his Bow.

He that sells upon trust, loses many friends, and always wants
   money.
Don't throw stones at your neighbours, if your own windows are
   glass.
The excellency of hogs is fatness, of men virtue.

Good wives and good plantations are made by good husbands.
Pox take you, is no curse to some people.

> *VII Mon.* September hath xxx days.
>
>   Briskcap, thou'st little Judgment in thy Head,
>   More than to dress thee, drink and go to Bed:
>   Yet thou shalt have the Wall, and the Way lead,
>   Since Logick wills that simple Things precede.
>   Walking and meeting one not long ago,
>   I ask'd who 'twas, he said, he did not know.
>   I said, I know thee; so said he, I you;
>   But he that knows himself I never knew.

Force shites upon Reason's Back.
Lovers, Travellers, and Poets, will give money to be heard.
He that speaks much, is much mistaken.
Creditors have better memories than debtors.
Forwarn'd, forearm'd, unless in the case of Cuckolds, who are
   often forearm'd before warn'd.

> *VIII Mon.* October hath xxxi days.
>
>   Whimsical Will once fancy'd he was ill,
>   The Doctor's call'd, who thus examin'd Will:
>   *How is your Appetite?* O, as to that
>   I eat right heartily, you see I'm fat.
>   *How is your Sleep anights?* 'Tis sound and good;
>   I eat, drink, sleep as well as e'er I cou'd.
>   *Well,* says the Doctor, clapping on his Hat;
>   *I'll give you something shall remove all that.*

Three things are men most liable to be cheated in, a Horse, a
   Wig, and a Wife.
He that lives well, is learned enough.
Poverty, Poetry, and new Titles of Honour, make Men ridiculous.
He that scatters Thorns, let him not go barefoot.
There's none deceived but he that trusts.

> *IX Mon.* November hath xxx days.

When you are sick, what you like best is to be chosen for a
Medicine in the first Place; what Experience tells you is best,

is to be chosen in the second Place; what Reason (i.e. Theory) says is best, is to be chosen in the last Place. But if you can get Dr. Inclination, Dr. Experience and Dr. Reason to hold a Consultation together, they will give you the best Advice that can be given.

God heals, and the Doctor takes the Fees.
If you desire many things, many things will seem but a few.
Mary's mouth costs her nothing, for she never opens it but at others expence.
Receive before you write, but write before you pay.
I saw few die of Hunger, of Eating 100000.

X Mon. December hath xxxi days. . . .
Maids of America, who gave you bad teeth?
Answ. Hot Soupings: and frozen Apples.
Marry your Daughter and eat fresh Fish betimes.
If God blesses a Man, his Bitch brings forth Pigs.

> He that would live in peace and at ease,
> Must not speak all he knows, nor judge all he sees.

Adieu.

Of the ECLIPSES, 1736.

There will be this Year six Eclipses, four of the Sun, and two of the Moon; those of the Moon both visible and total.

The first is a small Eclipse of the Sun, March the first, 35 minutes past 9 in the Morn. Scarcely visible in these Parts.

The second is an Eclipse of the Moon, March 15, beginning 30 minutes after 4 a Clock, P. M. the Moon being then beneath our Horizon, and rises totally dark, and continues so till 25 minutes after 7, and the Eclipse is not entirely ended till 20 minutes after 8. This Eclipse falls in Libra, or the Balance. Poor Germania! *Mene, mene, tekel upharsin*!

The third of the Sun, March 31. 30 minutes past 2 in the Morning. Invisible here.

The Fourth is of the Sun likewise, Aug. 25. 35 minutes after three in the Morning; no more to be seen than the former; the Sun at the Conjunction being under the Horizon.

The Fifth is of the Moon, Sept. 8. 18 minutes after 8 at Night;

Beginning of total Darkness 18 min. after 9. Time of Emergence 57 min. after 10. End of the Eclipse at midnight.

The 6th and last, is of the Sun, September 23 at Noon: Invisible here tho' the Sun itself be visible. For there is this Difference between Eclipses of the Moon and of the Sun, viz. All Lunar Eclipses are universal, i.e. visible in all Parts of the Globe which have the Moon above their Horizon, and are every where of the same Magnitude: But Eclipses of the Sun do not appear the same in all Parts of the Earth where they are seen; being when total in some Places, only partial in others; and in other Places not seen at all, tho' neither Clouds nor Horizon prevent the Sight of the Sun it self.

As to the Effects of these two great Eclipses, suffer me to observe, that whoever studies the Eclipses of former Ages, and compares them with the great Events in the History of the Times and Years in which they happened (as every true Astrologer ought to do) shall find, that the Fall of the Assyrian, Persian, Grecian and Roman Monarchies, each of them, was remarkably preceded by great and total Eclipses of the Heavenly Bodies. Observations of this kind, join'd with the ancient and long-try'd Rules of our Art, (too tedious to repeat here) make me tremble for an Empire now in being. O Christendom! why art thou so fatally divided against thy self? O Poland! formerly the Bulwark of the Christian Faith, wilt thou become the Flood-gate to let in an Inundation of Infidelity? O mischievous Crescent! when shall we see thee at the Full, and rejoice at thy future Waning? May Heaven avert these presag'd Misfortunes, and confound the Designs of all wicked and impious Men!

COURTS

For Gratitude there's none exceed 'em,
(Their Clients know this when they bleed 'em).
Since they who give most for their Laws,
Have most return'd, and carry th' Cause.
All know, except an arrant Tony,
That Right and Wrong's meer Ceremony.
It is enough that the Law Jargon,
Gives the best Bidder the best Bargain.

In my last Year's Almanack I mention'd, that the visible Eclipses of this Year, 1736, portended some great and surprizing Events relating to these Northern Colonies, of which I purposed this Year to speak at large. But as those Events are not to happen immediately this Year, I chuse rather, upon second Thought, to defer farther Mention of them, till the Publication of my Almanack for that Year in which they are to happen. However, that the Reader may not be entirely disappointed, here follow for his present Amusement a few

ENIGMATICAL PROPHECIES
Which they that do not understand, cannot well explain.

1. Before the middle of this Year, a Wind at N. East will arise, during which the *Water of the* Sea and Rivers will be in such a manner raised, that great part of the Towns of Boston, Newport, New-York, Philadelphia, the low Lands of Maryland and Virginia, and the Town of Charlstown in South Carolina, will be *under Water*. Happy will it be for the Sugar and Salt, standing in the Cellars of those Places, if there be tight Roofs and Cielings overhead; otherwise, without being a Conjurer, a Man may easily foretel that such Commodities will receive Damage.

2. About the middle of the Year, great Numbers of Vessels fully laden will be taken out of the Ports aforesaid, by a *Power* with which we are not now at War, and whose Forces shall not be *descried or seen* either coming or going. But in the End this may not be disadvantageous to those Places.

3. However, not long after, a visible Army of 20000 *Musketers* will land, some in Virginia and Maryland, and some in the lower Counties on both sides of Delaware, who will over-run the Country, and sorely annoy the Inhabitants: But the Air in this Climate will agree with them so ill towards Winter, that they will die in the beginning of cold Weather like rotten Sheep, and by Christmas the Inhabitants will get the better of them.

Note, In my next Almanack these Enigmatical Prophecies will be explained.

R.S.

15

William Pitt and the Empire (1739-1762)[1]

William Pitt (1708-78) was born in London into a wealthy family who provided him with a normal, upper-class education. Leaving Oxford without a degree, he served for several years in the cavalry. In 1735 he entered the House of Commons from the pocket borough of Old Sarum. Never a man to fit easily into an organization, Pitt joined the opposition to Robert Walpole's government. Walpole had grounded his political supremacy on a policy of peace. In doing so, he turned his back on the traditional anti-Spanish policy, but the old issue of trade with Spanish America remained. By the Treaty of Utrecht of 1713, Great Britain had won the right to supply the Spanish plantations with slaves, and she had also been granted a very limited right to trade in general merchandise. English merchants, operating through the South Sea Company, attempted to expand the trading opportunities. This brought them into conflict with the Spanish coast guard and produced a series of incidents. Opposition to Walpole's policy of peace grew. The merchant-inspired desire for broader trading rights came to be symbolized by the cry "No Search!" In the face of the opposition, Walpole negotiated the Convention of Pardo, which provided for Spanish reparations for some ship seizures, but did not expand trading privileges. In the first of Pitt's speeches printed below, Pitt expresses the extreme discontent of the opposition. In 1739 Walpole's policy collapsed and the War of Jenkin's Ear began; three years later that conflict was absorbed into the War of the Austrian Succession. During the war Pitt had his first experience with the executive side of government as joint paymaster of the forces.

The War of the Austrian Succession did not resolve the basic issues dividing Europe. Eight years after the Treaty of Aix-la-Chapelle (1748), the climactic war for empire, the Seven Years War, began. Pitt held office briefly as Secretary of State for the Southern Depart-

1. William Cobbett (ed.,) *Parliamentary History of England, from the Norman Conquest, in 1066 to the year 1803* (36 vols.; London: Longman's and Co., 1806-20), X, 1280-83; XV, 1260-72.

ment, was dismissed, but returned to office and greatness. Between 1757 and his resignation in 1761, he became the "Great Commoner," one of England's truly magnificent war leaders. Pitt found his genius in his capacity to identify and further the national interest in the context of English foreign and imperial policy.

Kate Hotblack, *Chatham's Colonial Policy* (London: G. Routledge & Sons, 1917) is an analysis covering the years from the War of Jenkins' Ear to the Treaty of Paris. For the conflict in the southern colonies read Verner W. Crane, *The Southern Frontier, 1670-1732* (Ann Arbor: University of Michigan Press, 1929, 1956), and for the West Indies, Richard Pares, *War and Trade in the West Indies, 1739-1763* (Oxford: Clarendon Press, 1936). The fullest modern work is Lawrence H. Gipson, *The British Empire Before the American Revolution* (9 vols.; Caldwell, Idaho: Caxton Printers, 1936-56). The classic, both as history and literature, is Francis Parkman, *France and England in America* (Boston: Little, Brown, 1902-1903). The relevant volumes bear the titles *A Half Century of Conflict* and *Montcalm and Wolfe.* Parkman is ably abridged by Samuel E. Morison in *The Parkman Reader* (Boston: Little, Brown, 1955). In reading "Speech on the Convention of Pardo" note (1) what Pitt thought about the manner in which the Convention was submitted; (2) what specific objections he raised against the Convention; (3) to what extent Pitt thought the honor of Britain was compromised by the terms of the Convention; and (4) why he thought the Committee should disapprove the Convention. In reading his speech against the preliminary treaty with France note (1) what complaints he voiced respecting the terms affecting the fishery and why; (2) why he disapproved of the proposal to surrender Cuba; (3) why he objected to restoring some of the West Indies to France; and (4) what four elements having to do with Britain's external relations he deemed necessary to English security and well-being.

Speech on the Convention of Pardo (1739)

Mr. pitt:

Sir; I can by no means think that the complicated question now before us is the proper, the direct manner of taking the sense of this Committee. We have here the soft name of an humble Address to the crown proposed, and for no other end but to lead gentlemen into an approbation of the Convention. But, is this that full deliberate examination, which we were, with defiances, called upon to give? is this cursory blended disquisition of matters of such variety and extent all we owe to ourselves and our country? when trade is at stake it is your last retrenchment; you must defend it, or perish; and whatever is to decide, that deserves the most distinct consideration, and the most direct undisguised sense of parliament. But how are we now proceeding? upon an artificial, ministerial question: here is all the confidence, here is the conscious sense of the greatest service that ever was done to this country; to be complicating questions, to be lumping sanction and approbation, like a commissary's accompt, to be covering and taking sanctuary in the royal name, instead of meeting openly, and standing fairly, the direct judgment and sentence of parliament upon the several articles of this Convention.

Sir, you have been moved to vote an humble Address of Thanks to his Majesty for a measure, which (I will appeal to gentlemen's conversation in the world) is odious throughout the kingdom: such thanks are only due to the fatal influence that framed it, as are due for that low, unallied condition abroad, which is now made a plea for this Convention. To what are gentlemen reduced in support of it? first, try a little to defend it upon its own merits; if that is not tenable, throw out general terrors; the house of Bourbon is united, who knows the consequence of a war? Sir, Spain knows the consequence of a war in America; whoever gains, it must prove fatal to her: she knows it, and must therefore avoid it; but she knows England does not dare to make it. And what is a delay, which is all this magnified Convention is sometimes called, to produce? can it produce such conjunctures as those you lost, while you were giving kingdomes to Spain, and all to bring her back again to that great branch of the house of Bourbon, which is now thrown out to you with so much terror? If this union be formidable, are we to delay only till it becomes more formidable, by being carried farther into execution, and more strongly cemented? But be it what it will, is this any longer a nation, or what is an English parliament, if with more ships in your harbours than in all the navies of Europe, with above two millions of people in your American colonies, you will bear to hear of the expediency of receiving from Spain an insecure, unsatisfactory, dishonourable Convention? Sir, I call it no more than it has been proved in this debate; it carries fallacy or downright subjection in almost every line: it has been laid open and exposed in so many strong and glaring lights, that I can pretend to add nothing to the conviction and indignation it has raised.

Sir, as to the great national objection, the Searching your Ships, that favourite word, as it was called, is not omitted, indeed, in the preamble to the Convention, but it stands there as the reproach of the whole, as the strongest evidence of the fatal submission that follows: on the part of Spain an usurpation, an inhuman tyranny claimed and exercised over the American seas; on the part of England, an undoubted right by treaties and from God and nature, declared and asserted in the Resolutions of parliament, are referred to the discussion of plenipotentiaries, upon one and the same equal foot. Sir, I say this undoubted right is to be discussed and to be regulated. And if to regulate be to prescribe rules, (as in all construction it is) this right is, by the express words of this Convention, to be given up and sacrificed; for it must cease to be any thing, from the moment it is submitted to limits.

The court of Spain has plainly told you (as appears by papers upon the table) you shall steer a due course, you shall navigate by a line to and from your plantations in America; if you draw near to her coasts, (though from the circumstances of that navigation your are under an unavoidable necessity of doing it) you shall be seized and confiscated: if then upon these terms only she has consented to refer, what becomes at once of all the security we are flattered with in consequence of this reference? plenipotentiaries are to regulate finally the respective pretentions of the two crowns, with regard to trade and navigation in America; but does a man in Spain reason that these pretensions must be regulated to the satisfaction and honour of England? no, Sir; they conclude, and with reason, from the high spirit of their administration, from the superiority with which they have so long treated you, that this reference must end, as it has begun, to their honour and advantage.

But gentlemen say, the treaties subsisting are to be the measure of this regulation. Sir, as to treaties, I will take part of the words of sir William Temple, quoted by the hon. gentleman

near me, 'It is vain to negociate and make treaties,' if there is
not dignity and vigour to enforce the observance of them; for
under the misconstruction and misinterpretation of these very
treaties subsisting, this intolerable grievance has arisen; it has
been growing upon you treaty after treaty, through 20 years of
negociation, and even under the discussion of commissaries to
whom it was referred. You have heard from captain Vaughan at
your bar, at what time these injuries and indignities were continued; as a kind of explanatory comment upon the Convention
Spain has thought fit to grant you; as another insolent protest,
under the validity and force of which she has suffered this
Convention to be proceeded on. 'We will treat with you, but we
will search and take your ships; we will sign a Convention, but
we will keep your subjects prisoners, prisoners in old Spain; the
West Indies are remote, Europe shall be witness how we use
you.'

Sir, as to the inference of an admission of our right not to be
searched, drawn from a reparation made for ships unduly seized
and confiscated, I think that argument is very inconclusive. The
right claimed by Spain to search our ships is one thing, and the
excesses admitted to have been committed, in consequence of
this pretended right, is another; but surely, Sir, reasoning from
inferences and implication only, is below the dignity of your proceedings, upon a right of this vast importance. What this reparation is, what sort of composition for your losses, forced upon
you by Spain in an instance that has come to light, where your
own commissaries could not in conscience decide against your
claim, has fully appeared upon examination: and as for the
payment of the sum stipulated, (all but 27,000 £ and that too
subject to a drawback) it is evidently a fallacious, nominal payment only. I will not attempt to enter into the detail of a dark,
confused, and scarcely intelligible accompt; I will only beg leave
to conclude with one word upon it, in the light of a submission,
as well as of an adequate reparation. Spain stipulates to pay to
the crown of England 95,000 £ by a preliminary protest of the
king of Spain, the South Sea Company is at once to pay 68,000 £
of it; if they refuse, Spain, I admit, is still to pay the 95,000 £:
but how does it stand then? The Assiento contract is to be suspended: you are to purchase this sum at the price of an exclusive

trade, pursuant to a national treaty, and of an immense debt of God knows how many hundred thousand pounds due from Spain to the South Sea Company. Here, Sir, is the submission of Spain by the payment of a stipulated sum; a tax laid upon subjects of England, under the severest penalties, with the reciprocal accord of an English minister, as a preliminary that the Convention may be signed; a condition imposed by Spain in the most absolute imperious manner, and received by the ministers of England in the most tame and abject. Can any verbal distinctions, any evasions whatever, possibly explain away this public infamy? To whom would we disguise it? To ourselves and to the nation: I wish we could hide it from the eyes of every court in Europe: they see Spain has talked to you like your master, they see this arbitrary fundamental condition, and it must stand with distinction, with a pre-eminence of shame as a part even of this Convention.

This Convention, Sir, I think from my soul is nothing but a stipulation for national ignominy; an illusory expedient to baffle the resentment of the nation; a truce without a suspension, as to Georgia, of the first law of nature, self-preservation and self-defence; a surrender of the rights and trade of England to the mercy of plenipotentiaries, and in this infinitely highest and sacred point, future security, not only inadequate, but directly repugnant to the resolutions of parliament, and the gracious promise from the throne. The complaints of your despairing merchants, the voice of England has condemned it: be the guilt of it upon the head of the adviser: God forbid that this Committee should share the guilt by approving it!

Debate on the Preliminary Treaty with France (1762)

Mr. Pitt rose in reply to Mr. Fox. He began with lamenting his ill state of health, which had confined him to his chamber; but although he was at this instant suffering under the most excruciating torture, yet he determined, at the hazard of his life, to attend this day, to raise up his voice, his hand, and his arm, against the preliminary articles of a treaty, that obscured all the glories of the war, surrendered the dearest interests of the nation, and sacrificed the public faith by an abandonment of our allies.

He owned, that the terms upon which he had consented to conclude a peace, had not been satisfactory to all persons; it was impossible to reconcile every interest; but he had not, he said, for the mere attainment of peace, made a sacrifice of any conquest; he had neither broken the national faith, nor betrayed the allies of the crown. That he was ready to enter into a discussion of the merits of the peace he had offered, comparatively with the present preliminaries. He called for the most able casuist amongst the minister's friends who, he saw, were all mustered and marshalled for duty, to refute him; they made a most gallant appearance, and there was no doubt of the victory on the main question. If the right hon. gentleman, (Mr. Fox) who took the lead in this debate, would risk the argument of comparison, he would join issue with him, even under all the disadvantages of his present situation. His motive was to stop that torrent of misrepresentation, which was poisoning the virtue of the country. [No answer being made, he proceeded.]

He perceived, he said, that the right Hon. gentleman and his friends, were prepared for only the present question. He would, therefore, take a view of the Articles, as they appeared upon the paper, on the table.

[Mr. Pitt was so excessively ill, and his pain so exceedingly acute, that the House unanimously desired, he might be indulged to deliver his sentiments sitting; a circumstance that was unprecedented. Hitherto he had been supported by two of his friends.]

The first important Article was the Fishery. The terms in which this article was written, appeared to him to give to France a grant of the whole fishery. There was an absolute unconditional surrender of the islands of St. Pierre and Miquelon, which, if France continued to be as attentive to her own interest, as we have hitherto found her, would enable her to recover her marine. He considered this to be a most dangerous article, to the maritime strength and future power of Great Britain. In the negociation he had with Mr. Bussy, he had acquiesced in the cession of St. Pierre only; after having, he said, several times, in vain, contended for the whole exclusive fishery; but he was overruled; he repeated, he was over-ruled, not by the foreign enemy, but by another enemy. After many struggles, he obtained four limitations to the island of St. Pierre; they were indispensable conditions; but they were omitted in the present treaty. If they were necessary in the surrender of one island, they were doubly necessary in the surrender of two. In the volumes of abuse which had been so plentifully bestowed upon him, by the writers who were paid and patronized by those who held great employments in the state, this cession of Pierre only, had been condemned, in terms of acrimony. He had been reminded, that the earl of Oxford was impeached, for allowing the French liberty to fish and dry fish on Newfoundland. He admitted the fact. But that impeachment was a scandalous measure, was disapproved by every impartial person. In one article (the seventeenth) the minister is accused of having advised the destructive expedition against Canada—Why was that expedition called destructive?— because it was not successful. Thus have events been considered by parliament as standards of political judgment. Had the expedition to Canada, under general Wolfe, been unsuccessful, there is no doubt it would also have been called destructive; and some of the gentlemen, now in office, would this day have been calling for vengeance upon the minister's head.

Of Dunkirk he said but little. The French were more favoured in this article of the present preliminaries, than they had been by any former treaty. He had made the treaty of Aix la Chapelle his guide on this point; but in the present treaty, even that requisition was disregarded.

Of the dereliction of North America by the French, he entirely approved. But the negociators had no trouble in obtaining this acquisition. It had been the *uti possidetis* in his own negociation, to which the French had readily consented. But Florida, he said, was no compensation for the Havannah; the Havannah was an important conquest. He had designed to make it, and would have done it some months earlier, had he been permitted to execute his own plans. From the moment the Havannah was taken, all the Spanish treasures and riches in America, lay at our mercy. Spain had purchased the security of all these, and the restoration of Cuba also, with the cession of Florida only. It was no equivalent. There had been a bargain, but the terms were inadequate. They were inadequate in every point, where the principle of reciprocity was affected to be introduced.

He had been blamed for consenting to give up Guadaloupe. That cession had been a question in another place, He wished to have kept the island; he had been over-ruled in that point also; he could not help it; he had been over-ruled many times, on many occasions—He had acquiesced, he had submitted. But at length he saw that all his measures, all his sentiments, were inimical to the new system; to those persons to whom his Majesty had given his confidence. But to Guadaloupe these persons had added the cession of Martinique. Why did they permit the forces to conquer Martinique, if they were resolved to restore it? Was it because the preparations for that conquest were so far advanced, they were afraid to countermand them? And to the cession of the island of Cuba, Guadaloupe, and Martinique, there is added the island of St. Lucia; the only valuable one of the neutral islands. It is impossible, said he, to form any judgment of the motives which can have influenced his Majesty's servants to make these important sacrifices. They seem to have lost sight of the great fundamental principle, that France is chiefly, if not solely, to be dreaded by us in the light of a maritime and commercial power. And therefore, by restoring to her all the valuable West-India islands, and by our concessions in the Newfoundland fishery, we had given to her the means of recovering her prodigious losses, and of becoming once more formidable to us at sea. That the fishery trained up an innumerable multitude of young seamen; and that the West-India trade employed them when they were trained. After the peace of Aix-la-Chapelle, France gained a decided superiority over us in the lucrative branch of commerce, and supplied almost all Europe with the rich, commodities which are produced only in that part of the world. By this commerce she enriched her merchants, and augmented her finances. The state of the existing trade in the conquests in North America, is extremely low; the speculations of their future are precarious, and the prospect, at the very best, very remote. We stand in need of supplies, which will have an effect, certain, speedy, and considerable. The retaining both, or even one of the considerable French islands, Martinico or Guadaloupe, will, and nothing else can effectually answer this triple purpose. The advantage is immediate. It is a matter not of conjecture, but of account. The trade with these conquests is of the utmost lucrative nature, and of the most considerable extent; the number of ships employed by it are a great resource to our maritime power: and what is of equal weight, all that we gain on this system, is made four fold to us by the loss which ensues to France. But our conquests in North America are of very little detriment to the commerce of France. On the West Indian scheme of acquisition, our gain and her loss go hand in hand. He insisted upon the obvious connection of this trade with that of the colonies in North America, and with our commerce to the coast of Africa. The African trade would be augmented, which, with that of North America, would all center in Great Britain. But if the islands are all restored, a great part of the benefit of the colony trade must redound to those who were lately our enemies, and will always be our rivals. Though we had retained either Martinico or Guadaloupe, or even both these islands, our conquests were such, that there was still abundant matter left to display our moderation.

Goree, he said, is also surrendered, without the least apparent necessity; notwithstanding it had been agreed in the negociation with M. Bussy, that it should remain with the British crown, because it was essential to the security of Senegal.

In the East Indies there was an engagement for mutual restitution of conquests. He asked, what were the conquests which France had to restore? He declared that she had none. All the conquests which France had made had been retaken, and were in our own possession; as were likewise all the French settlements and factories. Therefore the restitution was all from one side. We retained nothing, although we had conquered every thing.

The restitution of Minorca he approved: and that, he said, was the only conquest which France had to restore; and for this island we had given the East Indies, the West Indies, and Africa. The purchase was made at a price that was fifty times more than it was worth. Belleisle alone, he affirmed, was a sufficient equivalent for Minorca.

As to Germany, he said, it was a wide field; a tedious and lengthened consideration, including the interests of many hostile

powers; some of them immediately, and other eventually, con-
nected with Great Britain. There might, sometimes, be policy
in the construction of our measures, to consult our insular situation only. But while we had France for our enemy, it was a
scene to employ, and to baffle her arms. Had the armies of
France not been employed in Germany, they would have been
transported to America; where we should have found it more
difficult to have conquered them. And if we had succeeded, the
expence would have been greater. Let any one, he said, make a
fair estimate of the expence of transports and provisions to that
distant climate, and he will find, in the article of expence, the
war in Germany to be infinitely less than in the wilds of America.
Upon this principle, he affirmed, that the conquests made in
America, had been owing to the employment of the French army
in Germany. He said, with an emphasis, that America had been
conquered in Germany. . . .

The German war prevented the French from succouring their
colonies and islands in America, in Asia, and in Africa. Our
successes were uniform, because our measures were vigorous. . . .

Upon the whole, the terms of the proposed treaty met with
his most hearty disapprobation. He saw in them the seeds of a
future war. The peace was insecure, because it restored the
enemy to her former greatness. The peace was inadequate, because the places gained were no equivalent for the places
surrendered.

Mr. Pitt was so ill and faint, towards the end of his speech,
that he could scarcely be heard. He intended to have spoken to
some points relative to Spain, but he was unable. He spoke
nearly three hours; and when he left the House, which was before the division, he was in the greatest agony of pain.

The following are the principal Arguments which were offered
in favour of the Treaty:

That the original object of the war was the security of our
colonies upon the continent; that the danger to which these
colonies were exposed, and, in consequence of that danger, the
immense waste of blood and treasure which ensued to Great
Britain, together with the calamities which were, from the same
source, derived from the four quarters of the world, left no sort
of doubt that it was not only our best, but our only policy, to

guard against all possibility of the return of such evils. Experience has shewn us that while France possesses any single place in America, from whence she may molest our settlements, they can never enjoy any repose, and of course, that we are never secure from being plunged again into those calamities, from which we have at length, and with so much difficulty, happily emerged. To remove France from our neighbourhood in America, or to contract her power within the narrowest limits possible, is therefore the most capital advantage we can obtain, and is worth purchasing by almost any concessions. The friends of the ministry insisted that the absolute security derived from this plan, included in itself an indemnification: first, by saving us, more effectually than any other method could, from the necessity of another war, and consequently by giving us an opportunity of increasing our trade, and lowering our debt: secondly, by permitting our colonies on the continent to extend themselves without danger or molestation. They shewed the great increase of population in those colonies within a few years. They shewed that their trade with the mother country had uniformly increased with this population. That being now freed from the molestation of enemies and the emulation of rivals, unlimited in their possessions, and safe in their persons, our American planters would, by the very course of their natural propagation in a very short time, furnish out a demand of our manufactures as large as all the working hands of Great Britain could possibly supply. That there was therefore no reason to dread that want of trade which their adversaries insinuated, since North America alone would supply the deficiencies of our trade in every other part of the world. They expatiated on the great variety of climates which that country contained, and the vast resources which would thence arise to commerce. That the value of our conquests thereby ought not to be estimated by the present produce, but by their probable increase. Neither ought the value of any country to be solely tried on its commercial advantages; that extent of territory and a number of subjects are matters of as much consideration to a state attentive to the sources of real grandeur, as the mere advantages of traffic; that such ideas are rather suitable to a limited and petty commonwealth, like Holland, than to a great, powerful, and warlike nation. That on these principles, having made very large demands in North America, it was necessary to relax in other parts. That France would never be brought to any considerable cession in the West Indies; but that her power and increase there could never become formidable, because the existence of her settlements depended upon ours in North America, she not being any longer left a place from whence they can be supplied with provisions; that in losing something of the sugar trade, we lost very little else than a luxury; as to the other produce of the West Indies, it might be in a great measure, and in part already was, supplied by our possessions on the continent, which daily increased not only in the quantity, but in the kind of its produce.

At length the House divided, when there appeared 319 for the Address, and 65 against it.